Christmas '97

Jerry

The *Best* of
HERB CAEN
1960-1975

Books by Herb Caen

THE SAN FRANCISCO BOOK
BAGHDAD-BY-THE-BAY
BAGHDAD '51
DON'T CALL IT FRISCO
ONLY IN SAN FRANCISCO
HERB CAEN'S GUIDE TO SAN FRANCISCO AND THE BAY AREA
SAN FRANCISCO, CITY ON GOLDEN HILLS
(WITH DONG KINGMAN)
THE CABLE CAR AND THE DRAGON
ONE MAN'S SAN FRANCISCO
THE BEST OF HERB CAEN 1960–1975

★   ★   ★

The Best of
HERB CAEN
1960-1975

SELECTED BY IRENE MECCHI

CHRONICLE BOOKS • SAN FRANCISCO

First Edition 1991.

Copyright © 1960 et seq by the Chronicle Publishing Company.
All rights reserved. No part of this book may be reproduced in any
form without written permission from the publisher.

Printed in the United States of America.

Library of Congress Cataloging-in-Publication Data

Caen, Herb, 1916–
    The best of Herb Caen, 1960–1975 / edited by Irene Mecchi.
        p.   cm.
    ISBN 0-8118-0020-2
       1. Daily morning chronicle (San Francisco, Calif.) 2. American
newspapers—Sections, columns, etc.   I. Mecchi, Irene.   II. Title.
PN 4874.C2A25   1991
070.4' 44—dc20   91-11453
                                           CIP

Book and cover design: Kathy Warinner
Composition: On Line Typography

Distributed in Canada by Raincoast Books,
112 East Third Avenue, Vancouver, B.C. V5T 1C8

10 9 8 7 6 5 4 3 2 1

Chronicle Books
275 Fifth Street
San Francisco, CA 94103

PREFACE

I began writing a daily column for *The San Francisco Chronicle* on July 5, 1938. It was a magic time in a faraway city that has largely disappeared and may have existed only in foggy myth.

A curly-haired wide-eyed open-mouthed 22-year-old gee-whizzer from Sacramento, I felt like a kid who had been turned loose in a candy store. I was unreservedly in love with everything in the city and wrote about it with the unabashed and often excessive enthusiasm of the newly smitten.

"City of the world, a world in a city," I rattled on, glorying in the genuine excitement of the old waterfront, "The Roar of The Four" streetcar lines on Market Street, the dance bands in the big hotels, the round-the-clock nightlife, the ornate sidewheeling ferryboats that even then were fading into the mist as the great bridges were completed.

A world depression was on but San Francisco never seemed busier. Prices were low and wages were high in this strong union town where Harry Bridges strutted like a king. Row after row of almost identical but highly efficient houses, built by a colorful entrepreneur named Henry Doelger, crept across the sand dunes from the Sunset District to Ocean Beach, where an amusement park named Playland entertained thousands each weekend for peanuts and a few coins.

Give or take a strike or two, the city had been a tranquil place for many years. From 1912 to the time I began my column, San Francisco had only two mayors, the legendary "Sunny Jim" Rolph, who served from 1912 to 1932, and florist Angel J. Rossi, who emulated his predecessor, down to the toothbrush moustache and the winged starched collars. For an amazing decade (1930–1940), the population remained almost exactly the same, around 630,000. Racism was a growing problem largely overlooked because there were so few minorities. The city was dancing on the edge of a war at the end of a charmed life, almost cut off from the rest of the world, but it was about to change forever.

World War II brought thousands of "outsiders" (old-time native San Franciscans were intensely xenophobic) who discovered the secret place and couldn't wait to return to it. When the war ended, they did return, by the thousands, and a delicate balance was destroyed, through no fault of anyone. The United Nations Charter was signed in San Francisco, validating the city's historical importance.

Still fairly snug and characteristically smug, San Francisco drifted into the 1950s, prosperous and changing only slowly. It was not until the rise of the Beat Generation that the phlegmatic natives became a little restive. The old bohemians had been perfectly acceptable—even welcome in some of the better houses—but the scruffy beatniks were different. A little threatening, even. Against the system and all that. And the worldwide publicity they were getting—why, complained the Chamber of Commerce and convention bureau types, they were giving the city a bad name.

We come now to the time of great changes, bits and pieces of which are chronicled in my columns of the years 1960 to 1975. As the Beats phased out, the hippies and rock 'n' roll came on with a roar that shook up any old-time San Franciscans who were still complacent.

At the same time, the skyline, once one of the most gracious in the world of metropolises, began disappearing behind walls of look-alike high-rises. The very weather changed as sunlight disappeared in the cold canyons of "progress," that thing you can't stop, and icy winds swept debris along the shadowed sidewalks. "Progress" was stopped in the "freeway revolt" that killed the Embarcadero Freeway at the halfway point, but that didn't solve the growing problem of heavy downtown traffic. In fact, it added to it.

Still, San Francisco remained at the cutting edge of much that was new, daring and outrageous. The hippies died out, too many of them literally, but their influence would be felt for years among the young. San Francisco rock 'n' roll artists were high in the world hierarchy. The protests against the war in Vietnam produced "peace marches" of vast proportions that played a significant role in ending the conflict. In the more conservative parts of the country, San Francisco was looked upon as sort of a "kook capital." We who knew the essential conservatism of this outwardly liberal city looked on with amusement.

Fifteen years in the life of a young-old city, a place of careless enchantment that grew up overnight and had long preferred to face the dawn, bottle in hand, than the hangover of cold reality. The assassinations of the Kennedys and Martin Luther King sobered even pleasure-loving San Franciscans. Racial tensions increased. Nightlife withered as the streets became more dangerous. The flight to the suburbs began and the face of the city kept changing, sometimes overnight.

Through it all, I sat at the keyboard of my loyal Royal, trying to make sense of at least some of it, or, failing that, making the jokes that are also part of all serious problems. In these columns of 1960 through 1975, I hope I captured a little of the kaleidoscopic nature of the city I long ago dubbed Baghdad-by-the-Bay. That Baghdad was out of the Arabian nights, a place of myths and fables told by seductresses far into the night.

It is an atmosphere that still exists, thank God or Allah or whoever it was that blessed this small, special, annoying, irresistible place at the tip of a peninsula and the end of the world.

Herb Caen
San Francisco
June 6, 1991

1960

GEE, WHAT A CRAZY TOWN

Historic parks being sold down the drain for a mess of parkage, bearded Beatniks seeking peace of mind by chewing Zen-Zen, grown men fighting like kids over a multimillion-dollar stadium dedicated to a child's game, Gray Line buses hauling gray-faced tourists through the gray city on a gray day, a City crew washing the Broadway Tunnel as the rain splashes outside, Chinese selling Japanese trinkets to South Americans carrying German cameras . . . Gee, what a crazy town.

★ ★ ★

Police cars bearing "No Riders" stickers prowling around in search of somebaddy to pick up, a splendid example of Greek Revival architecture (the Old Mint) being used for little more than a pigeon roost, Tom Sawyerish kids washing a fire engine while the coffee-sipping firemen lounge against a wall, derelict buildings being torn down along Skid Road to leave the cold and homeless even colder and more homeless, fur-clad women huddling under umbrellas to peer at resort clothes in the downtown shopwindows . . . Golly, what a mixed-up place.

★ ★ ★

Two hundred people standing in a row at the Zoo to watch four Teddy-bears from Down Under chew dully on eucalyptus leaves, a cable car waiting in a lot at the foot of Hyde like a windup toy whose key has been lost, an $85,000-a-year baseball star searching in vain for an apartment to rent at any price, $7,000 cars parked outside all night because their owners' $500-a-month apartments have everything but garages, Coit Tower going dark at midnight because that's late enough now in the city that once stayed up all night . . . Jeepers, where do we go from here and what do we do next?

★ ★ ★

Crippled newsboys cheerily shouting the headlines of tragedies less poignant than theirs, bay-windowed beauties of the Western Addition disappearing to make room for concrete blockhouses that will solve the population explosion in explosions of monotony, Symphony musicians standing around the rear of the Opera House after a concert like kids with no place to go when school's out, at 6 p.m. the flowers hanging their heads in the sidewalk stands as though they know it's time to call it a day . . . Wow, so many bits and pieces of nothing and everything adding up to the whole which is equal to the sum of the encircled squares.

★ ★ ★

Jobless men killing time by watching afternoon shows designed for women in the window of a Market St. TV shop, a blind man humming a tune as he taps his way along Montgomery with a transistor radio plugged into his ear, a dear old lady (bedridden) living all alone in a 14-room Fairmont penthouse across the street from a mansion that was once her home, the world's greatest disc jockey doing his bit for culture by promoting a Haiku poetry contest whose winner will get a trip to Japan, ships from the seven seas neatly filed away for the night along the Embarcadero—their deck lights on as though afraid of the dark . . . Endless odds and ends of the endlessly odd wetropolis under the rainy skies of Drabuary.

★ ★ ★

Stone cold new Hall of Justice standing bare and square against the Freeway running wild with lawbreakers, little old Chinese lady teetering up the California St. hill on once-bound feet to feed bread crusts to the boundless seagulls, Sterling Hayden's romantic schooner lying tethered to the shores of Sausalito like a free soul brought back to earth, the sea lions back from their mating at last and sprawled in brown blobs on Seal Rocks—every now and then slithering into the icy water to escape the warm tourist stares from the Cliff House . . . Animal, vegetable, mineral in the soaring city built on stone and dredged-up dreams.

★ ★ ★

Well-clipped poodles walking well-polished chauffeurs along the well-manicured pathways of Lafayette Square, Beniamino Bufano doodling a pat of butter into a tiny masterpiece of a statue while

10

lunching at Veneto's, enchanted natives gazing with ah-struck eyes through the windows of Top o' the Mark while the visitors they've brought along glare around for a waiter, the Zellerbach building looking as delicately flimsy as a house of glass cards as it teeters on its stilts against its concretely staid neighbors, the old men of Union Square sitting rain-soaked on their benches with soggy newspapers over their heads and soggy squabs at their feet . . . Ah, Baghdad-by-the-Bay, where the living is easy for pigeons who get their Square meals from Union men.

★   ★   ★

A bored cashier yawning a gum-sticky yawn in the lobby of a Market St. movie palace festooned with photos of nude ladies who look even more bored, a Filipino barber on Kearny sawing away on his fiddle in the window as though to lure in a customer for a trimming, a few cars parked forlornly on the lot that once held the Montgomery Block's thousand priceless memories, dead seagulls strewn in nightmare profusion along Candlestick Seaway while their more fortunate mates hover in a ravenous cloud over the dumps lining the way to the magic city whose towers shine in the distance . . . Look away, look away from the death and debris— look ahead to the gates of Paradise.

★   ★   ★

The timelessly San Francisco smell—clean and right—of wet eucalyptus in the Presidio that guards the past, two jet fighters climbing fast into the murky sky to guard the present that is always tense, midnight lights burning high in the downtown skyscrapers as yesterday's trash is cleared away in readiness for the future that will soon rise out of the East Bay Hills . . . What a town. Gee, what a crazy town.

January 31, 1960

To My Valentine

It's not always easy to find new words to express an old love—and I have been in love with you for such a long time, and you have had so many expansive lovers. It may even be that I feel a twinge of jealousy: more and more admirers are flocking around you every year, pouring out their adulation, pledging undying loyalty—and all the while seeking the same favors your older lovers have known. It's not that we feel rejected. You seem to have as much time for us as ever—almost—and, like all good lovers, we are understanding; we know how much you have to do these days.

Perhaps it's just that we who have loved you longest feel we love you best, and of course this is nonsense. It is the last refuge of the possessive ones who can't help feeling annoyed that your line is busy so often now, that you find so many places to go without us.

And so we sit back in a graying line and watch you, not always happily. Sometimes you are daring and impetuous, the way we always loved you best, and then we are pleased. But too often you move slowly and with incertitude, as though you are indeed getting old—and we feel old along with you. However, that's the way it has always been for those who find you forever captivating; first the joyousness of spring on Twin Peaks, followed by the sudden plunge into the cold, foggy depths.

Neurotic? Schizoid? Can people in love with a city be anything else?

★ ★ ★

Of course (ah, the abject humility of the doomed admirer) I came along late in your bewitching game and am hardly qualified to raise a voice.

You have been loved all your life, perhaps too extravagantly. You became world famous when you were nothing but a precocious child. With a reckless charm and not much else, you played hostess to Kings and Queens—and they found you fair to look upon. It was all justified: when disaster struck, you faced the crisis with style and surprising determination—and your fame leaped higher than the flames that threatened to destroy you. Ravishing beauty plus boundless courage; it would be hard to imagine a more compelling combination in one so young.

And yet it's wryly amusing, perhaps even comforting, to recall that some of your most ardent lovers, even then, said you had changed, that you would never be the same carefree hoyden of old. They were right, of course, but it didn't matter in the long run: there were still no rivals in sight.

★ ★ ★

I can understand why you sometimes act bored, petulant, even a little spoiled. Only your sister in France has had so many articulate devotees. Twain, Harte, London, Norris, Kipling, Stevenson, Irwin, Burgess, Dana, Dobie, all laying their hearts at your feet. And Poet George Sterling—he loved you as well and passionately as any, and perhaps he had lost faith even in you the night he killed himself in the Bohemian Club. Romantic Sterling. Today you, the object of his most consuming fires, show not the slightest sign that

12

you even remember him. I know there have been other lovers, before and since, but surely none as dedicated as he.

★   ★   ★

Well, now I am sounding harsh—the righteous, foot-stomping old suitor who wants you to be always as perfect as you never were.

But it's hard to blot out the memories of our young love, when the skies were endlessly bright (of course, they weren't) and the nights were endlessly gay (I'm sure they were). I loved the glimpses of you from the ferries, the easy way you moved, the way you danced down the years, with laughter on your hills and sunshine splashing all golden and ripe across the soft, green meadows of the Park.

And I loved your way with people. No matter who they were or where they came from, you met them with the same level-eyed graciousness and made them feel welcome. You had time for them, then, and you worried about them. It worked wonderfully: they felt happy and wanted.

★   ★   ★

I know, I know—it's not quite that easy now, love, and perhaps we're as much to blame as you. So much to do, so little time, so many people—where do they all come from—running in and out, sometimes without even bothering to knock, and where are you going to put them? Feelings get hurt, injustices are inevitable and it's so easy to make excuses in an exploding world that you really weren't made for, now, were you?

And your old glittering, imperious appearance: you'll forgive me if I tell you your tiara is slightly askew, and it saddens me to see you improvising to keep your once impeccable wardrobe up to date. Throwing out so many beautiful, old things—are you sure they weren't good for a few more years? And buying so many ugly and expensive new things: oh, I know they're modern and up to date, but they look just like the modern, up-to-date things they're wearing everywhere else these days. They don't look like YOU.

It's hard to bear—your soft, easy, inimitable lines, corseted by freeways. And, darling, all that bridgework!

★   ★   ★

Ah me. What started out to be an unalloyed love letter has turned a little sour (blame it on my crotchety middle age), but, then, true love isn't necessarily blind and we love you still, through thick and sin, for bitter or words. And when your Bay is shining with time-lessness and the daphne blooms in secret gardens to herald the spring that waits around the corner—then we are young again

13

and certain, with the confidence of lost youth, that there is no better place to be in all the darkling world. *February 14, 1960*

As It Must to All Men

At 10 a.m. tomorrow—while you sit at your desk or lie in your bed, while you wash your dishes or pound your typewriter, while traffic rolls along the freeways and schoolchildren sit at their desk to learn about truth and justice and equality under the law—a 39-year-old man named Caryl Whittler Chessman will go to the gas chamber in San Quentin, there to be thrown roughly into a metal chair by nervous guards, there to be strapped in like an animal, there to sniff the poisonous fumes and writhe in agonized aloneness for a few eternal minutes, and then to be pronounced dead by competent medical authority.

All this will be done—if not tomorrow, at some future date—to satisfy you, dear citizen, to satisfy the conscience of the sovereign State of California, to demonstrate that Society strikes down its attackers, thereby re-emerging pure and undefiled. None of these things will happen, of course. You, for whose protection this savage rite is being conducted, will feel deeply troubled or indifferent, depending on your sensibilities. The Golden State will be less golden for having plunged again into the Dark Ages. And Society will be as corrupt and exposed as ever.

I have heard their voices and read their letters—the proponents of capital punishment who cry like the cold-eyed fanatics of old. "It must be done, it is written in the Bible, an eye for an eye." There is also something in the Bible about turning the other cheek, but no matter. Neither argument is tenable.

* * *

The man, Caryl Chessman, is no longer the issue; now he is the worldwide symbol of the farce that is capital punishment in California. Even those who thirst most avidly for his death are no longer quite clear about his crimes, nor do they care: all they know is that he has made a mockery of the law for 12 long years—thereby casting doubt into the hearts of all men—and this is inherently Bad. A man should be condemned and go quietly to his death, in orderly fashion. Consigned to the gas chamber under an hysterical law that now seems as archaic as the Iron Maiden (his crime has been duplicated scores of times, with no talk of the death penalty), he used other laws to fight a fantastic fight against fantastic odds.

14

A good part of the world seems to be on his side; instead of demanding his death to salve the conscience of Society, they are applauding, as people will, the battle of an underdog. A voluble Frenchman I met in Paris got tearful over what he considered the unfairness of it all. "Here this Chessman has been gambling with Death for 12 years," he said, "and he wins every hand, and then at the last minute he finds out the cards were stacked and the game was fixed. It is all a bad joke."

★ ★ ★

"Oh, well," a man said the other night as he chewed on a filet in a fashionable restaurant. "It's not the worst way to die. It's all over in a few seconds, and it's comparatively painless, they say." Not the worst way to die? Can you think of a worse way: to have the time and place scheduled for you, to be the star in a hideous sideshow before goggle-eyed witnesses, to die a meaningless death at the hands of a State seeking to cancel out a crime by committing another?

I saw my first executions when I was a kid police reporter on the *Sacramento Union*. Three, in fact. The State, not having yet achieved the ultimate in refinement, was hanging them then. On a hot summer day, I drove up to Folsom Prison to cover the hanging of a young man who, in the course of his first holdup, had lost his head and killed a storekeeper. I talked to him in his cell many times during the trial. He was sad, sick and scared. So was I.

"Don't worry, kid," the warden affably told me before the execution. "It's all over in a minute. Doesn't hurt a bit." I wondered how he knew.

We, the witnesses and press, stood nervously together on the cement floor of a big room, looking up at the gallows. The new rope, scientifically tested, dangled in the sunlight streaming through barred windows. Suddenly the door behind the scaffold swung open and the nightmare scene was enacted in a flash: the murderer, his arms bound, was hustled roughly onto the trapdoor, the noose was slammed around his neck, a black mask dropped over his unbelieving face, the trapdoor clanged open, the body shot through and stopped with a sickening crack. For an eternity, the victim twitched in spasm after spasm, and one by one the witnesses began fainting around me. "Doesn't hurt a bit," the warden had said. One eon later, a doctor placed his stethoscope to the body hanging limply before us and announced that justice had been done.

And from that day on, having been made properly aware of

the State's awful vengeance, no holdup man ever again killed a shopkeeper? You bet.

★ ★ ★

That, after all, is the purpose of capital punishment: to set an Example. And if this is so, why isn't it done properly? Why isn't Caryl Chessman gassed in the middle of Union Square at high noon, so that thousands of people (plus millions of TV viewers) can witness the fate of wrongdoers and vow, then and there, never to step outside the law. But no, that would be an indecent spectacle, abhorrent to those who prefer to live by euphemisms. He must be done away with in a gloomy little room, surrounded by a protective nest of walls, before the eyes of a few select witnesses—as though the act itself, the final demonstration of the majesty of the law, were some dark and dreadful thing. And a dark and dreadful thing it is.   *May 1, 1960*

THE RESTLESS CITY

The light is eerie at midnight along O'Farrell, in the devastation and desolation of the Western Addition. A feathery film of fog floats endlessly across the moon, and the tough old city cats prowl through the shifting shadows, picking their padded way in and out of craters, over the rubble, between the skeletal trees. There is an icy silence, as of death.

★ ★ ★

The wreckers, with their swinging steel balls and their flailing axes, have done their job well. For block after block, the ground has been cleared: Berlin, during World War II, looked this way after the last bomber had vanished into the West. Here and there, a house still stands—looking slightly dazed, through broken windows.

The dark side of the moon: you stand on the edge of the emptiness and try to remember all the wonders and monstrosities that stood there—the sagging wooden steps, the stoops, the stained-glass windows and the bays, the quatrefoils, the dormers, the carved pillars, all the intricate gimcracks and gewgaws of Carpenter Gothic that gave a face to a city's golden age.

You poke around among the ruins, like a veteran home from the wars to find his home obliterated. A trace of foundation, the outlines of what must have once been soft green gardens surrounded by wooden fences, where people long gone sat and smiled

16

up proudly at their ornate new houses.

Well, it doesn't much matter. Soon even these traces will be gone, buried under row upon row of concrete blockhouses where life will be neat, orderly, square, efficient and electronic. New trees will be planted, looking sterile and anemic. There will be new lawn, sparse and pale. And many children, all looking oddly alike.

★   ★   ★

Midnight, in the wasteland of the Western Addition. Two blocks over, you can see the bright lights of Post St. with its jazz joints and barbecue pits, looking like the main street of a small Western town. And farther up the hill, the soft golden haze of Pacific Heights, its big houses, rich and secure; death for them is still a generation away.

At the corner of Franklin, a tall palm tree still stands, spared by the wreckers in some fit of sentimentality. Tired and old, it droops slightly over the street that once was the most stylish in town, as though mourning the mansions that died around it. And a block away, the revolving sign of the Jack Tar Hotel whirls merrily—the garish shape of things to come.

★   ★   ★

Well, there's no use crying over spilt milk, especially when it has turned sour. San Francisco's Victorian Age is over—bad riddance to the good parquetry, the brass chandeliers, the high ceilings, the iron gates. The city, despite its desperate clutch on the past, has moved up another notch in history.

Lately, I have been looking at the old downtown apartment houses with new and symbolic eyes. Now that all but a few of the boarded ancients have been destroyed, they are next in line. One by one, in the years to come, they will be tumbled down, and with them will go tumbling a whole new set of memories.

San Francisco's downtown apartments are unique. No other city has so many, clustered together in one area, looking as though they were designed by the same architect, all of a piece and era. They reek, some literally, of the tasteless Twenties, with their decorated stucco, their ironwork doors, their tile lobbies, their fluted columns, their vaguely Spanish influence (Spanish was very big in the Twenties, Heaven knows why).

And yet, I'll miss them, too, when they are finally gone. For the Typical San Francisco Apartment House has played a part in all our lives—and there will be nothing quite like it again.

★   ★   ★

If you lived in one, you lived in them all. Every man Jack among

17

us had a girl who lived in one at some stage of his love life. Rich and married lawyers kept (and still keep) their girls there. During Prohibition, they housed speakeasies. After Prohibition, they contained after hours (or after ours) joints. When the town was open, bookies and madams operated there. Widows, bachelors, young newlyweds, the whole Sanfrantasmagoria living cheek by jowl by howl by the skin of their teeth, trading cups of sugar (or marijuana) over the back stoops, above the garbage cans in the concrete court.

The old apartment houses, all smelling alike: cabbage, even when it isn't cabbage. The elevator creaking and swaying as it rises, with many a frightening click. The dimly lit halls with the drab, patterned carpet of indeterminate hue. The doors, each with a tiny peephole (Swordfish!). And the apartments themselves. You could walk through each one blindfolded and never stumble across a stick of furniture, so many times have you seen it all: the mousey sofa, the easy chair with the crocheted antimacassar, the pseudo Oriental rug, the footstool (one leg loose), the hexagonal coffee table (two burns), the slight smell of gas from the leaky kitchen stove. And the cracked plastic radio, held together with adhesive.

This is San Francisco, too—a big, stucco slice of it, of what we were and what we are. When the bell tolls at last for the old apartments, the planners will watch the carnage unmoved, and a lot of you will say "Good riddance," as you said good riddance to the Victorians.

But where then shall we look for the vanishing roots of a city? *September 25, 1960*

1 9 6 1

★ ★ ★

THINGS COULD BE WORSE, BABY

Mr. Kennedy promises us the American equivalent of blood, sweat and tears, the cost of living hits a new record high (hardly anybody can afford to die), and your favorite speculative stock hits a new low—but on a fine February day, with the wind and the fog (and soon the Income Tax Man) in your hair, who gives a fig for all that? I prefer to think about:

★ ★ ★

The girls with the beautiful legs sitting sidesaddle on the Powell cable, their skirts just above their knees;

Dollar-size pancakes with melted butter and hot syrup at the airport's Pancake Palace a few minutes before your jet takes off;

The expectant, absolutely palpable hush in the Opera House in the split second of eternity before Maestro Enrique Jorda gives the downbeat;

The first kids of a premature spring playing catch in Alta Plaza, reminding you that football is finally dead (long live McElhenny the King) and that baseball (the game for people who never grew up) is again on its lumbering way (ah, to be in England, now that Mays is here!);

Pink blossoms on the confused trees that, like all San Francisco, can't tell one season from another.

★ ★ ★

It's a drear, drab world—if the bomb blast don't getcha, the radiation must—but meanwhile, there's always:

Saturday lunch at Jack's, where (the weekday pressure off) it's perfectly okay to dawdle for three hours over your second bottle

19

of Chateau Magdeleine;

The good wood and leather smell of Brooks Bros.—like the interior of a new Jaguar;

The North Beach character who wears a campaign hat turned up on one side (like Teddy Roosevelt's) and marches proudly down Stockton St. to the beat of invisible drums;

Strolling alone through the damp eucalyptus smell of Golden Gate Park, feeling that the city is a million miles away and all the while knowing (with a secret, pleasant smile) that it isn't;

Searchlights waving their skinny white arms through the fog-banked night, in frantic counterpoint to the serene blinking of the bridge towers.

★　★　★

Headlines, breadlines, schmedlines—it's still these little things, and they count:

Al Trobbe's foot poundin' piano beat at 6 p.m. (and your first drink) in the Fairmont's Cirque Room;

The old-time candy store next to the Larkin Theater, everything in bulk and on display in proper glass jars. A sample? Of course;

The King Sisters, still singing loud and clear (and modern) after all these 25 years of keeping up with the times;

The old waiters who serve you lunch only if they're in the mood—in the Happy Valley, the last un-Sheratonized corner of the Palace;

The Ralph Stackpole statues in front of the Stock Exchange, reminding you that Big Business, in the proper mood, CAN give a bohemian artist a big job to do well;

The mournful midnight blast of a ship as it heads into the well-worn stream that leads through the Golden Gate to High Adventure; your mind's eye can see its white wake as it clears Fort Point and disappears, gathering speed.

★　★　★

You take the crises and I'll take:

The crazy cruise clothes (even if you're not going anywhere) in the downtown show windows;

The late movies on TV, especially when they're "For Whom the Bell Tolls" (and was there ever a smile like the young Ingrid Bergman's?);

The dental nurses rushing out of 450 Sutter to lunch, their white uniforms showing beneath their coats—and looking oddly sexy (considering their sensible shoes and thick stockings);

The tourists lined up at the velvet rope in El Prado while the regulars squeeze past, make a wide swing around the barrier (this is the way the Nazis turned the Maginot Line) and settle down at the tables the tourists are waiting for (you have to Know Your Way Around, especially Around);

Union Oil's pastel storage tanks dotting the otherwise drab countryside on Highway 40 near Richmond—the kind of public relations you'd like to be related to;

The patient, fatherly voice of the cop in the loudspeaker car warning the jaywalking ladies not to do what he knows dambwell they're going to do the second he turns the corner.

★ ★ ★

Being a big city hick, I still get a kick out of:

A young girl getting her first orchid at a sidewalk flower stand (how soon she'll outgrow the thrill, but now—);

The adroit way Maitre d'Hotel Bill Coleman shuffles the patrons at Trader Vic's—never (well, hardly ever) placing a guy next to his ex-wife, or a married couple alongside the lover everybody knows about except the husband;

Dick Hadlock's superlative discourses on the wandering roots of jazz on KJAZ—a program that never hits a clinker;

The clatter of the streetcars as they circle at the Trans-Bay Terminal, a distant echo (but an echo all the same) of the Roar of the Four around the long-gone Ferry Building loop;

Silly cartoons like the one showing a Princess gazing in horror at the big and ugly frog in her bed at daybreak and gasping, "But you said you'd be a Prince in the morning!"

The real estate firm of Hogan & Vest at Stockton and Washington in the heart of Chinatown—is this where East meets Vest in this city of laughter on the hills?   *February 5, 1961*

THE SAN FRANCISCANS

"San Francisco," I wrote some time back, "is like a club that isn't quite as exclusive as it used to be"—a statement that seemed to me more sadly obvious than explosive. (I can always tell when I have written something likely to backfire. As I hit the period, the typewriter starts jiggling, the ribbon turns red and bursts into flame, and the shift key begins dancing up and down like a mad thing.)

As I say, the statement didn't seem particularly offensive, but the mail that followed it was—highly. "You are a typical San Francisco snob," wrote a splenetic Sunset District housewife. "You don't think anybody is capable of appreciating the city except you old-timers who can't look in any direction but back." A gentleman with an educated hand, writing on embossed Bohemian Club stationery, noted a bit more evenly: "Only a Sacramento boy—the operative word is Sacramento, not boy—could write so naively about San Francisco. It's too bad you can't take the city in stride. You are obsessed with socialites, Pacific Heights and Rolls-Royces in your efforts to make San Francisco something it never was."

A third letter was more succinct. "San Francisco stopped being exclusive," said the anonymous vilifier, "when we let YOU in." Touché!

★　★　★

Like most people, I enjoy getting any kind of mail that doesn't turn out to be a bill, even when it's abusive and aside from the point. But then, maybe the point wasn't quite as obvious as I'd intended it to be, if it could bring charges of snobbery, naivete and a self-propelled lowering of values.

I remember writing once that "When I hear a Texan and a Chinese in conversation, it's the Texan who sounds like a foreigner." I consider that a valid statement that could be called snobbish only in Dallas or Houston, and, being a San Franciscan, I don't care WHAT they think there. The cadences of the Chinese, and their celestial presence, have been a part of the atmosphere since the city's Year One. The Texas drawl is comparatively recent, but, I hasten to add, that isn't the point, either.

I don't think that place of origin or number of years on the scene have anything to do with it, really. There are newcomers who become San Franciscans overnight—delighted with and interested in the city's traditions and history. They can see the Ferry Building for what it represents (not for what it is), they are fascinated with the sagas of Sharons, Ralstons, Floods and Crockers, they savor the uniqueness of cable car and foghorn.

By the same token, I know natives who will never be San Franciscans if they outlive Methuselah. To them a cable car is a traffic obstruction, the fog is something that keeps them from getting a tan, and Los Angeles is where they really know how to Get Things Done. A native San Franciscan who prides himself that his family has been in the real estate business here for three generations placed an avuncular hand on my knee one recent night and asked, "My boy, why do you take off on buildings like the Jack Tar? You can't stop things like that. It's new. It's modern. It's progress."

I don't object to the Jack Tar as such. I can think of a dozen cities where it would look right at home. Here—well, do you carry a plastic handbag with a sable coat? And speaking of native San Franciscans, a man who signed himself just that way wrote after I seconded a suggestion that the Embarcadero Freeway be torn down: "Far as I'm concerned, they can tear down the Ferry Building and COVER the city with freeways."

That day will come, old man, along with the leveling of the hills and the filling in of the Bay, and we will be indistinguishable from Peoria.

★　★　★

The San Franciscan, I submit, is anything but a snob. He is clannish, yes, but only about his city—every facet of it that delights him. In the old days, he was equally at home in the free-lunch counters of Market St., in Eddie Graney's billiard palace, at the Old Poodle Dog, and in Mrs. Spreckels' big house. He knew Jim Corbett and John L. Sullivan and Oofty-Goofty and Will Tevis, and greeted them all as equals in the egalitarian city. In a later manifestation he could hang out at the Black Cat or Izzy's and feel at ease in Anita Zabala Howard's drawing room.

Today he wears a sweater to Enrico's, a proper suit and vest to the Palace's Happy Valley, black tie to the Museum and tails to the Opera—and knows the best place in Chinatown to get jook, too. He realizes San Francisco has grown larger and stranger and away from itself, dividing into groups that are afraid to stray into the city's unbeaten paths, and for them he can feel only sorrow.

They are missing the far ranging excitement of being a San Franciscan who'd rather look at the Ghirardelli tower than the Jack Tar.

★　★　★

The other midnight, in a Chinatown bar, I met a real San Franciscan. He was a middle-aged longshoreman from the Mission, and he wore a zipper jacket and open shirt. While he quietly sipped a Scotch, he talked of Harry Bridges, Bill Saroyan and Shanty Malone. He was curious about Leontyne Price and Herbert Gold. He wondered if the Duke of Bedford's paintings were any good, he missed Brubeck, and he discussed Willie Mays down to his last spike. He seemed to know everybody in town, by first names—and it was only after he'd left that we discovered he'd bought a round of drinks for the house. For want of a better phrase, he had that touch of class—the touch of a San Franciscan.

March 12, 1961

23

1962

Cloak & dagger: Barnaby Conrad is back from his perilous one-week mission to the French Riviera, understandably done in but reasonably successful. His assignment, if you recall the preceding episodes, was to seek out Pablo Picasso and get his approval for a Picasso sweatshirt to be produced by the S.F. advertising firm of Weiner & Gossage, which first foisted or foist firsted Beethoven sweatshirts on an unsuspecting world.

Conrad never did get to see Picasso in person, for, as ill luck would have it, Picasso's Riviera houseguest at the time was Matador Luis Miguel Dominguin—and Dominguin has hated Barnaby ever since the publication of "Matador." In this novel Conrad makes Dominguin the villain mainly responsible for the death of Manolete. "I will not have that louse in this house," Dominguin is reported to have said, more or less, in reptilian Castilian.

However, Picasso's agents in Paris and New York approved the sweatshirt deal, in return for twice as much money as Weiner & Gossage were first prepared to pay. "You must understand," one of the agents said, "that Senor Picasso is interested in only three things—money, money and money. Along with his personal responsibilities—wife, ex-wives, children—he still contributes heavily to the Communist Party."

Capitalists, arise! Throw off your Picasso sweatshirts!

★ ★ ★

Proud beauties: The best thing about the Golden Gate Bridge's 25th birthday party Sunday, under blustery skies, was the parade of old automobiles. How handsome and distinguished they looked, these creations of an American pride of workmanship and design that has largely disappeared under the leveling pressure of a mass market.

There were Packards with hoods a block long and noble prows that seem to have gained in dignity through the years. There were Pierce-Arrows, their fenders blossoming into headlights, their tall radiators adorned with a lithe goddess of the chase. Wire-wheeled Cadillac tourers with huge headlamps, wide running board and side mounts. Graceful La Salles with narrow, sensitive noses. Old Buicks with sloping radiators and a dozen distinguishing touches. Even after all these years you could identify each one at a glance — and each one, from the standpoint of design and integrity, could hold its own with the dozen or so old Rolls-Royces in the parade.

As the beauties moved slowly along the outside lane, dowager-proud, the lookalike monsters of today sped past them, filled with lookalike families laughing, pointing fingers and poking fun. From a coldly scientific standpoint, I don't know whether you can tell anything about a generation by its conveyances, but if you can, the story was all too clear last Sunday.

I will have to cast my vote for the era that produced the Golden Gate Bridge — and the ravishing cars that matched it for vision and daring. *May 29, 1962*

SMOGVILLE-BY-THE-BAY

Today I'm going to write about the heat—as a public service. As soon as this edition of the Old Chron hits the streets, the foghorns will start blowing and all will be well again in this coolest of all summer worlds. It never fails. Don't ask me why. When I write one of those drippy things about the mist slithering through the eucalypti, and ships crying to each other like lost children, you can be sure that by the time the paper is out, the thermometer will be up around 100. Conversely, same thing. As a tribal rite, it's a better bet than washing your car to bring on the rain.

* * *

Yesterday morning, the smog was up before anybody else (does it all come from whatever the hell they keep burning on Treasure Island?). Steam rose from Coit Tower—the concrete silo where they keep the brown gravy that is piped by gravity to all the restaurants in North Beach. A ship was ploughing sluggishly across the hot Bay, leaving no more wake than a crouton in a bowl of lentil soup. The aroma from the Coffee Belt was so thick you could stir it with a spoon (do the cons on Alcatraz have to stir their coffee with their fingers these days?). The flags on the skyscraper roofs dropped listlessly against their staffs, and you could only hope they were drip-dry and colorfast. Downtown, everybody was wearing dark glasses, like celebrities who hoped to be recognized. Now we know why those three guys escaped The Rock. They were getting away from the heat.

★ ★ ★

"It's those damn H-bomb tests," said the perspiring bartender at Mike's Place. "It's changing the weather. I've lived here all my life, and it never used to be like this. Another thing, I'm tired of making lemonades. I've squeezed more lemons today than Betty Crocker in a cake contest."

I thought about that as I sipped my citron. On a hot day, I catch myself remembering "The Day the Earth Caught Fire," that fine English movie about the H-bomb tests knocking the earth off its axis, or something, and it gets so hot nobody can stand it, and pretty soon, curtains. That's why I'm always reassured when I read "It was the hottest day since 1887" or the coldest day since the blizzard of '88, and so forth.

Actually, the hottest day in S.F. (101.2) occurred on Sept. 16, 1913, and the second hottest (101) on Sept. 8, 1904, and heck, they were still fighting with crossbows back then. As the man once said about all the illegal goings-on in this "closed" town, "It ain't the heat, it's the cupidity."

★ ★ ★

If you're about my age, give or take a few lies, you might remember The Great Heat Wave of 1939. There's an old wives' tale in this town—started by a then young wife—that after three hot days the fog always comes in, but back in September, '39, the fog didn't come in for 12 long, steaming days. It was awful. In Chinatown, the people were sleeping on their fire escapes, and the Marina Green was covered with mattresses covered with groaning couples, many of them married. A nut in a sandwich board walked around hollering "The world will end tomorrow!" Everybody hoped he was right.

After about the 10th day of this misery, Mayor Angelo Rossi did an amazing thing. He declared a holiday—"as a humanitarian," he said. "Besides," he added off the record, "I don't feel like working

26

either." He closed the City Hall and told the kids they didn't have to go to school till it got cooler (cheers). Wily old Angelo happened to be in the middle of a hot re-election fight against Franck Havenner, and there's no telling how many votes this got him. He won by only a few thousand, many of them cast by the parents of schoolchildren wearing "Rossi for President" buttons.

Of course, it should be remembered that San Franciscans didn't know how to handle the heat in those benighted days. The women wore furs, come what may or June, and the men wouldn't be caught dead outside of a tweed suit, preferring to be caught dead in one. And the Man Least Likely to Succeed in S.F. was an air-conditioner salesman. Many were thrown out of windows by irate old gaffers, wearing vests and spats and thundering: "By Gad, sir, don't you know this is the city air-conditioned by God, by Gad?"

* * *

These days life goes on, swelter-skelter, and anyway, George Christopher doesn't strike me as the kind of guy who'd give you a day off just because it's hot. After all, he's a "progressive conservative," unquote, which must keep him going around in circles faster than an electric fan. "The best dressed women in the world," also unquote, don't mind being seen downtown in little white dresses, as long as they're wearing their little white gloves as a concession to the legend, and the men drive around in shirt-sleeves, their jackets hanging from the hook over the back seat, looking square.

The day's finest example of sartorial non-conformity was supplied by a woman who strode into United Air Lines' Postreet office to pick up a ticket. She was wearing a mink stole, sweatshirt, walking shorts, tennis shoes and no socks. Coke Infante, the leader of the North Beach kookpack, was also wearing shorts, plus hiking boots. Ken Crane, a Foremost Dairies milkman, made his deliveries in spotless white Bermudas.

However, let's be fair to warmer. Not everybody hates the heat. Yesterday morn a visitor walked out of the Palace Hotel in full tourist uniform—seersucker suit, sandals, straw hat, bandolier of cameras—and stood for a moment on Market, sniffing the hot air. "My," he beamed to his haltered wife, "isn't this just WONDERFUL?" I could've killed him.

* * *

I think I just heard a foghorn.   *June 21, 1962*

27

FINGERNAIL ON THUMB

I don't know what you did on Labor Day, but I sat and stared at the map.

It hangs on the wall above my typewriter—a large, yellow-and-blue, official-looking map of San Francisco executed by W. Elliott Judge, the cartographer. Yellow for land, blue for water, two arbitrary colors, and let us put the cartographer before the horse-laugh, for on this Labor Day morning, gray is the color of my true love. Mourning fog near the ocean, and are we not at all times near the ocean?

Every morning for the last 14 years, at least, I have sat and stared at this map while waiting for ideas that seldom come. It is as familiar to me as the back of my hand, which is even more precise than most cliches, for one of the earliest descriptions of San Francisco suggested that you think of the Peninsula as a thumb, and the city as the fingernail . . .

Of your right hand, of course.

★   ★   ★

A good map, and this is a good one, is a fetching piece of work, as impartial as the stars. It tells you everything, and nothing. Scales, grids, coordinates, compass (bold arrow pointing North), intersections, elevations, tunnels, parks in swatches of green: a city laid flat and bare, without comment. With this excellent map unrolled before you, skipper of the chartered streets, you would never get lost and never find anything. A cartographer is not concerned with the soul of the city.

★   ★   ★

This jagged fingernail, this tiny tip of a miniscule Peninsula, this boundless tightly bound world—the map reminds you how small it is without so much as suggesting how much it contains. Here a duel was fought, there a man was hanged, down the street a fortune was made, and off that shore an empire builder drowned, his empire having vanished into the even murkier depths of high finance . . . but the map is not interested in these things, being only a skeleton. It is up to you to flesh it out.

There is, however, deadpan humor in a map. At eye-level, my map shows me De Boom St., and every morning I ask the same question. Is there a Lower De Boom? Does a Casey live on it? There is a Hyde but no Jekyll, and why is that, since Jekyll was the respectable and respected? The stranger may locate Drumm without knowing there's a Fife Building on it, and if he did, he would think it a gag, whereas the building honors a person named Fife. There are no treats on Treat, De Long is short but Short is shorter. And Broad is narrow.

The hollowest joke of all, of course, is the mean slash of Market St., the obtuse angle that no traffic plan can ever solve. A pioneer engineer named Jasper O'Farrell laid it out, naming it for Philadelphia's Market St. He selected a less controversial street to bear his own name, a street that runs straight and true and gets in nobody's way.

★   ★   ★

San Francisco, a neat thumbnail, well-kept except for the snaggle-toothed piers along the Embarcadero, odd-numbered North of the Ferry Building, even-numbered South, and then on down the clean cuts of China Basin and Islais Creek, just above India Basin. More jokes there. If somebody asks you to meet him at the corner of India and Contra Costa, don't do it unless you're wearing a diving suit. An underwater city exists in that area, its streets already named, awaiting only the dredges to bring it to life.

★   ★   ★

The map makes no comment, but the street names tell their story nevertheless. The early ones honored contemporary heroes, as they should have—the city was young and proud. Then the Presidents found their way onto the signs—the city was patriotic. Streets were named after those in the great cities of the East (Broadway, Chestnut, Walnut)—San Francisco longed for respectability. Popular and easy-living ladies were immortalized in shady alleys (Jessie, Clara, Annie)—the city didn't give a hoot for respectability.

Now the city had an international reputation, and it paid homage to its exalted sisters. A nest of streets was born far out in the Mission: London, Paris, Lisbon, Madrid, Prague, Munich and even Moscow, which intersects with Russia. Of all the Nation's metropolises, only Chicago and Baltimore seem to have made good, dangerously close to the San Mateo line. Naturally, there is no Los Angeles Ave., but there is a Hollywood. Movies are universal.

Perhaps the city was growing too big and impersonal. The Ingleside District, being young and friendly, picked some first names: Harold Ave., Lee Ave., Vernon, Randolph and Jules. Jules? A Frenchman in the Ingleside, so far from his native soil. World War I was ignored, World War II is still being fought in the streets near Mission and Amazon: Cassino, Kasserine, Moselle, Rapido, Ploesti—tough campaigns with heavy losses. The Admirals are remembered at Hunters Point: King and Nimitz. And in the Bay View District, those faraway places with strange-sounding names, where GIs never expected to fight, broil, freeze and die: Guam, Kiska, Attu.

★ ★ ★

The city's most popular Mayor, Jimmy Rolph, is there on the map. He runs into Lapham, who runs into Robinson, and can Christopher be far behind? Somebody in the Sunset had a bright idea: naming streets in alphabetical order (Kirkham, Lawton, Moraga, Noriega and so on). Somebody across the city followed suit (Armstrong, Bancroft, Carroll, Donner, Egbert). Egbert? I say! Urbano Drive, being oval, looks like a racetrack, and it was: Ingleside Track. And if a big city is one in which the street called Main is not the main street, San Francisco qualifies.

. . . . And so, on Labor Day, I sit and stare at the map, knowing that it contains an awful truth. Too much for a book, not enough for a column. *September 4, 1962*

WORLD SERIES

Well, folks, it was just another ball game. Except that all around the place people were lighting the wrong ends of their filter-tip cigarettes. And squirting mustard on their popcorn. And drinking beer through soda straws. And stepping into phone booths when the call they had to make was in the men's room. Yes, it was just another ball game, except that it happened to be the first game of the first World Series ever played in San Francisco, and so many people were hollering "Kill those Yankees!" you'd have thought you were in Oxford, Miss., instead.

★ ★ ★

Even Candlestick Park, which sometimes gives the uncomfortable impression that a giant had taken the Embarcadero Freeway and bent it into a horseshoe, looked brighter than usual. Flags, banners and splashy clothes on the overflow crowd, which included both people and politicians, gave the place the touches of color it too often lacks. The sun was shining, but the predominant color was gray—the Yankee gray that has given so many teams the blues. The Yanks have twice as many prima donnas as the S.F. Opera Co. and more polish than Shreve's, and yet they deliver. United Parcel should do so good.

★ ★ ★

I was surprised the day dawned at all, after the rioting and booz-
ing of the night before, but dawn it did, with many fascinations.
There hasn't been so much bloody scalping since General Custer
was a buck private. A guy outside the Palace was unashamedly asking $100 per ticket, and getting it. The champ was a feller who sold
four reserved (not box) seats for $720 to a sucker from N.Y. who
was happy to pay the $180 per. The sucker had a big bet on the
Yankees and came out ahead anyway. During the morning hours
cab drivers were getting rich. By game time several were seen pric-
ing real estate in the financial district.

★ ★ ★

It was a hard game to get into, unless you were Mickey Mantle or
Willie Mays (Orlando Cepeda should have paid his way), and yet
a lot of people were there who obviously had never been to a
Giants' game before. The lady in front of me kept pronouncing
Kuenn as "Coon," and a city official who shall be nameless had to
read the numbers off the scoreboard and consult his program
before he knew which Giant was at bat. The gates were clogged
with ticketless characters listening on their transistors—"I wanted
to get as close as I could," one of them said, touchingly. Half the
people inside were listening to transistors, too, to make sure who
was playing. Like music lovers at the opera's opening night, baseball lovers at a World Series game are rare.

★ ★ ★

The Yankees beat the Giants, but it was baseball that shut out the
world. The only way Cuba and Berlin could have crossed anybody's
mind would have been if the Giants sent up a pinch-hitter named
Felipe Cuba, and if the Yanks had a Whitey Berlin warming up.
Market St. looked emptier than Chavez Ravine. H. Liebes' had a
color TV set on every floor. Saks Fifth Ave. excused every employee
who had even a grandmother going to the game. The Bit of Paradise at 61 First St. had five TV sets around the room, and one in
the men's room. What makes this an item is that the place is owned
by Bernard Mirandette, a Basque, who knows only one thing about
baseball, and that's that he doesn't know anything about baseball
except that he hates it.

★ ★ ★

Chinn Ho, the Chinese millionaire who owns everything in Hawaii
that Henry Kaiser doesn't, flew in from Honolulu with orchid leis
for everybody who wasn't smoking a cigar. Lyndon Johnson, who
happens to be the Vice-President of the U.S., covered the game
briefly from a helicopter (one Oakland moneybags tried to hire

31

an SF-Oakland Helicopter to hover over the ENTIRE game, and was turned down). John Parsons, gen. mgr. of the Mark Hopkins, found himself with two extra tickets in the morning, pondered a while, and then gave them to the houseman-janitor, Marcellus Givson. Any man who would do that probably likes dogs and children, too, and can't be all good.

★　★　★

New York's Aly Cohn, Horace Stoneham's best friend, packed his bags Wednesday, went out to N.Y.'s Idlewild Airport and watched the final Giants-Dodgers playoff game on a TV set there. Clutched in his hand were two airline tickets—one for L.A., one for San Francisco. At the end of the ninth he ran for the S.F. plane, sobbing happily and crazily. In his abandoned joy he tore up the L.A. ticket, good for a refund, and used it for confetti. Meanwhile, the teletype between Macy's N.Y. and Macy's S.F. was crackling. David Yunich, President of Macy's there, made a bet (a matched set of golf clubs) with Ernie Molloy, President of Macy's California, and Yunich, the winner, couldn't keep from heckling the loser inning by inning.

★　★　★

Still and all, the Giants looked great during the first few innings. "Yankee, Go Home!" was hollered 11,987 times in 30 minutes by 11,987 wits. After Whitey Ford was nicked for two runs, Nick Geracimos hollered, "Ford is washed up!" Which is natural, since Nick sells Chevies. Mugsy Spanier, the noted Dixieland trumpeter, insisted, "I'm the best baseball fan here. I can tell you the names of the 1919 Chicago Black Sox, where they played and how much they got." And the girls at College of the Holy Names in Oakland called to report that Giants Hall is the name of their dormitory, replacing Durocher Hall—named not for Leo but for (Sister) Mother Marie Rose Durocher.

★　★　★

The cry around here used to be "Wait till next year!" Now it's "Wait till tomorrow," which is today when we'll tie it up or drop two behind. You could bet on it. *October 5, 1962*

Aftermath—What?

The town seemed strange and silent yesterday. "Back to normal," commented Honest John Gehring, the good cop at Five and Mission, but was it? After the longest baseball season in history, and one of the longest World Series, it was eerie not to hear the transistors crackling away, up and down the streets. The TV sets in lobbies and bars looked blank and sullen; they had enjoyed being the center of attention for so long, too.

★ ★ ★

It was hard to remember what life had been like in the old days. What did people do then, what did they talk about? It might be true that there's nothing deader than a season, the day after it's over, but the whole city had lived with it so long. Yesterday all was emptiness and letdown. The tension was gone, the air was out of the balloon, even the hills seemed flat.

But surely there is more to life than a baseball season, even one that had risen to fictional heights and had left its mark on everybody in town, whether they wanted to be marked by it or not.

Before all the strange madness began, our little world had been full of a number of things. Hadn't it? There was Cuba and Berlin and Vietnam and "Oliver!" and the opera season and even that business between—let me see, oh yes—Pat Brown and—uh—Dick Nixon? Well, they are still with us, it seems, now that the sports are back in the sports sections, but it will take a while to get readjusted.

★ ★ ★

After the last out of the last game of the Series on that crackling clear Tuesday afternoon, a man stood up in his box and cried out in agony: "It's all over! What'll I do tomorrow?"

There must be something left to finish out a life. There's the United Crusade and the fight to save Twin Peaks from the outdoor desecrators, and the restoration of the Palace of Fine Arts, and the Muni's 50th anniversary celebration (ride the iron monster) and even the 49ers, who play something called football and seem to be getting better at it. There's Harry Bridges versus Fred Schwarz, and the gripping new book by Eugene Burdick and Harvey Wheeler, "Fail-Safe"—a book that'll keep you up late nights till you finish it.

There are other seasons than baseball season. The opera season is still on and the ballet season begins tonight—the great Bolshois from the Land of the Bolsheviks, at the Fox Theater, and we will find out whether the Fox is worth saving.

★ ★ ★

All these things are eminently worthwhile, and certainly as important as baseball, which, in the deathless words of F. Scott Fitzgerald, is nothing more than "a child's game played by a few dozen

33

illiterates," after all. Isn't that so?

Then why in our childish, illiterate way does one's mind keep going back to that Tuesday afternoon, with the skies a startled blue, the pennants snapping in a lip-cracking North wind, and 44,000 childish illiterates huddled together as one? When one should be thinking of young Mr. Kennedy or, at the very least, Maya Plisetskaya, why does one recall Tom Tresh's fabulous catch, Willie McCovey's great-hearted hitting, Willie Mays' perfect shot to the right-field corner, the failure of Felipe Alou and Hiller to lay down the all-important bunt in the ninth, Jack Sanford's cardinal sin that cost him the game (he walked the opposing pitcher)?

I can't explain it. F. Scott Fitzgerald, a serious man who came to grips with serious problems, never could have explained it, either.

★　★　★

Those pictures you sometimes see in the papers of grown-up people actually crying after their team loses a game or a pennant or a Series or whatever—well, I used to think most of 'em were fakes, too. You and I, being skeptics if not cynics, know better than that. Grown people don't cry over something so trivial, so meaningless.

That's what I thought till late Tuesday afternoon, but here were all these people at Candlestick, actually sobbing. Tears running down their cheeks. Not just the women, either. Women go to the tear ducts fast and easy, like a 6–4–3 double play. These were grown men, crying. Even little Billy Pearson, the pint-sized ex-jockey, was blubbering. "Anything I can't stand," said Jimmy Buffa, "is to see a half-grown man crying."

A lot of other things went on. Take poor Charlie Stuart Jr., advertising boss of Bank of America. In the fourth inning he was hit just over the right eye by a Roger Maris foul ball and is in St. Mary's Hospital for three days with stitches and slight concussion, besides which he lost 10 bucks on the game. Ralph Terry of the Yankees pitched so well that all the hypocrites in the stands gave him a hand on his last turn at bat—"but," pointed out Ardath Borba, "only hypocrites get World Series tickets." Which is true. Even Don Sherwood, who hates baseball because it's beyond him, was there.

Mickey Mantle was playing so deep for McCovey that Del Courtney offered him a seat in his band, stationed in center field. At the Old Clam House on Old Bayshore, one of the finest old-time saloons in town, a disgruntled Giant fan kept playing Danny Kaye's "Dodgers Song" on the juke box till he almost got kilt. At

Imperial Palace in Chinatown, a mob of Chinese fans were rooting wildly ("Today," explained owner Kee Joon, "we are scrutable"). At game's end Grace Cathedral's carillon tolled a death-slow funeral march. And at midnight Willie McCovey was sadly sipping a ginger ale at Pack's, while Duke Ellington's band rose to salute him with one of Duke's classics, "You Hit It Good, and That Ain't Bad."

★   ★   ★

Now let's forget the whole thing and settle down to the business at hand, wherever it is. But first let's look at the whole instead of the doughnut: over the seven games, the Giants scored 21 runs, the Yankees only 20. And another thing. . . .   *October 18, 1962*

THE VERTICAL EARTHQUAKE

Henry Park has invented a parlor game—fun for young and old alike—called City Planning. The equipment is relatively simple and any number can play. All you need is a grid map of San Francisco (with numbered co-ordinates), crayons in various colors, and a dice box.

The player who wins the toss rolls the dice, locates the corresponding co-ordinates on the map, and "destroys" or "improves" that square with his crayon. If he colors a beloved landmark, such as the Palace of Fine Arts, he gets 10 points. A theater—the Fox, for instance—is worth 9 points. If the numbers he rolls fail to intersect, he may draw a freeway—15 points—between two spots and pick up any number of points in between, depending on the buildings in his path (a pre-1906 house is worth 5 points, as is a restaurant where Jack London is known to have eaten).

The players may give themselves various titles—State Highway Engineer, City Architect, Eastern Capitalist, and so on—and the one who destroys the City Hall for a parking lot, with a freeway overhead, is declared the winner. To add a final note of verisimilitude, all the players are blindfolded.

★   ★   ★

Well, city planning, like Monopoly, is just a game—a dangerous game that San Francisco is playing every day with great recklessness. It contains an added hazard that Mr. Park failed to deal with: the players are not only blindfolded, they are masked, and the masks aren't necessarily black or white. It's hard for us—the public—to tell the good guys from the bad guys, and sometimes even the players themselves aren't sure. If you want to build a 33-story skyscraper on a slope of Nob Hill, are you a Hero or a Villain? Not too long ago the answer would have been simple. Now there is a muttering in the marketplace.

* * *

A few days ago we were delighted or chagrined, according to our various tastes, to read that another 20-story apartment house will rise on Russian Hill—in a so-called "sacred enclave," complete with ramps, walls and the ghost of Willis Polk. For years the general feeling in that area has been that nobody would dare desecrate it with a towering slab of concrete. Good taste and an ingrained love for San Francisco would prevail, and so on.

Well, we learned something—again too late. Nothing is sacred in San Francisco any longer, and traditions taken for granted are soon turned into granite, as it were. The Russian Hillers who opposed that 20-story building expressed a great, if not necessarily exclusive love for San Francisco and made vain appeals to ethics and morality. The lady who is going to build that skyscraper probably loves San Francisco, too, in her own fashion, and would like to make a buck, besides. That is also a sacred tradition.

Which brings us to the Nub Hill of the problem: the lady who owns the Russian Hill property is not breaking any laws by building a glassy-eyed monster there. The Hartford Insurance people, who are taking sort of a beating because they want to build a 33-story filing cabinet on the edge of Chinatown, are perfectly within their legal rights, too (the design of the building might be open to esthetic question, but no laws apply there).

* * *

If what's left of the physical character of San Francisco is to be preserved—like Topsy, it "jes' growed," and it accidentally grew handsome—the law has to be changed. (Frank Lloyd Wright once said "San Francisco is the only city I can think of that can survive all the things you people are doing to it and still look beautiful." Then, reverting to his role of curmudgeon, he snickered that "What San Francisco really needs is another earthquake," which overlooked the fact that we are having an earthquake—a vertical one.)

Changing the law to provide for zones that are indeed sacred and untouchable—for reasons of history, beauty and just plain breathing space—is not going to be easy. There are people in the City Hall who would tear down the City Hall without a qualm in the name of that magic slogan: "Get it on the tax rolls!"

And we have powerful groups who would rise in anger if, say, Hartford Life, offended at what little opposition has been raised, announced, "All right, if you don't want us we'll build our building in Oakland or Los Angeles." A high Chamber of Commerce official said the other day: "We WANT big buildings here. We want this to remain the business capital of the West." So does everybody—as long as the buildings add to, rather than detract from or even obliterate, the surrounding areas.

"Don't let that ghost-town talk start up again," warned another official. "We don't want people to say San Francisco is dying."

★   ★   ★

When can a city be said to be dying? In the journal called *Christianity and Crisis*, Howard Moody answers that question this way:

"A city is dying when it has an eye for real estate values but no heart for personal values, when it has an understanding of traffic flow but no concern about the flow of human beings, when we have competence in building but little time for ethical codes, when human values are absent at the heart of the decision-making and planning and governing of a city—it is dead and all that is left is decay."

Then he quotes T.S. Eliot, in "The Rock":

> *Though you have shelters and institutions,*
> *Precarious lodgings while the rent is paid,*
> *Subsiding basements where the rat breeds*
> *Or sanitary dwellings with numbered doors*
> *Or a house a little better than your neighbors';*
> *When the Strangers say: "What is the meaning of this city?*
> *Do you huddle close together because you love each other?"*
> *What will you answer? "We all dwell together*
> *To make money from each other"? or "This is a community"?*

November 11, 1962

HOW NOW, CITY THAT KNOWS?

On a bright October day in 1911, a jovial gentleman with fine moustaches, twinkly eyes and a considerable paunch made a short speech here, in the course of which he got off a remark that, to his own surprise, became part of the deathless love of San Francisco.

He was President William Howard Taft, and, at a banquet in his honor at the Palace Hotel, he raised his arms Heavenward and said "San Francisco knows how!" Taft was no phrasemaker the same Heaven knows but this one caught on, capturing, as it does, all the homely virtues that were to be exploited later by our advertising geniuses. It is short, elliptical and, although open to a variety of interpretations, designed to offend no one.

The 1911 audience ate it up, of course. They cheered, stomped their feet and looked at each other with happy nods and shining eyes. They were good and they knew it, and now the President of the United States had confirmed it with a string of pearly Words to Live By.

(Some years later a San Franciscan newspaperman met Taft in Washington and remarked, "San Francisco will never forget what you said." When Taft looked blank, the reporter reminded him of his magic phrase, and then asked: "What did you mean by it exactly?" Still looking vague, Taft shrugged, "Oh, I guess I meant San Francisco knows how to do things right." Then he smiled. "So they still remember that out there, do they?" he chuckled. "Well, well.")

★   ★   ★

The city that knows how—how well it sums up that era of good feelings. The 20-year reign of Sunny Jim, The Man in the Palm Beach Suit, was just beginning in the city that had dug itself out of the ruins to rise even more shiningly than before. Jimmy Phelan and Rudy Spreckels had smashed the graft machine of Abe Ruef. The Barbary Coast was roaring, the French restaurants bubbled with champagne and cinq-a-septs in their upstairs bedrooms, and the Bay was speckled with ferries. The streetcar service was the finest, if noisiest in the world—from the Ferry Building to the Cliff House for a nickel—and if the city seemed overly in love with itself, so was everybody else.

Old windbags like Irvin S. Cobb were getting off shades-of-Will Irwin speeches about "the happiest-hearted, the gayest, the most carefree city on this continent," somehow able to produce "a greater number of native-born, or anyhow home-grown, actors, distinguished fictionists, sculptors, landscape painters, silver-tongued orators, dramatists, wits, and—oh, yes—pugilists than any other city, great or small, in the Union."

San Francisco knew how, whatever that meant. When the cops closed a bawdy girlie show as "immoral," a San Francisco Judge slapped down the prosecution with a statement that delighted the city. "This smacks of Los Angeles thinking," he roared. "Case dismissed!" Only Novelist Frank Norris, who had once described San Francisco as "one of America's three storybook cities," seemed embittered. "This," he said, "is the city that never thinks."

History might prove him to have been more precise than the cryptic Mr. Taft.

★   ★   ★

Nobody knows the city's official slogan—"God in peace, steel in war"—but everybody remembers "The City That Knows How." It has come back to haunt us. Every time one of our "world-renowned restaurants" serves Crab Louis on a plate containing more potato chips than crab, somebody throws Mr. Taft's words in our face. When the price is too high and the hills too low, when the Symphony hits a clinker and the night club show's a stinker, when Skid Row is laid bare and racial tensions flare, the auslander is always there to sneer, "This is the city that knows how?"

★   ★   ★

I don't know what Mr. Taft meant any more than Mr. Taft did, but would a city that really knew how have allowed the last of the beautiful, old ferries to disappear from the Bay? Or stand by while the Fox is torn down? Or let anybody put up any kind of vulgar sign anywhere? Or permit our first, last and always final asset—our views—to be gradually walled off? Or confess it has no plans for Alcatraz, Treasure Island and the Presidio, should these become available? Or allow the State to slap a freeway anywhere it feels like it? Of course, planning is a dangerous thing, but other cities seem to have plans, and, as they say around the racetracks, you can't beat a horse with no horse.

Take so simple an item as Christmas decorations. We were barely able to raise enough money to light the yew trees in Union Square. Los Angeles has put $12,000 into its Pershing Square, and has gaily decorated streetcars that haul shoppers around for a dime, children free. (The streetcars are called "Santa Twinkle Liners," and if you think you can afford to laugh at that, go ahead.)

Chicago's Christmas decorations, in the State and Randolph area, are so lavish and stunning that the Midwestern apple-knockers—still laughing?—come in droves from hundreds of miles just to gawk (and buy). New York's Fifth Ave. is an unending delight at Christmas time, and the block after block of stately, lighted trees along the plazas of Park Ave. are a tribute to that city's imagination—and, again the ugly word, planning.

Even Washington, a city that one hardly ever thinks of as a city, has its Caroling Streetcar—a trolley filled with singers that rolls around the downtown streets during the season. We have

39

clanging cable cars, limping past the sounds of clicking cash registers, but where are the singers?

★   ★   ★

Thank you, William Howard Taft, wherever you are. You stuck a label on us. And now we're stuck with it.   *December 9, 1962*

1963

HORACE GREELEY WAS A BUM

I think it's fair to decide, at this point, that the Governor's attempt to create an atmosphere of jubilation over California's new eminence as the Nation's most populous State was something less than an unqualified success. You might even describe it as a qualified pain in the disaster. It may even have been eligible for Federal aid.

I wouldn't presume to say that most Californians are in favor of border guards to keep the outlanders where they belong— out—but most San Franciscans (a group I propose to speak for till shouted down) would not look amiss if we turned our bridges into drawbridges—open most of the time—and built a deep moat between us and San Mateo County. We could get along very nicely as an independent city-state, like the Venice of old.

The way it is now, United Statesers are infiltrating us to a frightening degree, and threaten to take us over in a bloodless coup. A bloodless coup is an anemic two-seater automobile.

★ ★ ★

Meanwhile, we of San Franciscans First—rallying cry: "Mendocino Is Losing Population, Why Can't We?"—can do very little except fight a crafty war of propaganda. Why, we have deviationists in our very midst, who know not what they do. Just the other day a big man in our Chamber of Commerce was quoted as saying "San Francisco is fast getting a reputation as being against progress," which the newspapers described as "a warning." Although he didn't mean it that way, I look upon his statement as a ringing declaration of our aims. Perhaps he is an unconscious San Francisco Firster.

41

The propaganda war, first phase, must be waged in the following manner: You are in New York, say, and you come face to face with the enemy—the Incipient San Franciscan. "Well, well," he says, "so you're from that marvelous city. I was only there once, years ago, but I've never forgotten it. Y'know, I was saying to my wife just the other day, let's get out of this Godforsaken place, load the old car and move to San Francisco."

"Sure you could pass the fruit inspection?" you say. "We've got a very rigid fruit inspection at the State line. Too many as it is, especially in San Francisco."

After you pick yourself up from the floor, you smile, "Only kidding. Boy, you New Yorkers are touchy. Actually, I always come to New York this time of year. Earthquake season back home, you know. Pretty scary. And all those new buildings—the way they sway. Phew. Gimme New York. Solid. Safe.

* ★ *

After he thinks about that for a moment, he says, "But what a beautiful city. The views, the cable cars, the Bay and those hills—."

"Views?" you say. "What views? I can tell you haven't been there lately. The way our City Planners are going, they'll have the place looking like Toledo any day now. Something funny's been happening to the Bay, too. Tremendous waves—tidal, almost. Most people don't know this, but the reason is that it's too dangerous. Waves are cracking the walls. Personally, I think they're caused by all those people jumping off the Golden Gate Bridge."

"Uh—yeah," he says. "I've read about your suicide rate. Why is it so high?"

You smile a sad, sweet smile. "Ask me that same question after you've lived there a few weeks," you sigh.

* ★ *

He breaks the ensuing silence by asking "How about another drink," at which you shake your head: "No, thanks. Another reason I come East every year is to dry out. Gotta stay drunk most of the time in San Francisco. Fog day after day—gets depressing. And then there's the snow. That's the only reason we keep those rickety old cable cars—they can get up and down the hills in the snow. Of course, cars can't make it and all those horses falling down, breaking their legs, and—."

"Snow?" he asks, astounded. "I didn't know you had snow."

" 'Course you didn't," you nod. "Chamber of Commerce won't let a word get printed, even in the local papers. They've got such power you wouldn't believe it."

★   ★   ★

"You're putting me on," he says sharply. "Why, I remember going on a picnic in Golden Gate Park in January."

"Ah, the good old days," you respond with false brightness. "We put up a helluva fight, but it went. They covered the whole park with cement and turned it into a parking lot, all the way out to the beach. Did I say beach? That's a laugh. You can't even swim there—the undertow—and then the water's like ice." Shake of the head. "You can forget all that stuff about sharks not liking cold water. So many fins out there it looks like the Fulton Fish Market on Friday."

"I don't care," he says. "I'd still take a job there at half my salary if I could get an apartment with a view."

"Yeah, I used to feel that way, too," you nod. "If you get a view to the East, the sun wakes you up too early, and if you get a view to the West, the glare is terrible and your curtains fade. That's another reason I'm here. Lost my house in San Francisco. State's putting a freeway right through it. You never saw so many freeways. From the air, the city looks like a plate of spaghetti."

You arise and shake his limp hand. "Let me give you a little tip," you say confidentially. "If you have to come to California, the really 'in' place is Stockton. Then you can come to San Francisco on weekends—that is, if the drawbridge is down."

January 13, 1963

End of The Character

Some of us old newspaper hacks were sitting around at the Nam Yuen in Chinatown the other night, eating stuffed chicken legs and discussing Topic A, as usual, which is not what you think. Sex may be Topic A in most places, and food is certainly Topic A in Paris, but in San Francisco Topic A is—San Francisco.

After we'd covered the usual high spots (Things Ain't What They Used to Be, but were they ever?), a former Front Page Farrell who has been put out to pasture as an editorial writer sighed a wine-laden sigh. "When I was covering a beat," he said, "I knew the town pretty well—and most of the characters. Now I feel like a stranger in my own city. Out of touch. The old characters are fading out, and I have no idea who's taking their place. Take Jake Ehrlich, for instance. Hardly ever goes to court any more. Who's

43

the new Jake Ehrlich?"

A youngish lawyer who had joined the table shook his head. "There isn't one," he said, "and there won't be. Jake'd be laughed out of court today if he tried that Edward G. Robinson act on a jury—and he's smart enough to know it. Old hat. You never hear about the smart lawyers today—the ones who make the big dough." He rattled off a list of names that the old newspaper hacks listened to blankly. "Never heard of 'em, right?" went on the lawyer. "They do their best to stay out of the papers, not get into 'em."

★　★　★

The former Front Page Farrell fiddled with his chopsticks. "Everything's different," he said (ah, the sadness of temple bells and aging men). "Take these two murder cases going on right now. In the old days, we'd have splashed them all over the place—pictures, pages of testimony, sob-sister stuff. I couldn't believe my ears the other day. The news editor on our paper wanted to put the deKaplany trial inside—on page NINE. And that Grandmother Kroeger thing. They tell me it isn't selling papers worth a damn."

"TV," suggested a novelist. "The people can see better trials right in their living rooms than they can read about in the papers. They go to a real courtroom, they're bored to death."

"Not when Jake Ehrlich was operating," said the Front Page Farrell stubbornly. "He had color. He was a real character. Still is. Cocky little guy, with that straw hat and those big French cuffs and that starched handkerchief sticking up like Mt. Shasta."

★　★　★

The youngish lawyer looked skeptical, "Sure, Jake had color," he conceded, "but he was living in a different world. They don't pay off on color any longer. Don't forget, this was a small town when Jake and Johnny Taaffe and Les Gillen and all those guys were really swingin'. I don't mean they did anything wrong, but they and the Judges—there weren't many of them, either—were like one big family. Hell, they all drank together and ate together. Everybody was a character, and the newspapers treated 'em like part of the family, too. A small town run by cousins."

"I disagree," said an amateur psychiatrist, proceeding to dredge up a platitude. "It's the age of conformity. People are afraid of characters, and afraid to be one themselves. The only thing to be is neutral—think neutral, dress neutral, talk neutral. Don't be red, white or purple, be gray."

"There's something to that," agreed another newspaperman.

"Character used to be a term of endearment—'boy, what a wonderful character.' Now it means some kind of a nut, and we have a whole new vocabulary to go with it. Characters don't exist, per se. We call 'em paranoids or schizoids or psychos, we write 'em off as sado-masochists, and we can tell at a glance whether their complex is Napoleonic, Narcissistic, Oedipal, edible or soluble in straight whisky."

★ ★ ★

"It doesn't do to examine a character too closely," put in an ancient columnist. "They're delicate. You start pulling them apart, they die on you. And once they become aware they ARE characters, they're no good at all. Take Emperor Norton. The more you read about him the more he sounds like a dreadful old bore. If you saw him walking down Montgomery Street today—with those two seedy dogs of his—you'd run a mile to avoid him."

"Maybe so," grunted the former Front Page Farrell, "but how about a William Ralston—or, to come up to date, Lucius Beebe?"

"Ralston seems to have had real color, all right," nodded the columnist, "and so has Beebe, because he doesn't try. He's just what he is, like it or lump it. But remember Tiny Armstrong and Barney Ferguson? The last of the real City-wide characters, and they worked too hard at it.

"I was as guilty as anybody. Gave 'em plenty of ink, and they soaked it up. But the more you knew about them the more pathetic they became. Tiny, with his bad legs and bad pump, wheezing around the streets, blowing that bird whistle till it killed him. And poor old, toothless Barney, dancing a jig in Jack's to make the millionaires laugh—and then, after they'd had their laugh, being shoved to the last table in the place to eat his lunch alone. They were sad enough to break your heart.

"People keep saying how come we don't have any characters around like Barney and Tiny anymore? Well, we probably do, and I hope they're where they belong—in a rest home—instead of being laughed at on the streets."

★ ★ ★

We filed out of the Nam Yuen into the Chinatown night. "People, people everywhere, but not a character to drink with, eh?" said the former Front Page Farrell, shouldering into an overcoat. I watched him trudge up Washington St. and disappear into a bar. Quite a character.   *January 20, 1963*

45

Quirk? Shmirk: Well, I read another long piece in a learned journal the other day about "the mysterious psychological phenomenon" of our suicidal bridge jumpers—"who invariably leap from the San Francisco side, their last sight being that of the siren city that lured them to destruction," and further blah. What's so mysterious? As Don Taggart pointed out long ago, most suicides approach the bridge from San Francisco, which puts them in the right-hand side heading North. You think they're going to swerve to the Pacific side and risk getting a tag? Or walk across the roadway and take a chance on getting hit by a car? Jumping is one thing, but let's not lose our heads.   *February 13, 1963*

Mutter & mumbles: Several letter writers, describing themselves as "REAL San Franciscans" (as opposed to what?), have been on my tired old back for not hollering louder against the death of the aforementioned Fox. Well, as I've said before, nothing and nobody could've saved this outsized dog; being simply (or, rather, baroquely) a monument to a movie mogul's megalomania, it contained the seedy seeds of its own destruction. When the outlandish era that conceived it was over, its usefulness came to an end, too. The long, final wonder of the wonderful Fox was that it stood as long as it did; the shadow of the steel ball has been darkly discernible for years.

If we are going to fight a realistic battle against that steel ball, a line has to be drawn between a kind of neurotic nostalgia (don't touch anything I remember as a child) and a reasonable appreciation of what works and what doesn't (the Montgomery Block, a real loss, was a living, usable link with the past right up to the day it died).

A case can be made for the cable car because it still functions as part of the transportation system—most of the time, anyway—although the California line has been dangerously foreshortened; the manic-progressives (the other side of the neurotic nostalgic coin) will soon be able to argue that it's not packing its weight—a fact they provided for themselves by shortening it in the first place.

* * *

The trouble with the Fox was that it was always impossibly big. It was too big even in the days when that 100-piece orchestra rose grandly out of the pit, and Franchon & Marco put on the stage shows that weren't all that good, if you're being honest with yourself. When the novelty wore off, the Fox stood revealed for what it was—a truly monumental novelty. As a showhouse, it simply didn't work, as the Bolshoi Ballet demonstrated last fall.

What San Francisco needs is a modern performing center—the kind they're voting on up in Sacramento today—where, say, the Actor's Workshop can appear and where a Royal Ballet can play when the Opera House is being used for the Broadway musicals it was never intended for. The civic disgrace is not that we're allowing the Fox to disappear but that in all the years since its decline we never made plans for something better (perhaps the remodeled Auditorium will fill the gap; we shall see).

Or, maybe Louis Lurie can be cajoled into tearing down his Curran and Geary and replacing them with a single, up-to-date playhouse of flexible size. He may even call it The Lurie Center of the Performing Arts. The man deserves a lasting monument, even if he has to build it himself. *February 19, 1963*

To each his own: A few years ago I printed the following letter from a Mrs. Freeman Pepper, who, with her husband, was about to move out of the Bay Area:

"We hate to leave our place. The climate is wonderful—very little fog—and beautiful plants and flowers grow very nearly everywhere. There are lots of little night-singing birds, seagulls, cormorants and a few pelicans. But the best thing is our million-dollar view. From our windows we can see from the Gate Bridge to the Bay Bridge, and the sunsets are spectacular. And at night, with the lights aglow, San Francisco is indeed a glamorous city. We shall miss our lovely home very much."

For 21 years Mr. and Mrs. Pepper lived on Alcatraz, where he was a guard—and they left only because he was retiring. Her letter might help to explain why, as the final group was leaving The Rock Thursday, another guard's wife glanced back for a last look at the grim prison—and hastily hid her tears behind a pair of dark glasses. To some it may have been hell on earth. But to others, obviously, it was Paradise Isle. *March 24, 1963*

Scene: On Monday afternoon the portly figure of Mr. Alfred Hitchcock was to be seen emerging, with a definite "thwuck," from

47

a large black limousine on Powell. He waddled over to a bench in Union Square and spread himself out like a roly-poly pudding. Some nut with a paper bag sprinkled grain at his feet, attracting pigeons by the hundreds.

Kicking at them good-naturedly, the director of "The Birds" admonished: "Get thee to Ernie's—I'll see you under glass at 7."

A cunning little blonde girl, dressed in blue and shoved from behind by an elderly lady, approached him. "There he is," said the lady, "the man you see on TV." The little girl burst into tears, and Mr. Hitchcock made a face at her. "That's right, dearie," he said. "I'm the bogey man."

As the pigeons fluttered about our heads and shoulders, we talked about "The Birds," which Mr. Hitchcock described as "a fowl epic, if I ever made one. Biggest cast of extras I ever had, too. Over 28,000 birds. Of course, they all worked for chicken-feed except for the buzzards, which had agents.". . . "The ads," I said, "quote you as calling it 'the most terrifying picture I have ever made.' Is that true?"

"Oh, indubitably," he replied. "I financed it myself, and I'm terrified at the thought of losing all my money." He batted a pigeon off his bald head. "Very dirty birds," he mumbled. "Spread disease. It's a little-known fact that you can even get rabies from a pigeon."

Herbert the Furrier walked up and greeted the director. "I understand that 'The Birds' is for adults only." When Mr. Hitchcock looked bland, Herbert cackled: "No mynahs allowed!" As Mr. Hitchcock was digesting this, one Herb Ligier cut in: "They tell me you're a bear for detail. I hear you left no tern unstoned." Mr. Hitchcock sprinkled a little grain among the pigeons. "They're not so bad after all," he decided.

The Union Square character who walks around with a sandwich board reading "Eat No Pork or Fats!" arrived. Patting his stomach, Mr. Hitchcock growled: "I didn't come here to be insulted. Why, on June 1, Santa Clara University is giving me an honorary degree in the humanities. I was hoping for ornithology, of course. You see, I went to a Jesuit school and I lived nearby in the Santa Cruz mountains. Perhaps someday I will be known as the Birdman of Santa Cruz."

He got up to leave, picking his way daintily through the pigeons. "Forget what I said about pigeons giving you rabies," he smiled roguishly, "unless you start foaming at the mouth in a day or two, of course." With another "thwuck," he squeezed back into the limousine, on the rear of which was a sticker reading "The Birds is Coming."

"So long," he waved. "I are going." *April 3, 1963*

THE TERRIFIC TRIANGLE

The clean old man was lounging against a wall at Taylor and Ellis, watching the new Hilton rise in all its sterile glory. "Well, that's it, kid," he said with a resigned smile. "That's the end of the Tenderloin."

As he spoke he was rhythmically flipping a $20 gold piece, that talisman of the old crowd. "Of course," he went on, "the Tenderloin has been dying for years. But that thing there"—he jabbed a finger at the monumental blockhouse—"that's the gravestone." He chuckled without amusement. "Sort of looks like one, too."

I glanced around. There were more parking lots and fewer places to go. Nearby, a new jewelry shop was being installed. A streamlined branch of the world's biggest bank was already in business. A small hotel once noted for all-night revels has become a "residence" for "senior citizens," that irritating euphemism.

His purple-veined face shadowed under the pearl-gray fedora. The Clean Old Man squinted into the late afternoon sun. Two hard-looking blondes in linty black slacks and high heels gave him a brief "Hi, baby" as they walked past. His eyes followed their rears down Ellis. "Won't see much of that any more," he said. "The old Tenderloin is about to get as square as that hotel. Now tell me about all the conventions Mr. Hilton is gonna bring to town, and I'll ask you—where they gonna go for laughs when they get here?"

* * *

The old Tenderloin—the "Terrific Triangle" bounded by Jones, O'Farrell and Market. Tenderloin: a peculiarly American term, born in New York. The lexicographers aren't too sure about its origin; the most educated guess surmises that the cops on a certain beat in Manhattan were able to afford tenderloin steaks. In San Francisco, the juice was rich enough for filet mignons, sparkling burgundy, apartment houses and places in the country.

* * *

In the few blocks of the "Terrific Triangle," for a comparatively few years as a city's time is reckoned, there was more action than anywhere else in the country. There were fine restaurants: the

49

Techau Tavern at 1 Powell, Newman's College Inn, the Bay City Grill, Herbert's Bachelor Grill. There were the "French" places—Blanco's, the St. Germain—with utter respectability on the ground floor, shady booths on the second, "riding academies" (as they were known) on the third.

You could drink till dawn in Dutch White's at 110 Eddy, and at Chad Milligan's Sport Club on Ellis. Franchon & Marco danced at Tait's Pavo Real on O'Farrell, where a kid named Rudolph Valentino was a busboy. Frank Shaw and Les Poe reigned at Coffee Dan's. It was unthinkable to miss a Sunday night at the old Orpheum, and if the bill there was a little weak (Jack Benny and Sophie Tucker), there was always the Tivoli, the Warfield, the Capitol, the Alcazar or Will King's Casino, with Will singing "I've got a girl who paints her cheeks, another with a voice that squeaks, they both ran away with a pair of Greeks—I wish I owned a restaurant!"

Girls, girls, girls. Every theater had a line, with Stage Door Johns to match. Every other small hotel was a house (the old Drexel alone had 30 girls). A doll with the marvelously San Francisco name of Dodie Valencia was a legend. Even the manicurists at Joe Ruben's barbershop were "as beautiful as Follies girls," the supreme accolade of the era.

★　★　★

But the lifeblood of the Old Tenderloin was gambling. The cars shuffled and the dice rattled through the smoky nights at the Menlo Club and the Kingston and at Chad Milligan's. The high rollers—Nick the Greek, Titanic Thompson, Joe "Silver Fox" Bernstein, Eddie Sahati—faded in and out with the foggy dawns. At Tom Kyne's in Opal Place, the cul-de-sac alongside the Warfield, you could bet on anything from the Mayor's race to the St. Mary's-Santa Clara football game to how many passengers the ferries would carry the next day.

The gamblers were the kings of the Tenderloin, and their names rang true, straight out of Runyon and Lardner. Carnation Willie and Benny the Gent, Bones Remmer and Siggie Rosener, Freddy the Glut, and Jelly and Marty Breslauer. At 10 a.m.—the end of the day that started at midnight—the bookies gathered at John's Grill on Ellis. Over the corned beef hash and the eggs sunnyside up they counted the cash and paid off the winners. Enough long green was scattered over the tables to carpet Ireland. Marty Breslauer alone packed $100,000, and one night a kid he'd befriended gunned him down for his roll.

But violence was rare. It was an underworld with class, a closed corporation. The cops, who were getting their share, kept it that way, and the hoods of the Organization never had a chance to move in. When they arrived at Third and Townsend they were met by the two toughest Inspectors on the force, who put them right back on the train.

The cops knew a good thing, and they had it. The mother of a Captain on the Force was the biggest madam in the area. One day at Bay Meadows a rookie cop who didn't know the score told her: "One of these nights I'm gonna come into your place and close you down." "And when you do," she replied coolly, "you'll find your boss in the kitchen drinking coffee."

★　★　★

It was a world we'll never see again. Godliness and purity now reign—don't they?—and the final long shadow is being cast over the Tenderloin by the Rising Hilton. The section is about to become infinitely more respectable. And infinitely duller.

June 2, 1963

Babylon revisited: If you children will form a circle around grampa's knee, I will tell you about the old Black Cat saloon on Montgomery. Oh, I realize it's still there, but it has undergone a subtle, or perhaps not so subtle, change the past decade. The pitch of the customers' voices seems to have gone up several octaves. From basso profundo to mezzo soprano.

In the mid-Thirties the Black Cat was the hangout of the True Bohemians. For one thing, it was across the street from the late lamented Montgomery (or "Monkey") Block, a rabid warren for starving artists. For another, there wasn't much competition, except for the nearby Iron Pot and Izzy Gomez's. A place called Mona's thrived in the cellar now occupied by the Purple Onion, but, although the pitch there was basso profundo, too, it was supplied by ladies in pants.

The Black Cat was the class spot of this classless society. You could usually find the shouting young Bill Saroyan there with Writer John ("Dago Red") Fante. And good artists like Dong Kingman, Bob Howard, Matt Barnes, Luke Gibney, Ralph Stackpole and Maynard Dixon. When Steinbeck would walk in, a respectful hush would settle over the place. The Nob Hill crowd came down on "slumming" parties (what are they called now?). The young wits who published a weekly called the Montgomery Street Skylight did their editing there, led by John Wright, who coined the Cat's deathless slogan: "We Reserve the Right to Serve Refuse to Anyone."

★   ★   ★

Nobody knew why the Black Cat was so popular. Owner Charlie Haberkorn's drinks ranged from fair to awful, but awfully cheap. The decor was Early Dirt, and the music, pounded out on a broken-down piano by anybody who came along, was pathetique, but not Tchaikowsky's. Nevertheless, the Black Cat somehow achieved the flavor of Paris in the Twenties—who can tell what alchemy makes a place live?—and it was totally lacking in self-consciousness, which its fake successors abound in.

What brings all this to mind is that last Saturday afternoon a reunion of Black Catters (1937–1946) was held there, and some of the survivors braved the bright sunlight to relive their youth. Unlike the Beats, they looked like people. There were Emerson Adams and Marie Breuner, Stanley Gough in his beret (Gough St. was named after one of his forebears) and Henri Lenoir without his beret (in the old days Henri didn't wear one, being a cigarette salesman). There were Bumble Bee Johnson, the elegant Robin Kinkead and John Horton Cooper, Jose Ramis and Karl Barron and dozens more. There was even an old-timer who kept announcing proudly "I was 86'd in '36!" (86 is a bartender's term meaning no more drinks for that drunk.)

It was a fine party, full of ghosts, memories and reminiscences of long-forgotten and oddly innocent scandals. We gingerly toasted the departed and congratulated each other that so many excellent people had survived the late Haberkorn's booze in the Black Cat of yesterday.   *July 2, 1963*

ONE SCORE AND FIVE

Anniversary columns are perilous undertakings. They turn out either sentimental, corny, sticky, icky, falsely humble, humbly proud or flatly arch. Today I shall make a sensational attempt to combine all these qualities, or lack of them, into one piece—a feat that shouldn't be too difficult for a reasonably bad writer. Come, watch the man fall on his face.

★   ★   ★

Exactly 25 years ago today—July 5, 1938—this column was first foisted on a properly suspecting world. A silver anniversary, any way you polish it—and please, no congratulations. All it proves is a rather peculiar knack for staying in one place. Other columnists have managed to escape long before this, but they probably had a strong alibi or a good lawyer. Besides, you don't get anything for 25 years. On your 50th anniversary, they hand you a gold watch, empty. By then, you've had the works.

*　*　*

A quarter of a century of columns (it's the dailiness that gets you, as somebody once said). That's some 7,200,000 words, or about 10 deadly words for every man, woman and child in San Francisco. Talk about overkill! Placed one atop the other, they would make quite a pile, which I haven't.

*　*　*

I wouldn't want you to think I became a columnist just like that. Before achieving this pinochle, I had made a name for myself—no matter what kind—as a sportswriter, police reporter and radio columnist. Actually, I didn't make my name at all. Steve George, then sports director of the Sacramento Union, made it for me in 1932.

After I had written a long and intolerable piece about high school football, he said: "Put your by-line on it. I wouldn't want anybody to think I wrote it." I scribbled "By Herbert Caen" at the top of the copy and handed it to him. "Good God," he said irritably, crossing out the last three letters of the first name. "Who ever heard of a sportswriter named Herbert?"

I wish to take this opportunity to thank Mr. George for turning me into a four-letter word.

*　*　*

Well, editors can't resist writers with short names, so in 1936 I was summoned to The Chronicle as radio editor, although the only radio I'd heard in Sacramento the previous three years had been the police radio. That sinecure lasted only two years, after which the paper decided to defeat radio by ignoring it. Shortly before July 5, 1938—a date that was to live in infamy till Pearl Harbor—the editor, a daring young man with red hair, asked me what I wanted to do.

"Write a column about San Francisco," I said. "About SAN FRANCISCO?" he replied incredulously. This may come as a surprise to you, dear reader, but there were no columns about San Francisco in those pioneer days. There were news columns and behind-the-news columns and City Hall columns and editorial columns, but was SAN FRANCISCO worth a full column every day?

53

It was a pretty trivial thought, and the editor was not impressed. "I see," he said doubtfully, "and what would you call it?" Not having thought about a title, I blurted the first thing that came to mind. "Uh—'It's News to Me,'" as what wasn't and isn't. "Well, let's see how it goes," shrugged the editor. "I'll give you three weeks." I never heard from him again. Maybe he's still trying to decide which way it's going.

★   ★   ★

The first column was so bad, I'm surprised there was a second. "It's News to Me, Says Herb Caen," read the heading on Vol. 1, No. 1. It began: "Yesterday was the Fourth of July. Today, here we are. This probably adds up to something or other, but I'm not quite sure what; isn't very important, however you look at it." As you can see, I was still young enough to take *The New Yorker* seriously, to the point of imitation.

After that sparkling first paragraph came a longish mishmash about the impending visit of FDR. Would he stay at the Palace, which had a Presidential Suite ($35 a day in those days), or at the Mark, whose owner, George D. Smith, was a big Democrat? The question remains unanswered to this day. (I think he stayed at the St. Francis.) That was followed by a perplexing paragraph about a woman, lighted cigarette in hand, jumping aboard a moving streetcar—an item fit for inclusion in a book titled, "Return of No Point."

The hypothetical reader was next treated to an anecdote involving the late Wayne Morris, a reigning movie star of the time, and I must say that this is of more than passing interest. His name was printed as "Mayne Morris," and this is historic since it marked the last time a typographical error was ever to appear in The Chronicle. And the point of the story, if any, was that Mr. Morris had been mistaken, in the St. Francis lobby, for a young S.F. press agent named Jerry Bundsen.

Shortly thereafter, Jerry Bundsen came to work for me as assistant, a job he has held ever since, proving that he is as stubborn as I am. Since his name appeared in the first column, it seems fitting that it should be mentioned 25 years later. But what really makes this a Funny Coincidence story—the kind I hate the most— is that his salary is the same now as it was then.

★   ★   ★

And so a quarter of a century has drifted past in a welter of items, tritems, slightems, and almost-rightems. As I said in Vol. 1, No. 1, it "isn't very important, however you look at it." But if you've been looking at it anyway, all those years, I thank you from the bottom of my column. *July 5, 1963*

Most Happy Fella

Happiness, says Charlie Schulz, is a warm puppy (it is also a warm bun on your dog at Candlestick Park). Happiness, says Logan Pearsall Smith, is a wine of the rarest vintage (it is also a jug of Mountain Red at Stinson Beach, when the sun is out; or, suggests Jimmy Price, the third martini on an empty stomach). Happiness, says George DuMaurier, is just a thing of contrasts (a Little Old Lady kicking a pigeon, Harry Bridges lunching at the Pacific Union Club). Happiness, says Francis Thompson, is the shadow of things past—the smell of a ferryboat, the faithful light on Alcatraz, eucalyptus leaves crunching underfoot on a quiet path in Golden Gate Park.

*　*　*

For a San Franciscan, happiness is many things: the first glimpse of the skyline as you drive in from the airport after a long trip, speeding through the Broadway Tunnel (where no cop can hide), passing a cable car on the wrong side, finding a good little restaurant where the lights and prices are low, overhearing a tourist say, "Boy, this city is even better than I'd heard"—and then discovering he's from Los Angeles.

*　*　*

Happiness, sang Frances Wayne on that great Woody Herman record, is just a thing called Joe. It is also a thing called a tree, newly planted and thriving on an otherwise hopeless expanse of concrete. It is a handsome new skyscraper in the Mission, a parking space with 40 minutes left on the meter, a candle-lit dinner in an old house whose dining room looks out on the Presidio, a girl with handsome legs climbing the wooden stairs to Macondray Lane, a Longshoreman in a white cap who walks along the Embarcadero with a rolling swagger.

*　*　*

Happiness, beams Charlie Brown, is finding Albania on the map. It is also finding a letter in your mailbox from the Internal Revenue, notifying you of a refund. It is finding a faded photo you never saw before of the winding railway on Mt. Tamalpais, tousled Jack London on the Snark, the "John D. Spreckels" with her studding sails out, an Arnold Genthe picture of a pigtailed Chinese, in baggy black pantaloons, watching the '06 fire boiling at the foot of California St. Happiness is finding a first edition of "The Maltese Falcon," autographed by Dashiell Hammett, and then finding the tale as exciting as you remembered it.

* * *

Mr. Webster is strangely materialistic. "Happiness," he begins, perhaps scratching his head: "1. Good luck; good fortune; prosperity." Happiness, a less literal-minded friend once observed, is living just beyond your means and getting away with it. Happiness is having friends who would never describe you and your wife as "a fun couple" and who never say "It's a gas." Happiness is a Bastian cartoon showing Goldwater carrying a sign reading "Bomb the Ban!", is John F. Kennedy acting like a statesman rather than a politician, is a Tahitian girl protesting French nuclear tests, is Dr. Teller being named Ambassador to Ruritania. Is a test ban.

* * *

"The world is so full of a number of things," said RLS, "I'm sure we should all be as happy as"—kings? How about a cable-car gripman, clanging his gong in triple-time. A scavenger with an old derby on the back of his head, a fresh rose behind his ear. A kid with a fishing rod walking down Van Ness toward the Aquatic Park pier. The tillerman on a hook-'n'-ladder, weaving through the Market St. traffic, a thousand admiring, childlike eyes following him. A chauffeur snugly asleep behind the wheel of a Rolls outside the Opera House, while his employer sleeps uncomfortably inside. A newly married young couple finding a little wooden house on Telegraph Hill, the Bay Bridge stretched neatly across their front window.

* * *

"A number of things." Happiness is flipping your cigarette butt at a cable slot and scoring a clean hit, is slapping a lamppost and getting a loud and clear "Bong!", is your dentist saying "No cavities, see you in six months," is a motorcycle officer saying, "Well, OK this time, but watch it," is Desiree (in Alexis' Gypsy Cellar) singing the score from "Irma La Douce," is the first bite of Cold Dollar Chicken (in a sweet bun) at Johnny Kan's, is wearing an overcoat to work in the morning and having the weather stay miserable all day, is the sidewalk photographer no longer bothering to take your picture, is browsing through Gump's without being tailed by a salesman, is a theater poster promising "Original Broadway Cast," and having it turn out to be true.

* * *

"Who says happiness is necessary?" growl the psychiatrists. Be well-adjusted, that's the thing. OK, so being well-adjusted is a button-down collar that flares properly, an old tie that still dimples in the center (no matter how you tie it), your wife wearing a dress you picked out (and her friends enthuse over), the woman seated in front of you (at the Curran) removing her big hat while you were still screwing up courage to ask her to, a broken TV tube that nobody seems to mind, "Bye-bye BABY!", lighting a cigarette as your doctor (on the phone) is telling you your chest X-ray looks fine, "This round is on the house," a bridge hand with 23 points (and a void in your opponent's suit), Sinatra singing "At Long Last Love," the Gate Bridge from the Legion of Honor courtyard, getting the first Kleenex out of the box without tearing it . . .

★　★　★

Happiness is a restored Victorian house, is a perfect hamburger, is Leon Fleisher playing the Brahms First, is a shared experience—like still getting a kick out of being a San Franciscan.

August 4, 1963

I have been flying up and down this dog-legged State via PSA, the people's airline. Cheap, fast and on time. They have only six Electras, but they shuffle 'em around so fast you'd think it was 600. "We try to keep all our planes in the air," explained an exec. It's a worthy thought for any airline. When you fly PSA you can forget those slick ads showing a couple dressed by Brioni and Dior and carrying $5,000 worth of alligator luggage. Your fellow passengers include the barefoot young men wearing Bermudas and nothing else, ladies in slacks and high heels, electronics execs with attaché cases containing a change of socks. The principal baggage is box lunches. Next they'll have passengers standing in the aisle, hanging on to overhead straps. I like it. August 27, 1963

City of Golden Windows

Indian summer arrived with such a vengeance this week you'd have thought the Indians were getting even for something. "The City Air-Conditioned By Nature" needed a little help from mechanical gadgets, and a new batch of smog arrived every hour on the hour from L.A., the West Coast distributor. The newsboy at Powell and

Geary wore a large lapel button reading "Yes, It's Hot Enough for Me."

The early mornings are magnificent. As the sun cocks an eye over the East Bay hills, San Francisco becomes The City of the Golden Windows. It is World Series weather without the World Series (a billboard on El Camino in San Carlos reads "L.A. Dodgers vs. Del Webb Construction Co."—or is it Destruction?). The natives dress like tourists and the tourists look as if they came to the wrong San Francisco, if you can imagine such a place.

The Bay is a big bowl of lentil soup, with ships wallowing around in it like croutons. Saloons have their doors propped open, and bartenders keep running out of Tom Collins mix in this normally Scotch-and-martini town. Excellent weather for girl-watching, especially at Aquatic Park, where Miles Harrison Doody was heard to say about a sunbathing cocktail waitress: "She looks terrific in a bikini except for two little things . . . "

*　　*　　*

Life unfolds in a warm dream. Over at the Berkeley Tennis Club, where the world's best amateurs are playing this week, they can't believe their good fortune. At the California Tennis Club, Supreme Court Justice Hugo Black and his wife play again with Ursula and Jerry Stratford, who keep saying "Good serve, Mr. Justice" and "Nice shot, Mr. Justice," and finally, "Isn't there SOMEthing we can call you besides Mr. Justice?" "Call me Hugo," says Mr. Justice Black.

*　　*　　*

North Beach is the place to be on a hot day. The green of Washington Square is strewn with bodies, like a battlefield. You can't get an outside table at Enrico's, the only coffee house in the world where you can sip iced tea and get hit by a passing truck at the same time. "Man, it's too hot to protest, even," yawns a Negro musician. "Oh, I dunno," replies Dick Robertson. "I need some clothes. Let's organize a Freedom March on Brooks Brothers."

The dandy Italian housewives of North Beach are out in force, with their string bags—shopping European style, from store to store. First to the butcher shop, then the vegetable stand, then the fruit store and the bakery and the fish market. In the supermarket age you don't find this kind of shopping anywhere else. But supermarkets are nice, too. Especially the Marina Safeway, with its wide view of the Marin hills and the leafiness of nearby Fort Mason.

The naked city shrinks to small town size as Old Blazer oozes through the blue. Cops and cabbies shed their jackets, and only the furriers look furious. At Herbert the Furrier's an 86-yr-old groom buys a mink stole for his 72-yr-old bride, as the wizened janitor leans on his mop, shaking his head: "These May-December marriages never last."

★ ★ ★

You wander around the town, spearing items with a pointed stick. Giorgio Tozzi, who starred in "Mefistofele" at the Opera House Tuesday night, pushes his way through a crowd of well-wishers— in a hurry to make a 12:30 a.m. plane to New York for his first rehearsal at the Metropolitan yesterday. "And with my luck," he grins, "I'll be the only one on time for it."

Mary Costa, the most beautiful girl in the opera world, dines alone in a dark corner of Trader Vic's "other" room (her husband, a movie director, is stuck in Hollywood). At Alexis', Mrs. Walter Keane celebrates her 35th birthday, and her husband, funny boy, presents her with a cake containing 55 candles; she throws it at him, misses. In the Jack Tar's Lobby Lounge, Bill Juchnick requests "Don't Take Your Love From Me" and tips Pianist Bob Surabian $500 for playing it. Surabian sits there counting the money over and over. He can't believe it.

In the St. Francis Grill, a customer orders a Bullshot (beef consomme and vodka over ice); "We don't call it a Bullshot," says Bill, the Captain. "Now it's Ox on the Rox." Dr. Robert Cahan, the psychiatrist at S.F. General, smiles that he will name his new boat "Freudian Sloop." And at Rocca's, Hostess Martha Price, wearing a bubbletop, boasts that her measurements are 34–34–24–34— the first 34 is my hairdo."

★ ★ ★

The Indian summer sun heads for Seal Rocks. At Steinhart Aquarium in the Park, a skin diver lowers himself into the dolphin tank, and kids whoop "He's gonna play with the dolphin!" But he doesn't. He's an underwater window-washer, and he busies himself wiping off the smudges put on the glass by the big fish as it noses around.

Comedian Ronnie Schell phones from Washington, D.C.: "I'm a big hit here. The critics are comparing me with Chaplin—they think I oughta be deported." On Powell, a gripman shoos a gaggle of tourist ladies off the outside step: "You women have taken over all the rides from us men, but this is one ride you haven't got and will never get." The sun dips a toe into the Pacific, and in a flash the East Bay becomes The City of the Golden Windows.

Artist Mel Jones, a newcomer from Colorado, looks around at the purple dusk and murmurs in wonder: "You know what San Francisco says to me? San Francisco says 'Mel Jones, you're going to STARVE . . . but beautifully.' " *September 26, 1963*

On Sunday I attended the only cocktail party in the world where, when you asked "Who won?" the answer was "Portland, 9–4."

It didn't matter that the Smodgers had just scored an unprecedented sweep over the Yankees, or that the 49ers had lost their 11th straight—also, unprecedented (the score in that one was Sadists, 26, Masochists, 3).

At the cocktail party I speak of, "Portland 9–4" was the only result anybody talked about. The party was in the glorious $250,000 mansion of the Fremont Bodine (Peter) Hitchcocks Jr., out there at the lush end of Broadway, and it followed the polo matches in Golden Gate Park.

Portland had defeated Santa Rosa, a team badly crippled by the loss of Luther Burbank. And San Francisco—the team for which Mr. Hitchcock leads a chuckered career—lost 8–7 to Central Valley, a name more identified with public ownership than private polo.

However, the party, in that beautiful old house overlooking the Bay, made everything worthwhile. Not since the golden age of Hollywood had I seen dashing young men in polo attire—white riding breeches, boots, artful smudges on the face—stride into a mile-long drawing room. Butlers with silver trays of drinks moved through the crowd. Pianist Shelley Robin and Bassist Vernon Alley tinkled in a corner. The only people missing were Gloria Swanson and Pola Negri. Scott and Zelda were there in spirit.

As somebody said long ago, "If Jack Kennedy gets elected, we'll have Little League Polo." Sunday we had it. *October 8, 1963*

Classic: Well, Perry Como will do his TV show here next Thurs., and of course he will sing "I Left My Heart in San Francisco." This innocuous ditty is now sort of the official S.F. song, as Irving Berlin's "God Bless America" has become the roadshow National Anthem, an eminence it scarcely deserves. Therefore, we will now tell you more about "I Left My Heartcetera" than you care to know:

It was written in 1954 by George Cory and Douglass Cross, now in their late 30s, who met in the Army 15 years ago and have been writing songs together ever since. Before entering the service, Cory lived in S.F. (his father is still here) and Cross in Oakland, but they wrote "I Left My Heart" in Brooklyn Heights, N.Y., where they live now. It would be nice to say they wrote it because they were homesick, but actually, says Cory, "we were sick for a little money."

That came slowly. The song went begging for eight years till Tony Bennett's conductor decided it was worth recording—but only as a single. The single sold 500,000 copies in a hurry, and then went into a Bennett album, "Heart," that grossed over a million dollars. Since then the song has been recorded by 200 different artists in eight languages, is still No. 1 in sheet-music sales and has never been under No. 20 among national best-seller recordings.

Songwriters Cory and Cross now split $50,000 annually in royalties on this one song alone, and are not about to rush back to San Francisco. "We might have left our heart there," says Cory, "but the money is here, man."   *November 14, 1963*

BLACK FRIDAY

After the first newsflash on the radio there wasn't much reality to Friday. The morning had started out cold and gray, and the young ladies of Montgomery St., on the way to their first coffee break, were wrapped in their own arms (and thoughts) and saying "Brrrrr" in exaggerated tones. A few people were chattering about something known as the Big Game. The saloons were getting ready for a big night. The inevitable cliche expert, in the office hallway, was heard to say "Thank God it's Friday." At that point Dallas was still most renowned as the home of Neiman-Marcus, a fancy department store; the fact that Adlai Stevenson had been spat upon in Dallas was still remembered by only a few. Dallas. "Big D," they call it. D as in Death.

★   ★   ★

The radio was playing a thin, insipid record by an English dance band—the kind of music you listen to unconsciously, if at all—when the first bulletin was announced. Like all such things, it had a fictional ring. The announcer sounded stunned and confused, and for a moment you felt sorry for him. His careful training in

61

voice and diction went out the window, and he stumbled over the words. "There is a report—a bulletin—there is word from Dallas that . . . " You snatched fleetingly at the hope that it was only an unconfirmed rumor as you spun the dial through the networks.

*   *   *

Slowly a stillness crept over the city. A paralysis was setting in as a million minds focused on a city in Texas. Cars pulled over and parked—it seemed impossible to drive and listen at the same time. The only sign of life on the Bay was a gray Army transport inching past Fort Mason; no flags shown on her, and she seemed like a ghost ship. I picked up my telephone. No dial tone.

*   *   *

Now there was a steady flow of radio bulletins, the announcers sounding breathless, as though they had just been slugged in the stomach. "He is at least gravely injured—." ABC quoted a Secret Service man as saying the President was dead, "but this is unconfirmed, we repeat, this is unconfirmed." But all the while a lump was forming in your throat, and your heart was sick. NBC had the President dead, while ABC said "He is still alive, we repeat—." Flash: Two priests entered the hospital. You found yourself praying for the first time in years. Oh, God.

*   *   *

Your thoughts rambled in the most confused way as the news tickers clattered in the background. You remembered Arthur Godfrey sobbing on the air as he described FDR's funeral, and the peculiar, choked phrase, "God bless his gaudy guts." And "the drums are playing slowly, ohhh sooo slowwwly." You remembered France, 1945, and the first announcement of FDR's death—tears glistening on the stubbly cheeks of combat GIs. Zangara firing at Roosevelt and killing Mayor Anton Cermak of Chicago; just the other day Westbrook Pegler, that paragon of journalists, had said again "Zangara killed the wrong man."

*   *   *

You sat by a window and stared out at the empty street, your mind still as cloudy as the skies. Odd, nagging thought: Gavin Arthur, grandson of the 21st President of the United States, had refused to vote for Jack Kennedy in 1960, although he is a Democrat. Arthur, the expert on horoscopes, had cast one whose signs, he said, indicated only one thing: the 35th President would die in office. You smiled condescendingly at him—then. There was a brief, terrible silence on the radio. And then the announcer, clearing his throat, said the simple words you could scarcely bear to listen to.

* * *

"John Fitzgerald Kennedy, the 35th President of the United States, is dead." There was a brief interlude of recorded classical music that sounded like Beethoven and then the "Star-Spangled Banner" came on. The great Flag on the Telephone Building was slowly lowered to half-staff, where it rippled briefly in the cold air and then sagged.

* * *

And so you cried. You cried for the young man and his wife and his family. You cried because you hadn't realized how much the young man meant to you. You cried for every stupid joke you had ever listened to about him, and you cried for the fatuous faces of the people who had told them. You cried for the Nation, and the despoilers of it, for the haters and the witch-hunters, the violent, the misbegotten, the deluded. You cried because all the people around you were crying, in their impotence, their frustration, their blind grief.

* * *

By early afternoon the city had collected itself slightly. The sun tried to force its way through the overcast, but it was a feeble effort. Downtown, the Salvation Army bells were ringing on the street corners—mournfully. A cable car rattled over distant tracks, sounding like firecrackers far away. Now the radio announcers had regained their aplomb, and a few commercials were creeping back on. One Senator said, "Words are of no use at a time like this," but other politicians had their statements prepared. A San Mateo lady I know took her son in to the dentist, and said, "Isn't it terrible?" "Oh, I don't know," said the dentist. "I didn't like him or his politics." She managed to walk out into the hallway before she became ill.

* * *

The President is dead. Long live the President.

November 24, 1963

HOLIDAY AT HALF-MAST

It has been a week of unparalleled tragedy and irony, and today, in the crowning irony, the Nation is summoned to give thanks. Thanksgiving Day, one of our oldest observances, with the Flags

63

at mourning for the youngest President—and the families will gather from here to Hyannis Port, where there will be an empty chair at the table, and who among us will not be thinking of that?

* * *

But, as the bishop said hopefully in Grace Cathedral, out of so much evil, surely some good must come. And perhaps he is right—although the price was too terrible. We, all of us, paid bitterly for our smugness, our selfishness, our foolish pride. A shot in Texas warned us that it CAN happen here, as Sinclair Lewis predicted so many years ago, and during those four dark days of November we learned new lessons about ourselves and each other. That is a small thing to give thanks for, for we still don't know whether the lesson came too late, but it is something.

* * *

For the past week the world has been looking at us perhaps more critically than ever before, but the picture that emerges is not totally black. We are the Nation of monstrous error, as illustrated by the events in Dallas, but we are also the country of Jacqueline Kennedy, an enduring figure of nobility. The great mass of Americans reacted with such dignity and restraint that the man in the pulpit on Nob Hill could assert with confidence: "As a people we are united as never before." If that is so—and again the cost was prohibitive—it is something to give thanks for, too.

* * *

And where do we go from here? Well, for one thing, we go back to work, but not as though nothing had happened, because everything has happened. An age vanished in a week. Values were shaken up so brutally that they can never be measured by the same yardstick. It is the age of speed, but even so the speed with which everything changed is staggering in itself. The Nation has grown older, and perhaps wiser. Over and over again the past few days I have heard people begin: "Say, have you heard that—did you know—oh well, it isn't important anyway." The old lines of communication are shot. Nobody at the moment is quite sure what is important, and the fact that we are even thinking about that—Americans are not strong for introspection—might be a hopeful sign.

* * *

A vanished age. Can you even recall what seemed of paramount concern a short week ago? The headlines were large with a coed who had disappeared, the turmoil in Vietnam, the marksmanship of Y.A. Tittle, the decline and fall of a local football team whose

64

name has not crossed many lips recently. The election of a Mayor was still being discussed and analyzed—"an amazing upset, fantastic thing," a lot of people were saying. The rebuilding of a dilapidated temporary building would, it seemed, cost a couple of million more than anticipated, and even then it wouldn't look as gloriously temporary as before. Mr. Burton and Miss Taylor, giants last week in the public consciousness, have suddenly been reduced in size to ordinary human beings with quite ordinary problems. Let us give thanks for that, at least.

★   ★   ★

One week ago, seven days in the past, 168 short hours back in the golden age of a young and confident leader, Texans were still vaguely comic characters who had too much money (have you seen the new Neiman-Marcus catalog?), a man I went to school with phoned from Washington with a new anti-Kennedy joke (I forced a laugh, because I had heard it before) and a small stack of neatly printed cards arrived from a humorous printer in Minneapolis ("Don't Be a Bigot," they read. "Hate Everybody!"). Only a week ago hate was still something to joke about, because everybody knows that Americans don't really hate. Seriously, that is.

★   ★   ★

In a week we have learned too much, and much of it too late. A week ago we were all fully prepared to give thanks that we are the best-fed, best-housed, best-paid people on the face of the earth, that we lived amid peace and plenty, that we were the acknowledged leaders of the free world (our God-given right) and that, in contrast to events in South America and Southeast Asia, this was not a land of terror and violence. A week ago we could have sat down to our turkey with an easy conscience, and the jokester at the table would have drawn a laugh by giving thanks that we are not turkeys. We would not have given much thought, probably, to the young man in the White House, and not too many of us would have read this Thanksgiving proclamation. That's one of the things you take for granted. Will we ever again take for granted a good man in the White House?

★   ★   ★

And so we enter the new age, this Thanksgiving Day, brutally shaken, but more aware than ever before of the dark forces around us—and within ourselves—that can still be controlled. If we have learned anything, we have learned that there is no such thing as security. When anarchy reigns—and anarchy begins when you stop caring for your fellow man—then not even the most valuable man

65

in the land is safe. All the guns in the Secret Service could not keep him safe, and all the weapons of destruction at our command will not keep us safe. The only shield is compassion and understanding, firm in the face of hate.

★ ★ ★

If we have learned that, let us this day give thanks.

November 28, 1963

1964

O TIME IN THY FLIGHT

This year marks the 25th anniversary of a lot of things (naturally), among them the World's Fair on Treasure Island, the Nazi invasion of Poland, the first Woody Herman band and the opening of Top o' the Mark. This might seem like a random set of examples, but actually they all tie in, as we shall endeavor to demonstrate. Watch out for loose ends and flying hyperbole.

★ ★ ★

There was a reunion last week of some of the people who helped launch the '39 Fair, and they all stood around saying things like "I can't believe it was 25 years ago, can you?" I can. It might as well have been 250 years ago, so dim is the memory. Like everything that happened before the Atomic Age, it seems like ancient history, far away and touched with innocence. The very idea of throwing a World's Fair while half the world was about to explode seemed a little unreal, even then, but we were determined to stay out of it, and I guess a Fair was one way of showing it.

Actually, the '39 Fair got off to a frosty beginning. On opening day only about 30,000 people showed up, shivering in an icy wind that knifed through the unfinished buildings. The roller-coaster was a bore, Sally Rand's Nude Ranch was embarrassing (a lot of girls who didn't have the figure for it stood around naked), and the Japanese, so soon to become our enemies, supplied a lovely dreamlike building that came across the Pacific, piece by piece. The Brazilian Pavilion immediately became known as the Brazilian Pazilion. Harris Connick, boss of the Fair, signed up Edwin Franko Goldman's military band under the impression he was getting Benny Goodman, and an un-Fair gag was born: "The Fair is suffering from Connick indigestion." Mr. Connick was a nice man, to whom one big band was much like another.

*   *   *

Still, the Fair at night was a brave sight, especially from the windows of the new Top o' the Mark, and we were at peace, although several countries that had promised to exhibit had to renege, since they were about to be swallowed up and knew it. To demonstrate how long ago all this was, Jake Ehrlich was a young lawyer defending madams, murderers and assorted hoods, whereas today he is representing the Chamber of Commerce in the fight for taller buildings. Respectability ages a man faster than late hours and bad champagne.

*   *   *

The Fair rolled on through '39 and '40, while the German armies rested up for the invasion of France and, they thought, England. In all frankness, it wasn't a great Fair, although it mellowed as it went along (and the hot toasted scones were magnificent from the start). The architecture was somewhere between late Mayan and early Pacifica Modern, neither here nor there: it was not one of the golden ages of design. In comparison with the 1915 Exposition, ALL of which should have been preserved in Saranwrap, it was a poor thing. Some day you should look up the photos of the '15 Fair and marvel at the grandeur. I realize it is pointless to compare prices, but that one cost only $18,500,000 to build, right down to the last shrub. It will cost almost that to restore properly the Palace of Fine Arts, but—pointless.

*   *   *

Benny Goodman, with one of his inferior bands, finally arrived at the '39 Fair and drew great crowds of what were known as hepcats. It was the era of the big bands, and if you'd heard his greatest, the one with Bunny Berigan (playing with a pitcher of gin under his chair) you were ahead of the game. Woody Herman, who closes at Off-Broadway tonight, emerged from the Isham Jones band to form his first group (Jones' singer, Al Morris of Oakland, left at the same time and changed his name to Tony Martin). Artie Shaw came into the Palace with a band that included ten fiddles, a cello and Johnny Guarnieri on harpsichord. I don't know how they could afford it, but all the hotels had big bands. In terms of today's dollars (again, pointless), it was like the St. Francis hiring the San Francisco Symphony for tea dancing.

*   *   *

Well, 25 years is a long time, but it's hard to get nostalgic about that Fair on the dredged-up island in the Bay. Only on closing night, at the end of a particularly warm, clear day (smog hadn't been invented yet) did some of us realize sharply that the lights were going out on our youth and that war lay ahead. The Top o' the Mark was jammed with people pressing their noses to the glass, and when the last light was extinguished, a long sigh ran through the crowd and you sat there looking silently at your highball. When war came, the corners of the Top were filled with young wives watching transports sail out of the Gate, and behind the bar the collection of "last survivor" bottles grew and grew. The big bands blew themselves out, until today (save for Woody, the Count and the Duke) they are as rare as the whooping crane. And Treasure Island, its real and spurious treasures removed, became the dark and far off blob it is—a place where people once laughed and sang while fire flickered on the horizon.

★ ★ ★

Tonight, if you're in the mood, you may listen to Woody Herman, visit Top o' the Mark and drink a toast to Treasure Island, thereby celebrating three silver anniversaries in one. Like most anniversaries, it will be a little sad.   *February 23, 1964*

YOUR CITY—AND MINE

"They're ruining this city," said my cab driver as he gunned across Fifth and Market, grazing a frightened covey of pedestrians, cutting in on a truck and forcing a car to the curb. He was one of the rudest drivers I've ever been marooned with—a true anarchist of the traffic wars—but it is always "they" who are at fault.

"Market Street is a disgrace," well-intentioned ladies are forever writing to newspapers. "Why don't they clean it up?" Some of these ladies probably feed the pigeons and walk their dogs on your sidewalk, but that's all right. "They" are wrong.

And so it goes, the livelong day. Why don't "they" do something about civil rights demonstrators, freeways, high-risers, Alcatraz and teen-agers? I've seen teen-agers and the motorcycle gangs stop on the highways to change flat tires for old ladies—the same ones who cluck-cluck about "teen-age punks" and "what is this world coming to?"

★ ★ ★

It's not "they" who are responsible for what pains or delights us about the city and our life in it. It's us. Anarchy is a strong word, but it begins at home; if you define it as a breakdown in law and order—and a disregard for your fellow man—there's plenty of it around. There's a little anarchy in all of us who complain about freeways and insist on driving our cars to work; let the other guy take the bus. There's a touch of anarchy in the pedestrian who walks against the "Wait" signal, and plenty in the nut who runs a red light. As for the man whose new building robs thousands of their view, or levels a green hill in the sacred name of free enterprise—well, maybe that's the divine right of economic royalty.

★   ★   ★

A city, any city, is always in a state of anarchy, more or less controlled. For a city is the world—or the jungle—in microcosm, and the laws of the jungle prevail. Let me get mine, and then we'll worry about the common good. As for what constitutes "mine," it's every man for himself.

The old-timers think the newcomers are ruining the city, and the newcomers regard the old-timers as a bunch of fuddy-duddies intent only on preserving a distant dream. There are people who believe, in all honesty, that San Francisco should have as many skyscrapers as can be crowded onto the existing space, "because that's what makes New York exciting, isn't it?" What makes (or is it made?) San Francisco exciting is a unique expanse of sea, sky and hills; when that is gone, at last, this will be a mini-Manhattan.

There are those who can't understand all the fuss about freeways. Young people born in the Freeway Age can't see anything wrong with a device that takes you where you're going as fast as possible—no matter how much beauty was sacrificed in the process. There is even something to be said for the Embarcadero Freeway: it affords a brief glimpse of ships at dock, something few people could see before.

As for the Highway Engineers, their problem is simply to build a straight line between two points at the lowest possible cost (in millions), and if something like Golden Gate Park gets in the way, too bad for Golden Gate Park. In the hierarchy of anarchy, the car is God, and a place to park is Heaven.

★   ★   ★

Well, there are a thousand viewpoints in the viewtiful city—and a view is sacred only to him who has one and is in danger of losing it. The Negro marching in a picket line couldn't care less about the Fontana, and the worker who lives in Deep Mission isn't likely to shed any tears over a freeway that nips off a corner of a Park he never visits.

Albert Schlesinger, a dedicated civic leader, says that "If we allow the Palace of Fine Arts to disappear, San Francisco will have a black eye all over the world"—which may be stretching it a little. It won't matter a whit in Ghana, Guiana or Genoa, or even to the Skid Rowgue on Third St., crouched in a doorway with his bottle of muscatel.

However, the Palace has become a symbol in the cold war raging in San Francisco. Somewhere the line must be drawn in the battle for beauty and tradition—even if it smacks at times of unreality—and apparently the Palace of Fine Arts is to be the line. Thanks or no thanks to William Howard Taft, San Francisco has been stuck with a label, "The city that knows how," and the know-how is somehow concentrated in a poetic structure that was built to fall down.

(I have the feeling that 50 years from now some savage satirist in the mold of Evelyn Waugh will write a screaming novel about a millionaire giving two million dollars for the restoration of a temporary building—only to find it is not enough by far. As war, pestilence and famine wrack the world, the red tape grinds inexorably until at last, out of the ashes of a dead city, rises a gleaming $50 million palace, built by the skeletal survivors of the memory of a man long dead.)

★   ★   ★

Franklin Murphy, Chancellor of UCLA, said the other day: "If we do not return beauty of the environment to a position of the highest priority, we shall have made of our growing megalopolises a major force for human brutalization." He wasn't speaking of the Palace of Fine Arts, but the words apply to what it symbolizes as a counterbalance to Neo-Box building and the stranglehold of freeways.

Brave words, Dr. Murphy's, but they are only words, and a city's people will not respond to stimuli that have no meaning for them. There will always be those who find a 50-story building more exciting than a Palace of Fine Arts. The challenge to "the city that knows how" is to find room for both, and it's not "they" who are going to solve the problem. It's little old anarchistic us.

March 29, 1964

SPRING'S OLD SWEET SONG

At this time of year I always remember the blind man on Market

St., with a sign around his neck reading "It is Spring and I Am Blind" (another blind man of the era, a quarter of a century ago, wore a button that announced, a bit too jauntily, "Long Time No See").

In the springtime it's hard not to think of the blind. There is so much to see in the burgeoning city, even two eyes seem hardly enough: the pale secretaries seated primly around the Mechanics Monument, faces turned to the sun, skirts drawn above their knees; the men with their hats in their hands, instead of their hands on their hats; daffodils in Maiden Lane and daft old dillies in Union Square. And always the blind.

In a few downtown blocks I counted five blind beggars playing those strangely tuneless songs on their accordions, as stoically patient as the dogs curled at their feet. Three of them have been working the area so long their faces are as familiar as those of John Gehring, the Good Cop, or Monk Fowler, the broken-nosed newsboy. Why are there blind beggars on the streets of a rich city?

But it is spring, and even they know it; for one thing, the wind is losing its bite. But it still has enough teeth to put a ripple in the flags at half-staff for the fallen General of the Army—the flags that send your memory racing back to the dark coldness of last November. On Third St. the pawnshops are again selling rifles with telescopic sights. Spring is the time for fresh starts.

*   *   *

The city is in full motion. Ladies in flowery hats jaywalking across Stockton, the tired voice of Officer Charlie Bates snapping at their heels. Children blossoming along the slanty side streets of Chinatown. Bodies sprawled on the green of Washington Square, the bells of SS Peter & Paul's floating over them like golden clouds. An aircraft carrier sliding past the foot of Leavenworth, crew lined on the deck, staring at the white city basking on its hills. New buildings rising stalk-straight, steel flowers growing out of deep, dark holes, and how will they look when they reach September? New paint, new signs, and the sun probing the decaying recesses of the Palace of Fine Arts where memories stir in dark corners.

*   *   *

The spring sun shines bright—on the ugliness of a city, as well as its beauty. The tough, tired old faces on Market St. look even more careworn in the glare; the touching faces of people who've known too many winters. The lonely men, lost under their hat brims, sit in the still darkness of small hotel lobbies, staring at nothing. In the cafeterias every other seat is taken at the long tables, for the lonely would rather sit alone than rub elbows with someone as far away as they.

From the top of a hill you can see the streets stretching for blocks, treeless as the Sahara. Everything is possible in this age of the cities—garages six stories deep or ten stories high, freeways that can dump a thousand cars a minute into a one-way, dead-end street, housing projects that spring up overnight on land that came from nowhere—and yet the planting of a single tree (of decent size) on a downtown street seems a project beyond the grasp of our finest minds. Money doesn't grow on trees—could that be the reason?

But street signs are a different story. They proliferate the way trees used to. Every fine spring morn a new batch seems to have grown—revolving, dangling, clamoring for attention, outshining the sun. There must be a giant Johnny Appleseed of the sign industry, and he scatters his seeds with fine abandon. Who's to stop him?

★　★　★

Spring in the city—the good life (convertibles and beer cans), the lush life (limousines double parked at I. Magnin), the hard life (see you at Candlestick Park on Tuesday). The nannies wheel their carriages in Lafayette Park, the doormen walk the poodles on Russian Hill, kites speckle the sky over the Marina Green, and there are all those people getting drunk in the Buena Vista, ignoring the fine view of Alcatraz, just across the watery street. The seasons come and go, the tides change, the stars swing in their orbits, but the same people are always standing there in the Buena Vista. Perhaps they were built in at the factory.

In the dark crevasse of Montgomery, where the sun makes only a brief appearance daily, an old man in a long overcoat is foraging in a trash basket. Well, he is not really old, you decide on a second look. Just defeated. Dress him in a suit from Ohlson & Holmes and he'd look like any mother's son of a Montgomery Streeter. But this mother's son didn't make it, and his mother probably had high hopes for him, like all mothers. Now, in the springtime of the year, he is rooting around in the garbage on the street where the money is grown—but never thrown away.

When it gets a touch warmer, old Mr. Whitehouse, age 81, will be back at the corner of Fifth and Market, handing out his Bible pamphlets. Once he owned 14 Littleman markets and sold them for $100,000. His wife gave her half to religious charities. He is spending his on the pamphlets he gives away—2,350,000 to date. Of his $50,000 he has less than $10,000 left. "God bless you," says

Mr. Whitehouse to the people who brush past him, ignoring the pamphlet he offers for nothing.

⋆   ⋆   ⋆

Another April in the city, and it is not only the blind who cannot see. *April 12, 1964*

SAN FRANCISCAENA

Whenever I feel I'm getting out of touch with the city—a fear that haunts all newsmen—I take a long walk along Market Street. As therapy this is better than a hot oil rub, picking up a 24-point bridge hand or flipping a cigarette butt at a cable car slot and watching it go in without touching the sides.

A few minutes on Market will convince anybody, even the oldest native, that he'll never get to know San Francisco. It's the street of broken dreams, of frozen screams, of strangers rubbing elbows—a main street a million miles away from the San Francisco the Convention & Visitors Bureau tries so desperately to portray in its magazine ads: the Tony Bennett city of tiny cable cars climbing to the stars that look down on seven-course dinners, nights at the opera and all that sort of kitschy-koo.

In many ways Market is the most sophisticated street in town, if by sophistication you mean weary, worldly and aloof. Its warmth is its coolness: you're alone, but so is everybody else. In a city that in too many ways is like a small town, it is blessedly impersonal. You can walk from Sixth to the Ferry without seeing anyone even vaguely familiar, and a foolish friendly smile gets exactly what it deserves: a darting glance on the edge of suspicion.

Market is teeming with San Franciscans you'll never get to know. It is quite clear that they don't want to know you, either. Nothing is given, nothing is expected—a truly civilized arrangement.

⋆   ⋆   ⋆

Market Street is the city in all its desperate vitality and glorious vulgarity—the Alcatraz of streets. It's there, but nobody knows what to do with it. Every traffic plan runs up against it and falls back, defeated. The dreamers talk vaguely of pedestrian malls and islands of shrubbery, but there is no doubt even in the pretty drawings; they will end up in the files (of the wastebasket) along with a thousand other plans bravely titled, "What to Do About Market Street." It is wide, long, stubborn and unregenerate—a true brute of a street. A dead end with a life of its own.

The image-conscious San Franciscan nervously warns the visitor: "Stay off Market. It's no more San Francisco than Broadway is New York." A specious argument. Might as well say Post Street is no more San Francisco than Fifth Avenue is New York. Market is mucho San Francisco—our main drag, and don't linger overlong on the second word. It's a drag only if you can't face the fact that San Francisco isn't all bankers at Jack's, Dolly Fritz at Trader Vic's—and No. 263 off the Golden Gate Bridge.

Market Street has broad sidewalks, beautiful lampposts, pockets of respectability and ugly realities. The delicate Zellerbach Building turns its back on it, but The Emporium faces up to it and beats it. The Flood Building maintains its dignity—brooding gravely above the biggest (and liveliest) Woolworth's in the world—and the PG&E Building, as handsome as any in the city, lights its face at night, as befits a face worth seeing.

But I see I'm getting off on the wrong tack, too. Buildings have nothing to do with the terrible fascination of Market. People have everything to do with it.

★ ★ ★

Market is old men spitting on the sidewalk and blowing their noses in the gutters. Women too broad of beam to wear slacks, but wearing them anyway, tucked into pointy boots. Girls with hair tossed a mile high over pouty faces filled with chewing gum. Old ladies smoking cigarettes and flipping them away expertly. Greasy-haired boys wearing pants so tight they must have been painted on, standing in silent knots, icy glance on passing girls. Young men in shiny leather jackets, trying to look insolent and dangerous, which they could very well be. Slim-hipped boy-girls piloting motorcycles with frigid efficiency, returning your stare with a contemptuous flick of dead eyes.

Market is rock 'n' roll blaring out of little record shops, $9.95 shoes and $19.95 dresses, the smell of hot dogs, men spooning crab cocktails into faces hidden inside upturned collars, schoolgirls eating ice cream sandwiches, dirty magazines with their pages Scotch-taped so you can't get a free peek, pinball games flashing their obscene lights, and bums in World War II overcoats who take your quarter without the thanks you didn't want anyway. Give thanks that you're able to give it.

First-run theaters and worst-run fleabags where bizarre rites are said to take place in the seats down front, blind men pausing for a look at the nude girls in the peep shows, religious fanatics hollering at the startled tourists waiting for the Powell cable, and little toy windup dogs running in circles on the sidewalk Pockmarket Street, the mass, the mess, the beginning and the end. You don't have to like it. It couldn't care less about you.

★   ★   ★

And what should we do about Market Street? The same thing we should do about Alcatraz. Nothing. However, you might walk along it once in a while, you people who are willing to concede only that the Ferry Building is at one end and Twin Peaks at the other.

What lies between is the San Francisco that San Franciscans will never know—the anonymous thousands who live their secret lives that no computer, no pollster, no newspaperman is ever going to get at. In their walled silence they make a mockery of the four-color posters we try to sell to the world as The Real San Francisco.

When you walk along Market you become just another face in the crowd—a crowd that takes you at face value. It might not be The Real San Francisco, but, brother, it's real.   *June 14, 1964*

I remember Papa: For thousands of San Franciscans yesterday was a day of mourning. Pierre Monteux was dead at 89: a living legend had gone to join the immortals of music.

For 17 golden years (1935–1952) he presided over the San Francisco Symphony—but there is more to it than that. He was part of the city's life and color in every way. A cuddly toy in a black overcoat, he walked his wife's beloved poodle, Fifi, daily outside the Fairmont Hotel as passing cable cars clanged a greeting. He and his Doris had a salon of friends and artists in their suite at every cocktail hour (Papa Pierre's favorite stunt: stealing the piano to play an exceedingly jazzy version of "Crazy Rhythm"). After a concert you could find him at the Blue Fox eating oysters and drinking champagne.

He was roly-poly, twinkly-eyed and humorous. To an ambitious young singer who whispered to him at a dinner party: "What would you say if I said I love you?" he chuckled: "I would say it is too late." When the ladies of the orchestra performed a can-can, in tights, at his birthday party, he observed: "I have been conducting them for years, and this is the first time I knew they had legs." He had black hair and a white moustache, and when somebody accused him of dying his hair, he smiled: "You are wrong—I bleach my moustache" (he delighted in being photographed with Novelist Charles G. Norris, who had white hair and a black moustache).

★　★　★

During his last few seasons with the Symphony the chronic complainers were heard to say that he had been here too long. He took it philosophically. "I don't blame them," he sighed one night during his last season here. "If I had to look at the same backside for 18 years I'd start complaining too."

It seemed as though Pierre Monteux would surely go on forever, but he began failing rapidly ten weeks ago after he fell in Rome, hit his head on a marble floor and suffered a concussion, followed by strokes. Ever since he has been in bed in his home in Hancock, Me., where he died about 4 a.m. yesterday. Among his last words were:

"When I see Brahms I really must apologize to him for the way I've played his beautiful music."

To those who loved Pierre Monteux, especially in Brahms, the apology will seem unnecessary. *July 2, 1964*

Doesn't anybody work in this crazy town? It's a question I often ask myself, in lieu of working. The financial district bars start filling up at 11:30 a.m. with executives bobbing for olives in martini buckets. At 2:30 the restaurants are still loaded, with customers to match. You phone a Civic Leader at 3 p.m., and his secretary loyally announces "He's in conference," meaning he's in wine. I guess it's like the Army. The Sergeants do all the work.

Case in point: I was driving along Filbert the other noon when I happened to pass the Marina Bowl. As in a cartoon, a balloon labeled "Idea!" appeared over my head. Somebody had told me once that here was a bowling alley that had good food, a piquant combination. So, casting my Diner's Club card to the wind, I went in—and confronted the biggest mob this side of a Sam Bronston production.

The bar was three-deep in Police Inspectors, Judges, doctors, lawyers and leaders of industry, whose names I dare not use for fear of rocking the city to its foundations. George Cerruti was standing in a corner, playing his accordian. Squealing girls were being pinched in the funniest places. A man in the salami business was buying champagne for the house.

Bewildered but fascinated, I sat at a table with three stout millionaires and ate the kind of lunch you'd expect to find in a bowling alley, especially if the alley is in San Francisco: minestrone, cannelloni, venison and risotto, salad and, for dessert, peaches in red wine—plus the champagne the salami man kept sending over. "Is it always like this around here?" I gasped to the owner Johnny Cardoni. "No," he admitted. "It's a little quiet today."

When I crawled out, at 2:45, the place was still jammed, and Mr. Cerruti was on the 17th chorus of "I Lost My Heart in San Cholesterol." The Marina Bowl, I discovered as I left, was formerly a car barn, and Filbert seemed an appropriately nutty street for the scene enacted within. But I ask again: Doesn't anybody work in this crazy town?   *July 27, 1964*

Crazyville: As my colleague, RJG, has pointed out, Broadway in North Beach is getting as honky-tonk as the Tenderloin was in its worst (or best) days, but it's the same old story. Nothing succeeds like excess, and as long as the joints are making money—and they are—there'll be no changes made.

I wandered through the area Tuesday night, and there were more people around than you'll find on a Saturday night in most cities. You had to wait for a table at La Strada, at least a hundred sidewalk gawkers were watching the dancers inside El Cid, and the line outside the Jazz Workshop stretched halfway down the block—not to see a bare-breasted Swim dancer, but to listen to the elegant bossa nova sound of Stan Getz, the man for whom the tenor sax was invented.

"Give 'em what they want" is the cry of the hard-eyed entrepreneurs, and it's nice to know that sometimes they want the best, which is what he is. Or maybe nobody knows what they really want—but Stan Getz 'em anyway.   *July 30, 1964*

THE TOTAL CITY

I saw an ad for men's shoes the other day that read "For Total Style!"—and it struck me that "total" has become a very big word in the current vocabulary. Total commitment, total annihilation, total nuclear response, total TV (as in the coverage of the political conventions) and inevitably, total mess. Which brings us to the concept of The Total City, which most San Franciscans fondly believe theirs is—and for good reason, in most cases.

But for a few days last week, when the opera season seemed doomed, the concept was badly shaken. Either a city offers everything, in return for the difficulties of living in it, or it doesn't offer enough. You take away one major attraction, and suddenly the crazy kaleidoscope is out of kilter. To force a bad pun, a city is more than the sum of its parties. And do not ask for whom the bridge tolls, it tolls for thee—a quarter at a time.

*　*　*

Well, why do we live in a city anyway? Certainly not for its total traffic, which has become so absurd as to be obscene. Not for its prices, which are high enough to make your nose bleed; or its salaries, which always seem one plateau behind.

We live in a city for total experience—the multifaceted life in microcosm—and in a city that is compact as well as total, the experience is particularly rich. San Francisco has hovels next to mansions, garish neon masking dreary tenements, magnificence and misery, wild tensions and wilder releases. And always the soul-cleansing fog and the wind-whipped banners on the skyscrapers, the cables crawling up the hills to yesterday, the flower stands making explosions of color on the street corners, the banker at his dry martini and the Skid Rowgue at his sweet muscatel.

It is all of a piece, and nothing can be removed without destroying the whole. For all its hardness, a city is a delicate mechanism, as we discovered last week when a vital cog—the opera season—was almost removed.

*　*　*

I suppose the majority of San Franciscans couldn't have cared less about the crisis (a Geary St. newsboy hollered the headlines, "Opera Season Dead," and added a sarcastic "Boo-hoo-hoo"). But the picture San Francisco likes to present to the world is that of "the city that has everything," and we aren't all THAT total.

We have major league baseball, played in a park that isn't in the same league with Los Angeles'. The less said about Kezar Stadium—right? We are about to spend $7.5 million to restore a building that made more sense as a ruin—and use it for what? We have an excellent Opera House that is being overworked, out of necessity and shortsightedness. We have a treasure of hills and views that is being squandered for lack of a plan.

"Culture" is a word we bandy about to a perilous degree. Our Symphony is only now being pulled back into shape by the energetic Josef Krips. Our private art collections are notoriously below the quality and quantity of Los Angeles', and our art buyers are picayunish. Our museums are not as bad as indicated by the nasty crack of an Eastern museum director—"San Francisco should amalgamate its three bad museums; then it would have only one bad museum"—but we have nothing to be smug about there, either. Our ballet company, acclaimed elsewhere, has to struggle here.

The hard fact is that when it comes to "culture," it is principally the San Francisco Opera Company we can boast of without qualification. A civic official, fair carried away, described it the other day as "the crown jewel in our cultural crown," and so it is. When the San Francisco detractors go to work, ticking off our shortcomings, it is always the opera company that stops them cold.

*　*　*

Well, we almost lost it, and once you lose anything as complex as this, there's a danger it will never be put back together. Los Angeles, which is about to complete a dazzling music and art center, most certainly would have moved fast to organize its own opera company—and they've got the money and ambition to do it. A few years hence, the Los Angeles Opera Company may have been playing here, instead of vice versa, and then where is The Total City?

A cheer at this point for Jack Shelley, who clearly saw the danger and was more determined than Robert Watt Miller to avert it.

And a cheer for the too often maligned Musicians Union. I admit to being partial to our musicians. They are the unsung heroes of many an opera performance, and the public villains in many a negotiation. Their salaries have not kept pace with the rising costs of opera production (nothing, it seems, is too much to pay for a star) and yet they are usually the first to be asked to compromise.

*　*　*

No thanks to the sometimes ridiculous coverage of the newspapers, the opera here has been made to appear a social bauble—and those who run it have not done enough to correct the image. As a tough but fair-minded City Hall official put it while the negotiations were on: "If they want to keep it their plaything, they'd better be prepared to pick up the tab."

The opera has been saved, but it was a close thing—not just for society, the merchants and the hairdressers, but for everybody who loves music and the concept of San Francisco as The Total City. Even those who never go near the Opera House would have had their life diminished, whether they know it or not.

August 30, 1964

SING ALONG WITH KURT

Well, the opera season is now in full swing, and it is already apparent that Dr. Kurt Herbert Adler has scored another triumph. The repertoire is longer than ever, and the operas themselves aren't getting any shorter, either; "Parsifal" went on so long that its last act carried over into a rehearsal for "Rosenkavalier," causing considerable confusion. The town's three distinguished music critics are demonstrating again that it is possible to attend three different performances of the same opera at the same time, and the Opera House's newest amenity—seat belts—is keeping more sleeping patrons than ever before from falling into the aisles, where they get in the way of walkouts.

However, there remains the problem of the synopsis of each opera. These are printed in tiny type in the program, sometimes on blue paper, which makes them even more illegible. You haven't time to read the story of the opera on the way in, because you're already late. During the intermission you're standing in line at the bar, hoping the bartender likes your face. It doesn't do much good to read the synopsis after it's all over and say, "Oh, is THAT what was going on?"

Therefore, as a public service, we are presenting our all-purpose synopsis to cover any opera in three acts, four languages and five hours. It is titled "Dristan und Clairol," with music by Giuglielmo Flavorzone, and a libretto by Samuel Sanskrit based on a book written by Y. A. Tittle derived from a word uttered in 1836 by Sir Edmund Bore. After memorizing, tear into small pieces and swallow. Oh, about that word of Sir Edmund's. It was "Eh?"

★ ★ ★

ACT I

As the curtain rises, Dristan makes a triumphal entrance, singing his famous hymn to Sol, king of the Bagels. Sol, the first basso (a role made famous by Orlando Cepeda), clasps him to his bosom and offers him the hand of his beautiful daughter, Clairol, in response to which Dristan sings the unforgettable aria, "Che bella, mais wo ist la miserare?" ("It's a nice hand, but how about a look at the rest of the girl?") Irium, knowing that Clairol is actually Prince Vasili Romanov in disguise, shouts the betrayal from the ranks of the peasants, and declares her love. Unfortunately, she herself is disguised as a donkey, being under a spell, and coughs constantly, having played the cigarette girl in "Carmen" once too often. She drops her handkerchief, which is picked up by Count Giuseppe DiMaggio, who has been discarded by Clairol, who has been rejected by Lentil, who in turn is seeking the mother of Dristan, who has been imprisoned in a high dungeon by Sol, a secret member of the Giovanni Birchio Society, who is jealous of Dristan's popularity. As the curtain falls, the skies darken, the plot sickens and the peasants are revolting, except for Clairol, who has fallen asleep in the arms of Nembutal.

★   ★   ★

ACT II
In the mountain hideaway of Dreft, the fairy king, who performs a suspiciously gay dance to the music of The Smugglers, a banjo band. Clairol, seeking her mother, Machree, has been rejected by Dristan, who has found her handkerchief in the possession of DiMaggio and has killed him in the same high dungeon where Machree is held prisoner. Clairol, still coughing, not knowing she has conspicuous consumption, sings "Come un bel di DiMaggio" and stumbles away, vowing to spend the rest of her life in Solitude or Penance, two active retirement centers near Coalinga. Dristan arrives with his faithful friend, Zinfandel, on a fishing expedition. Drawing a pike, he runs Dreft through, not knowing that Dreft is Irium in disguise. As Irium dies, she reveals that she is actually a prince and the son of Sol, king of the Bagels. Dristan plunges into Remorse, a small river near the Slough of Despond, and is heard off-stage singing "Ai Cosa Nostra." As the curtain falls, the peasants are revolting, except for little Vel, who sings the happy washday song, "Ou est la blanchisserie de ma Tante?"

★   ★   ★

ACT III
This act opens on a more relaxed note (B flat), since the morning newspaper critics have already left to make their deadlines. Dristan, miraculously saved from drowning by mouth-to-mouth resuscitation performed by his faithful Zinfandel, is on his way to join a convent, having been turned into a woman by the evil witch, Kreplach, who is actually Machree, who has escaped from the dungeon disguised as an Elk (although in the original libretto she is a Rotarian). Dreft reappears briefly, having forgotten he was killed in the second act, and does a gay dance with the peasants, who are still revolting, except for Clairol, whose attempts to enter a

monastery have been rebuffed. Dristan and Clairol declare their love for each other, after which Clairol reveals that she is actually Fluoristan, opening her mouth to show 33% fewer cavities (as she sings "Costa Diva," the aria rendered immortal by Mary Costa). As the revolting peasants begin to dance again, she is seized by another, and final, coughing spell, little knowing that help from Bowerman's is on the way. They vow to die together, and prepare a poisonous potion of gin and vermouth, which Dristan swallows first, singing in agony, "Troppo Cinzano!" ("Too much vermouth!"), in which she joins for the duet, "Chiedi all' aura Noilly Prat" ("So next time ask for something drier"). The potion having failed, they climb to the top of the nearest basso profundo and, clasping hands, leap into the orchestra pit, there to perish among the oboes, one of which is actually Sol, king of the Bagels. Onstage, as the final curtain falls, the peasants are still revolting, and the audience sounds a little menacing, too.   *September 27, 1964*

JUST FOOLIN' AROUND

People who see a Red under every bed must spend a lot of time down on all fours.

When a man says, "Well, things could be worse," you know he has given up the search for something better.

Why don't girls who say "G'bye now" also say "Hello then"? Makes just as much sense, if not more so.

The best restaurant in town is a good one in which you are known to the owner; the second best is the one that serves consistently good food whether the owner knows you or not.

Ballet dancers have pretty legs and show as much of them as the law allows, but have you ever seen a sexy-looking ballet dancer? Female, I mean.

The trouble with learning to yawn with your mouth closed is that you keep getting invited to dull dinner parties.

How long has it been since you've seen a movie that's too SHORT?

Shirley Temple still looks as though she might burst into "On the Good Ship Lollipop" any minute.

If you take a seat behind an open window on a Muni bus—to get the breeze on a hot day—the next passenger will close it. However, if you have a cold and sit behind the closed window, the next passenger will open it.

Men who wear white socks also wear two fountain pens in their breast pocket.

Columnists are forever printing items like "Bing Crosby was in the audience, completely unrecognized." Then how do they know he was there?

★　★　★

Little things that make the day: The tie you put on in the morning dimples perfectly on the first try . . . Both sides of your button-down shirt collar bellow evenly . . . A tourist, seeking directions, asks you a question you can answer in under 500 words . . . The girl standing next to you at the corner, waiting for the light to change, is wearing Hermes' Caleche . . . The bill from a store arrives with a self-addressed envelope; the bill itself shows a credit balance . . . 49ers, 31; Green Bay, 27 . . . You are the first to see Molinari-Pradelli entering the Opera House orchestra pit, and can lead the applause . . . "The next 30 minutes of Rodgers & Hart songs will be uninterrupted by announcements or commercials" . . . A Golden Gate Bridge toll collector greets you by name . . . You ask Information for a number, and she says "Klondike" instead of using the initials or a digit . . . The pretty stranger you smile at on Geary smiles back . . . A man in the Palace lobby smirks, "I'll bet you don't remember my name," and you remember to reply, "I'll bet you go around winning that bet all day."

★　★　★

Little things that ruin the day: The white tie you sent to the laundry, tagged "Do Not Starch," comes back starched, tag and all . . . You round a corner and find that a once-familiar view of the Bay has been blocked by an ugly new building that went up overnight . . . "He just stepped out, may I have him call you back?" . . . The toastmaster who says "The man I am about to introduce needs no introduction" gives him one anyway . . . "So what's new?" . . . Green Bay, 31; 49ers, 27 . . . The stranger who falls asleep next to you at the opera puts her head on your shoulder: her hair is lacquered . . . A lovely Victorian house being steel-balled to death . . . "The number you have reached is not in service at this time—" . . . You are driving across the Gate Bridge on a beautiful morning, and then you see, alongside, the Sheriff's van filled with prisoners on their way to San Quentin.

★　★　★

Every day, in every way, our advertising geniuses are getting better and better (and don't ask "than what?"—THEY don't care).

For example, I was charmed to learn just the other day that long stretch socks—the ones that come up over the calf—are "executive length"; the longer the sock, the higher the status. And the '65 Imperial has a gauge that tells you when the other gauges aren't working; what happens when that gauge fails is not stated in the ad, which DOES tell you that this is one of Imperial's "33 other standard luxury features" (when luxury becomes standard, what is there left?). A new Alcoa ad describes our Golden Gateway area as "an urban suburb," not to be confused with a suburban urb. However, on the brighter side, we have Mac McCoskey, who reminds us that before TV, nobody knew what a headache looked like. There's that.

★　★　★

Out of my mind: Now that the cable cars are officially a National Monument, I can think of a few other things that deserve permanent commemoration. For instance, the busted lamppost on Battery St. that Willie Britt would rather have been than the Waldorf-Astoria. Swan's Oyster Depot on Polk. The clock everybody is said to have met under in the St. Francis lobby. Freed Teller Freed. The Panama Canal Ravioli Factory. Normandie Lane in the City of Paris. The bathtub where Anna Held bathed in Almaden champagne. The warehouse at the foot of Telegraph Hill where Philo Farnsworth perfected TV, which hasn't been perfect since. And so on . . . Playing the odds: Seven out of ten people who never write fan letters eventually write fan letters beginning "I never write fan letters." Nine out of ten bridge players who ask "Who dealt?" just dealt. Four out of five tennis players look at their racquet after missing a shot. Four out of seven people who pronounce realtor as though it was spelled "realator" will take you aside to tell you "an interesting antidote." Eight out of ten people who think "Candy" is a satire don't know a dirty book when they've read one.

October 11, 1964

The View From the Heights

A reader writes: "As a newcomer to San Francisco, I am confused by the constant newspaper references to a district known as Pacific Heights, which I cannot find on any map of the city. Where—and what—is it?"

★　★　★

One is tempted to reply that Pacific Heights is a mythical faubourg that exists only in the minds of society editors, columnists and real estate agents, but that wouldn't be entirely accurate. For there really is a Pacific Heights, with its own peculiar view of San Francisco—perhaps the only view in town that looks inward rather than out.

Literally, Pacific Heights is a bit of a misnomer. Since it lies on the Northern flank of the city, it overlooks the Bay, not the Pacific. Physically, its boundaries are as loose as its restrictions are tight—let us say, from around Fillmore to Presidio, and from Clay to Union (westward from Presidio to about Arguello the section becomes Presidio Heights, with no marked difference in income or outlook).

However, as you may infer from these loose delineations, there is more to Pacific Heights than location, for many poor or socially unacceptable people live in the areas sketched above, and to be Really Pacific Heights you may not be either. But as long as you are neither, you may even live on Russian, Nob or Telegraph hills, and, in rare instances, Sea Cliff or even Jordan Park (VERY rare). Potrero Hill may make it yet, but never St. Francis Wood.

A further salient of Pacific Heights juts down the Peninsula into parts of Burlingame, Hillsborough and Woodside, somehow avoiding Atherton almost completely. The late Mr. Atherton would be astounded.

★   ★   ★

In sum, Pacific Heights is a point of view that points at itself with pride. Ideally, it is Old Money, which, as anybody knows, is much better than new, inflated stuff. It is Pucci pants, little Chanel suits, English bootmakers and an accent compounded of Ivy League schools, the proper upbringing and Old Forester.

Pacific Heights is "let's hop in the Jag and buzz down to Pebble for the weekend." It's knowing Paris much better than Los Angeles, New York better than Oakland, and the Right People in both. It's "couldn't be nicer, couldn't be more attractive, couldn't be more fun" and "couldn't have been duller," with or without the quotes. It's saying on long weekends, "Let's go away—EVERYBODY will be out of town anyway."

Pacific Heights is houseboys in white jackets walking poodles in clipped jackets, polished windows with shades drawn by polished butlers, indifferent dinners cooked by indifferent cooks ("good ones are SO hard to get"), surprisingly strong martinis and surprisingly bad wines. The houses are pleasant, whether done in Early Michael Taylor or Late Anthony Hail, and the mirrors are generally superior to, and looked at more often than, the pictures. As the finger bowls come, the ladies go to powder their noses.

Pacific Heights is an eternal cocktail party at which everybody knows everybody else, an endless bridge game involving the identical foursome, musical chairs to the same old tune, packages from Gump's, I. Magnin, Podesta and Laykin, Tuesday and Friday nights at the opera and a third-base box at Candlestick. If you're not With It, where are you?

Through all the changes it changes not. It is the city's power and sometimes glory, the Northern Lights and the Southern Cross, the day-and-night repository of all that is gilded and glamorous about San Francisco. It is Big Business and Big Pleasure, and it keeps a lot of money in circulation, occasionally its own. And if it sometimes appears to be out of touch with reality, weep not. Reality could very well be out of touch with Pacific Heights.

★　★　★

Without Pacific Heights—and let me stress again that I use the term loosely—San Francisco would not be what it is today, for better or worse. To the world of stylish travelers and slick magazine editors, it IS San Francisco—or at least the part of it that is thought of (and written about) as "sophisticated, gay and sparkling." When any distinguished visitor says, "I just adore San Francisco," you may be sure he isn't referring to picnics in Golden Gate Park or the English muffins at Foster's. He has been taken in by The Group, he has been given the Pacific Heights whirl, and this, forevermore, is San Francisco to him.

He is one of the fortunate few, for The Group is as clannish as its counterparts anywhere (visitors who say San Francisco is "cold" and "hard to get to know" didn't make it through the pearly gates). The cable cars, the bridges and Twin Peaks are fine to see, but if you haven't been invited into the hushed drawing rooms, where the minions of Thomas the Butler pass the canapes, you haven't been inside the San Francisco where names are dropped and unlisted phone numbers picked up.

So I say hail to Pacific Heights, wherever it may be. As the city grows away from itself, it grows more deeply into itself, perhaps in self-protection. It is the last of the constants, where children still curtsy, manners are excellent, the ladies are lovely, and drinking a bit too much is not only acceptable but almost mandatory. Life may be equally pleasant in the Deep Mission or the Far Sunset, but Pacific Heights has the panache and the postiche, not to mention the Beluga and the Malassol, and the Aubusson underfoot.

Whatever high style still accrues to San Francisco lives on in this glorious Never-Never Land of three cars for every two-car garage and Chicken a la Kiev in every pot. Long may it be preserved, sous cloche or on the rocks.   *October 18, 1964*

THINGS TO COME—AND GO

"You're lucky," nervously smiled a friend who works in a plant that is becoming more and more automated. "They'll never invent a machine that can do your kind of work."

"That's right," I agreed, just as nervously, my monkey mind meanwhile wondering whether "automated" refers to a couple making love in a car.

Could a machine perform such miracles of bad jokes as the foregoing, I wondered, fingers paradiddling on the desk. Any answer was not out of the question. After all, a computer known as the Ginsberg III had written some incredible poetry and even showed signs of sprouting a beard before it had been hastily unplugged. At this very moment hundreds of tape-fed typewriters are turning out business letters containing every cliche of the executive mind.

So why not a computerized column? Many of my own, I reflected sadly, already sounded machine-made, with only the names misspelled to confuse the libel lawyers. Perhaps I was becoming a machine myself, sitting dead-eyed and slackjawed at the typewriter, pounding out the same old familiar stories for years without end.

Well, we would soon see about that, I said mechanically. Gazing into the mirror, I found a satisfactory reflection of flesh and flab, presumably human. I started toward the door, only to be pulled nearly off my feet by a violent tug. I had forgotten to unplug myself from the wall.

*   *   *

The resident genius in charge of computers listened to my proposal with baited breath, having obviously had fish for lunch. His eyes, one red, one green, one amber, lit up and began blinking rapidly. "Certainly I've got a machine that can write a column, six days a week, without breathing hard," he said, leading me over to a metal monster in a corner.

"This little beauty right here," he went on, patting its pointy head, "is the Super Human Razzle Dazzle Linear Unit, otherwise known as SHRDLU. Properly programmed, it can put any number of people out of work—not only sensation-seeking columnists, such as yourself, but legmen, bust men, press agents, public relations engineers and even a pre-set number of restaurants and night clubs. Not only that, it automatically sets its own typographical errors, easy as pi. It never gets hangovers, is completely tax-deductible, and—."

"But is it funny?" I interrupted. "This machine," he replied, "is a scream." He pressed a button, and it screamed. "Here, I'll give you a sample," he continued, punching a button marked "East Bay." Wheels whirred, and a tape emerged, reading "Terrible accident the other day at the Oakland International Jet Airport—a plane landed."

"Doesn't crack me up," I said sourly, but he only shrugged. "First we have to program it," he pointed out. "You can't get more out of a computer than you put into it. After all, it's only superhuman."

★ ★ ★

We spent the next hour feeding a week's supply of column fodder into SHRDLU, a nice little machine once you got to know it. First we put in the staples—Golden Gate Bridge, Telegraph Hill, Coit Tower and so on. Then we taped a little corn: "Fog through harpstrings Gate Bridge," "Jampacked cable car waddling over Nob Hill like old woman with armful of packages," "Squirrels playing ring-around-rosy at dawn in dew-kissed glen Golden Gate Park," "Lovers necking unashamed in parked cars at Land's End as sun sinks slowly Westwise."

"Now some of those names you're always using," he said, so we ran the gamut from A (for Andy Lacbay) to Z (for Zellerbach), plus B for Conrad, J for Shelley and H for Bridges. "And don't forget your bed-and-butter items," he prompted, so we taped in "Headin' for a weddin'," "Going their separated ways," "Glimpsed at a tete-a-table for two," after which we programmed various punch lines: "And the stranger at the bar turned out to be long-lost brother he hadn't seen since 1909," and the ones about the Judge who has his car stolen and the cop who has his house robbed.

Under "Old San Francisco," we fed in "Fire-quake Emperor Norton, Bummer and Lazarus, six-bit dinners with wine at Sanguinetti's," and for "Critical Comments" we supplied the machine with "high-risers the lowest, bulldozing builders with one-tract minds, 49ers must go and why they don't, Giants midget, San Francisco slipping, wait till next year."

★   ★   ★

The computer man rubbed his hands in anticipation. "That's plenty of nothin'," he smiled. "More than enough for a week's columns in The Voice of the West." He slapped SHRDLU heartily on the back and said, "You are now a columnist. Write us a Monday column, you superhuman little beauty."

He pressed the "Start" button, and sure enough, the tapes rolled and it typed out "Caen colm for Monday." Then it neatly printed "Set all two colms," after which came a long silence as it whirred quietly. "That's odd," said the computer man, giving SHRDLU a kick. Slowly, it typed "J. Rolph and B. Conrad glimpsed at a tete-a-table for two in Sanguinetti's," a line it then exed out. After another silence, the machine wheeled around and began gazing out the window.

When the computer man kicked it again, SHRDLU lit a cigarette. Then it changed its own typewriter ribbon, and when it began sharpening pencils, the man got frantic. He pressed a whole lot of buttons and the machine lit up angrily. A wisp of smoke curled out of its top and a tape appeared, reading, "Think I'll run down to Hanno's in the Alley for a quick drink."

I went back to the office feeling better. A machine might replace a columnist someday, all right, but it won't get any more work done. Not if it's properly programmed.

November 15, 1964

1965

So we don't have Norton Simon—we have Cyril Magnin. When he built his store at Montgy. and Bush, he added a fancy, matching newsstand at the corner for Newsboy Albert Johnson. Couple of months ago, a truck came along and smithered it to smashereens, and poor Albert has been homeless ever since. So, having received hundreds of letters and calls from worried Albert-lovers, Cyril is rebuilding the stand, and it will be dedicated Tuesday with a ribbon-cutting, speeches and champagne. What has Norton Simon done for homeless newsboys lately?   *April 2, 1965*

Mutter & mumbles: "Why don't you write something about the outlandish clothes worn by the young people these days?" writes a crotchety old-timer. Can't do it. I remember too clearly the Uniform of the Day when I went to school: corduroy pants that were never, never washed—and were considered perfect only when they were stiff enough with dirt to stand by themselves. With these hideously filthy pants it was de rigueur to wear a spotlessly fresh white shirt every day—a bewildering combination that baffled our parents as deeply as we're baffled today.

   "Isn't San Francisco first in anything any more?" asks another old crotchet. Certainly. We're first in torn-up streets. I've never been in a city where so many helmeted crews were so busy each morning setting up red flags, taking off manhole covers and setting out these plastic hats for witches that were buried standing up, as St. Clair McKelway once described those markers. Second, we're first in dirty buses. In the ankle-deep debris on a Kearny bus the other day, I found a missing page from the Dead Sea Scrolls, a 1935 Chronicle (first edition) and Sonny Tufts playing gin with Judge Crater. Third, we're first in honkers, wheezers, sneezers, sniffers and two-fingered nose blowers on downtown streets. The computer that could calculate the germ count in any given block on Market has yet to be built. *April 11, 1965*

Moonlight becomes you: Nine cops stalked into the Moulin Rouge strip parlor on B'way Friday night to check the action—and each one had a highball. Satisfied that no laws were being broken, they then left, sticking Waitress Betsy Butzen with the $11.25 tab . . .

* * *

Technical note: Since the raids on North Beach (the greatest since Schweinfurt and Ploesti), several baffled readers have written in to inquire about "pasties," an item figuring prominently in the news. These pasties are not to be confused with Cornish Pasties, a meat pie with a flaky crust. In fact, the pronunciation is different, the edible pastie having the short "a," the other kind rhyming with "hasty." The pasties under consideration today derive from "paste," as in pasting on, and are designed to be pasted over the tip of the things that if you show them in public, you could get arrested if you aren't wearing them, and sometimes if you are. Serbin's on Powell sells them at $1.95 a pair and up; they come in various colors and three sizes, small, medium and how about THAT? They have adhesive on the back and should be removed "slowly," says a Serbin spokesman, who adds that despite the raids, business is brisk. "We sell most of them," he said, "to Peninsula matrons, many of them well-known socially. They are ideal for sunbathing in the nude." No further questions? *April 27, 1965*

It was a great weekend, any way you look at it (provided you weren't looking at it in Vietnam or Santo Domingo). Willie McCovey became Lovey-Dovey McCovey all over again. The deck of The Trident in Sausalito was jammed with San Franciscans trying to identify the new high-risers on S.F.'s skyline (our profile has changed). A toll-taker on the Gate Bridge, James Frisbie, said, "Have a nice day," which is above and beyond. The Bay was studded with sails—white flags on a blue map of peace. Arthur Hoppe celebrated his 40th birthday (I wish it had been his 80th—I hate competition). And I became a father.

★   ★   ★

The trouble with having a baby—if you're a man—is that you're always in the way. I haven't been told "Kindly leave the room" so many times since I was a small boy myself. Doctors, interns, nurses, nurses' aides, even janitors who happened to be passing by—before the event, they were all in my wife's room, conferring like mad. But not me. Oh, no.

So you sit in the waiting room, right? The waiting room for expectant fathers at Children's Hospital is like waiting rooms everywhere—a TV set and a copy of Life magazine in a plastic cover stamped "Do Not Remove Under Pain of Death." Since it was 5 a.m., there was nothing on the telly, not even Gypsy Rose Lee. But there were a couple of other fathers-to-be, and I felt like I'd been through the whole scene before. You've seen it all in the cartoons.

One of the guys was an old hand at this. He wore a leather jacket over his pajama tops, rubbed his stubble and kept groaning, "Jeeze, I feel like I didn't get no sleep at all." The other cat was a young one; he kept tugging at his cropped hair and pacing up and down, as you knew he would. The one ashtray in the room was soon overflowing with butts. Bring the cameras in tight on that ashtray, Mac. Let's establish the mood.

Soon running out of conversation with the old hand—at 5 a.m., what is there to say?—I picked up the Life. It happened to be the issue devoted to the birth of a baby, in color. What luck! Try reading that at 5 a.m. on an empty stomach and see what it gets you besides queasy. However, it did indicate that the age limit for making the cover of Life has been lowered to the irreducible minimum.

In short, everything was predictable except the unforgettable moment when a nurse walked in to beam, "Congratulations, it's a boy!" And the other moment, when your wife is wheeled out, looking brave and beautiful, as only a woman can in her finest hour. As for the baby, I still haven't seen much of him except under glass, in an area that Children's Hospital calls "Baby Show." That's not so bad; another hospital in town calls it the "Heirport."

He looks a lot like me, but with any luck he'll outgrow it. And he already has more hair. *May 4, 1965*

Grant Ave. in Chinatown: an old woman crosses the street, wearing black pantaloons, a long smock—and white tennis shoes. The guy with you grins: "A member of the Wong Birch Society?" You smile, too, the fatuous, chauvinistic smirk of the Caucasian in Chinatown.

Ah, we do make such sport of the Chinese; it's almost like the good old "Yellow Peril" days of Denis Kearney and William Randolph Hearst the Elder. Two Wongs don't make a white. The phone book is full of Wong numbers. The Tai Ping Company—do they teach the touch system? Mr. Pon Gee, the insurance man—no doubt with a silky manner. Some chop suey and flied lice, Cholly, and make it chop-chop, so solly.

As Charlie well knows, you don't have to go overseas to find the Ugly American. We may all locate him in the mirror.

★   ★   ★

Still, I suppose, you could say the little old lady has come a long way. Fifty years ago, she would have been tottering painfully along Dupont Gai on bound feet. The menfolk were wearing long robes and pigtails, heading toward the smell of opium in the Street of the Thousand Lanterns. Arnold Genthe, the noted photographer, was lurking in dark corners, snapping the pictures that would engrave forever the image of Chinatown that lives today only in the mind of Caucasians.

Most of us are still in the era of the "Chinaman's Room." You don't know about that? You still find them in the dark basements of old San Francisco houses—airless little wooden rooms where the Chinese manservant lived. And died. Lacking an identity, he was given the family's surname. "Meet Ling Murphy—wonderful character. Been with us for years."

In these enlightened days, the "Chinaman's Room" is used for storage, or the family dog, if it isn't too pedigreed and fussy.

★   ★   ★

Don't get me wrong: San Franciscans love Chinatown, as well they should. It's one of our most consistent tourist attractions—"the largest Chinese settlement outside the Orient" (a polite way of saying ghetto). Everybody has his favorite little side-street restaurant, "and we know it's good because you only see Chinese there" (this is more likely to mean it's cheap than good). For ads and photographs, it's hard to beat: the silhouette of a pagoda rooftop, a dragon-entwined streetlamp with a halo of fog, a jumble of neon

94

ideographs, vaguely sinister-looking men, eyes hidden beneath black hat brims.

To those who don't live in it, Chinatown is San Francisco's most frozen cliché. Clink of mah-jongg tiles behind drawn curtains in a back alley. Dried seahorses in an herbalist's window, winter melon and snow peas at the grocer's, meat-filled buns in the bakery. Memories of tong wars and "Little Pete," who wore a coat of mail but was killed anyway.

That's Chinatown—that and the great dragon snaking through the mobs on New Year's. That and the fortune cookies and the chopsticks and the Midwestern tourists who buy back-scratchers and complain that they "can't find anything from China in Chinatown." They don't realize that we don't do business with China because there is no China; all the Chinese come from Formosa.

*　*　*

If you live in Chinatown, you live in a slum. Behind the neon and the bars and the restaurants and the curio shops, that's what it is—one big tenement, dirty, overcrowded and diseased (the TB rate is the highest in town). Have you ever walked up those long narrow stairs, past all the mailboxes that the tourists find so colorful? I have. You climb into a musty past of tiny wooden cubicles. Today the "Chinaman's Room" is in Chinatown, not Pacific Heights.

But the message never seems to get through the impermeable wall of fortune cookies and guidebooks. Just the other day, a group of Chinatown leaders again complained to City Hall about the slum conditions, the need for a master plan, the fact that 90 percent of the buildings qualify for condemnation and should be replaced by redevelopment.

Redevelop a tourist attraction? Heaven forbid. Even so intelligent a man as Planning Director James R. McCarthy was as taken aback as a member of the Convention & Visitors Bureau. He said things like "We mustn't destroy the character of Chinatown—one of the city's prime tourist attractions." The narrow streets and old buildings "are important to the image of San Francisco as an urban and urbane place to live."

Especially if you don't live there. The Chinese aren't people, they're characters in a four-color billboard. The Chinese bankers, lawyers and architects who complain about the restrictions on Chinatown aren't typical; to the McCarthys and the Convention Bureau and most of the rest of us, the Chinese do your laundry, cook, wait on tables and show you how to use chopsticks.

When they aren't on tap, being smiling and servile to their betters, they disappear up those long stairs into their rabbit warrens—ghosts living in a tacky Disneyland.

★   ★   ★

I can hear it now: "Everybody likes the Chinese in San Francisco." Sure they (we) do, in a paternalistic way. "Besides, they like to stick together" (or are they stuck together?). The young, the quick and the smart are getting out of Chinatown, or as far out as they're allowed. They aren't taken in by the role they're supposed to play, nor will they, and they aren't fooled by the phony pagoda rooftops that look so picturesque on the skyline but merely cover a multitude of sins. That little old lady in tennis shoes is still one step behind. Her daughter is wearing high heels and looking for a way out of "dreamy, dreamy Chinatown." *May 16, 1965*

THE BAY AROUND US

Well, just how DO you convince people that they're in danger of losing their most precious heritage? At the moment, I'm not talking about life, liberty and the pursuit of Communists. I'm talking about the Bay, San Francisco's most precious heritage. If you haven't heard, it's disappearing. And if you don't consider it precious, just think, to make the most obvious comment possible, what Los Angeles would give to have it. In exchange, they'd offer Forest Lawn, Troy Donahue and the La Brea Tar Pits and throw in Buff Chandler to boot.

★   ★   ★

I agree, it's hard to think of the Bay as vanishing when there's still so much of it about (one of our most sacred boasts—"big enough to contain all the ships of the world"—is probably still true). Viewed from a hilltop, it remains "the greatest landlocked harbor," vast and majestic; freighters, liners and even carriers look lost in its huge embrace. If you're tossing around the Bay in a sailboat, it may even seem a little bigger than is strictly necessary.

But it's going nonetheless, to the point where all the talk about more bridges is beginning to seem academic: our not too distant descendants may be walking across the fill. Put a Cathedral on Alcatraz and we could have our own Mont St. Michel. (Plans for a

$500 million bridge to Tiburon always put me in mind of George Lemont's plaintive question: "Wouldn't it be cheaper just to put Tiburon on a truck and bring it over here?")

The statistics are frightening, but they don't seem to make an impact on anybody except the conservationists, who are so dedicated they'll probably be investigated soon by a congressional committee. Conservationists, as everybody knows, are troublemakers who obstruct the hard work of State Highway Commissions, lumber companies, garbage operators, developers and other empire builders. I'd suggest sending them all back where they came from except that where they came from is now a supermarket.

★　★　★

The doleful fact is that the Bay, for all its present amplitude, is half as large as it was only a century ago—in the words of Writer Bruce Brugmann "a vanishing wonder of the world." Of its 276 miles of shoreline, only four miles have been set aside for waterfront parks. Exactly 61 feet of Richmond's big waterfront are still accessible to the public. Forty fill projects are on the boards. Meanwhile, half a million gallons of raw sewage pollutes its waters every day (Brugmann's Law: "When the Filler Barons spit, councilmen swim").

Not that I'm against Big Business filling in the Bay: if it weren't for the moguls in league with City Hall, Candlestick Park wouldn't be where it is, a constant delight to us all. It's just that sacred cows are like any other kind of cow. Their virtues are many, but the end product is still dung.

Senator J. Eugene McAteer's bill in Sacramento is the last, best hope of saving what's left of our single most important asset—the raging, tide-torn torrent (or lake-like bowl of idyllic blue) that has kept San Francisco among the world's storybook cities. If the bill is defeated, there will still be plenty of Bay around for us in our lifetime, but our kids' kids, or THEIR kids, will wonder not only where the flowers went, but the water as well.

The lot of the conservationist, like that of the policeman, is not a happy one. Do-gooderism has always been suspect in this misanthropic society of ours, and large segments of the public are inclined to look upon the do-gooder as some kind of nut.

★　★　★

In fact, the conservationist stands in the middle of a fast-disappearing oasis, surrounded almost entirely by enemies. When he cries out "Save!" this and "Save!" that, he churns up the manic-progressive grumps who accuse him of being addicted to chintz & charm, and Victorian yesterdays. The great public is apathetic:

"How can they say our Bay is disappearing when I can look out my window and see it?" The strongest enemies by far are those who stand to make a buck out of grabbing as much of the Bay—YOUR Bay, by the way—as is grabbable.

These last have the hidden power, the lobbies, the friends in Sacramento. If anybody can defeat McAteer's bill, they can—and a mild sort of bill it is; all it calls for is a Commission to halt further filling pending a four-year study, while not affecting what's already under way or authorized.

If you'd like to say a word in behalf of Sen. McAteer, his bill is SB 309. He'd be overjoyed and even pleasantly surprised to hear from you.

★　★　★

It's difficult for the conservationists to illustrate their warnings with dramatic immediacy. The people stir slightly, if at all, to hear that a redwood grove is being decimated, a hill bulldozed to death to provide fill, the life-giving edges of a Bay inundated by garbage. These things happen in isolated places, mainly out of public view. It is only a few years later, when the conservationists have yelled themselves into exhaustion, that the people stand around, wringing their hands and singing plaintively: "Where Did All the Flowers Go?" Or the view. Or the trees. Or the picnic spot where once the wind blew fresh and free.

A few paragraphs above I mentioned the 500,000 gallons of raw sewage that spew into the Bay every day. It's not a pretty picture, but it doesn't tell you much, either; is half a million gallons a lot or a little, and anyway you can't see it from your Russian Hill window (by the way, it's a LOT of sewage). Harold Gilliam, most lucid of the conservation writers, tries this kind of illustration: if you took all the fills now in progress or planned for the Bay, put them together, and dumped them in the Bay, you'd have an island three-quarters the size of San Francisco itself.

In short, time—and the Bay—are running out.

May 23, 1965

Electronic note: If you have a radio-controlled garage door—and who doesn't—you could lose it one of these days. You could, that is, if the Fed'l Aviation Agency gets worked up about it (the FAA recently shut down 58 in L.A. for interfering with aircraft navigation signals—pointing out that "signals from some garage receivers are strong enough to be picked up by an aircraft 16 miles away"). "It would be possible," continues an FAA spokesman, "for a pilot to inadvertently 'home in' on a garage door signal and fly directly toward it with great accuracy." Hoo-boy, you just THINK you've got problems. Wait till a jet tries to park in your garage.

May 26, 1965

Little landmarks: Cyclops in the Bay—dead Alcatraz's live "eye," revolving nightly over the crumbling Palace of Dark Arts . . . The aged apartment house, its dry bones crying for a coat of paint, at the illustrious Nob Hill corner of Powell and California . . . The original Maxfield Parrish painting of "The Pied Piper" in the Palace's bar of the same name—insured for $50,000, worth twice that, seldom glanced at by the brokers peering into their martinis . . . The tiny cul-de-sac with the most elegant name in town: Ashburton Ave., fingering its way for a few yards between the walls of the dead White House (it was named for a long-gone employee) . . . At Sutter and Mason, the Francisca Club's immaculate white portals and polished brass fittings—a Little Old Lady still putting up a stiff and starchy front . . . At noontime, the medical building nurses, surprisingly sexy despite their white stockings and uniforms, fighting the pigeons for a spot of grass in Union Square . . . The late Bernard Maybeck's Corinthian-column'd palace of an auto salon at Van Ness and Ellis—designed for Packard when that car was King of the Road; a distant relative of his Palace of Fine Arts (last of the big splendors) but built to last . . . The old lead-fronted building at Sacramento and Laurel—once a hotel for traveling salesmen, now the home of Art Dealer Billy Pearson's Mexican treasures . . . The spectacular lighting fixture—like a huge chunk of rock candy—in the Bank of Calif. branch at Sutter and Stockton . . . The little electrified Dutch Boy painting away, night after night, on the National Lead Bldg. off Bayshore Freeway; he was removed once, but put right back after the female patients in nearby S.F. General Hospital wrote that they missed "our dear little boy—the only thing we can see from our windows."

June 18, 1965

Breath of Tskandal: One of the national TV networks recently aired a long interview with several politically active Cal students— boys and girls alike. Before the program was shown, one of the girls, a member of a rich and socially prominent Eastern clan, alerted her family to be sure and watch.

Well, it so happened that the night of the interview, her parents were hosting an elegant party, with dozens of guests. The proud father had extra TV sets installed, and, at the appointed time, a hush fell over the group as the guests gathered around to look and listen.

Well, as the interview progressed, it developed that the Easterners' UC daughter is LIVING with one of the young men who was on the program. She discussed the situation quite coolly: "No, we haven't decided whether we'll get married" . . . "Don't want to rush things" . . . "Depends on whether we want children," and so on. The party broke up in embarrassed confusion. The father, a member of a big firm, resigned. The mother has had a breakdown. A United States Senator, a close friend of the family, is looking into the mess, and all in all, it's a fair-sized disaster.

July 1, 1965

Lint from a red carpet: Jim Varcados, upon learning that Princess Meg arrived in S.F. with 2,000 lbs. of luggage: "Hey—the original Megaton!"

Most enjoyable part of the Royal Couple's stay in SF, by their own admission: The 45-minute Bay Cruise aboard Dan London's yacht; the Bay Area celebrity they were most thrilled to meet: Bing Crosby, at dinner in Hillsborough Saturday night; greatest disappointment; not getting to Sausalito and Belvedere . . . Sharman Douglas, dining at Ernie's with actor Kevin McCarthy shortly before the Royal Couple arrived: "Migawd, I'm exhausted and the trip hasn't even started yet!" . . . For the BOAC flight from London, the Snowdons and their entourage took over the entire first class section—thereby bumping four San Franciscans who had reservations: The Howard Gossages and the Larry Dunhams; they switched to Pan Am and arrived in time to welcome the Royal Couple to the airport.

During the English-Speaking Union's luncheon at the Hilton, the Princess pocketed a fairly pallid souvenir—a dozen sugar packets bearing color photos of various Hilton hotels (now why would she want those?) . . . Henri Lewin, the hotel's catering mgr., who invented the special dessert called Coup Princess Margaret, asked her: "Did you mind my naming it after you?" The Princess, smoothly: "If you hadn't, I'd have insisted that you do" (go beat HER) . . . As she walked out at the end of the luncheon, she got a burst of applause; but Carol Channing, in her wake, drew cheers and hollers . . . Women's Wear Daily's Al Morch, surveying the chapeaux in the crowd: "A hatful of reign?"

Dolly Fritz MacMasters stayed at her Huntington Hotel just long enough to welcome Meg and Tony—and then disappeared to Nevada, to avoid any possible incidents threatened by her estranged husband, Donald . . . (And yes, Harry Waters, who runs the Huntington, IS a little tired of being asked whether he placed a pea under the Princess' mattress) . . . Finally, in the crowd gathered outside the hotel, L'Etoile's Marcel Clavien heard this mother say to her noisy child: "Now be quiet or I'll have the Princess turn you into a frog."   *November 1, 1965*

With it: San Francisco no longer need feel ashamed in the company of her sister cosmopolitan cities. We now have a Playboy Club, which, along with major sports, proper culture, a mounting crime rate and lousy traffic, is an absolute MUST for any metropolis worthy of the name.

I wouldn't say that the building (at Montgomery and Jackson) is the prettiest in town, but neither is it the ugliest. "The first plans were horrible," said Hugh Hefner, the young man who first discovered that bunny rhymes with money. "One of those terrible concrete slabs. At least I got the place built in red brick, which sort of fits."

An imposing brick fithouse it is, and the 61 Bunnies on duty are built to match. They float through the five-level layout with the greatest of tease, but of course you may only look, not touch and never (if you're a member) date. The lights are low, the drinks are decent, the atmosphere is sort of dated hipness: young men whose neckties are a trifle too thin, snapping fingers to recorded Sinatra, Previn and Basie.

It's all so innocent and clean-cut (especially the Bunnies in their crotch-oriented costumes). Hefner, thin, drawn, tense, sucked on his pipe, sipped a bourbon and Coke, discussed politics and sexual mores with great seriousness and floated through the crowded rooms like the Great Gatsby—with it but not part of it.

Even the illuminated wall photos of bare-breasted, All-American beauties seem wholesome as Mom's apple cheeks. When I left, my libido still registering zero, I noticed a carful of cops parked across the street, keeping a watchful eye on the club.

They'd have been better off casing someplace really racy, like the YMCA.   *November 15, 1965*

Plug-a-lug: Some joker with a big sense of humor and a bigger can of gold paint has been gilding the fire plugs out there on Castro and Diamond Sts., which the fire dept. doesn't think is too funny. Now they have to send a crew around to repaint 'em, which, at the going rate, is something like repainting a Rolls-Royce.

Since fireplugs are suddenly the biggest local news since silicone—who'd have believed it?—maybe you'd like to know that they come in various sizes and colors. Most low-pressure jobs are painted all white. The high-pressure ones feature red or blue bonnets, apparently by Mr. John. A green bonnet means it's over a cistern, and the plugs in the Twin Peaks area, with black bonnets, draw their water from the Twin Peaks reservoir.

As for the few that are painted all green, they get their water from lakes and swimming pools. The color does NOT mean that they are owned personally by Mr. Greenberg. Along with him, I'll be delighted when this whole hoo-ha brouhaha goes down the drain.   *December 3, 1965*

1966

The unforgettable: We shan't see her like again. Kathleen Norris, who died Tuesday at 85, was wise, witty, warm, wonderful—and all the other glowing adjectives in the lexicon . . . Most of all, she had humor. The last time I lunched with her, a few years ago at the Fairmont, a waiter asked her if she'd like a drink. "I brought my own," leered Aunt Kate, a teetotaller. "I've got a bottle of Four Roses stashed under the table" (this at 80!) . . . Her late husband, Novelist Charles G. Norris, who had white hair and a black moustache, was a crony of Pierre Monteux, who had black hair and a white moustache. Laughed Mrs. Norris, years before the famous ad: "Only their hairdresser knows for sure!" . . . Once, when she was a guest of Eleanor Roosevelt's at the White House, she heard that her then nine-year-old niece, Kathie Thompson, had been misbehaving. Grabbing a piece of Presidential stationery, Aunt Kate wrote to Kathie: "The President is shocked at you!" . . . A few years ago, an old friend told her of the death a few days earlier of a mutual friend, a dowager: "Happened on a Wednesday. She got up early and spent the morning with her nieces and nephews. Then she had lunch at the St. Francis, went to a matinee, had tea with her family, took a little nap before dinner—and never woke up." "Gosh," sighed Aunt Kate, "Doesn't it just make your mouth water?" . . . Goodbye to a great lady. *January 20, 1966*

THE DOUGHNUT AND THE HOLE

You take the substance, I'll take the shadow—sometimes. In the case of a special city like San Francisco, maybe the dream is more important than the reality; it is, after all, among the most romantic of places, and what does it matter that we're no longer sure about the color of our true love's hair?

On Montgomery St. the other day, I saw two gentlemen wearing real Chesterfield overcoats—velvet collars and all—swinging their tightly furled umbrellas with military jauntiness, and I began thinking that maybe all isn't lost after all. They cut a fine figure, a sort of idealized picture of what you want Montgomery Streeters to look like.

So perhaps you CAN go home again, Kathleen, back to the dreams of youth and the days of innocence, when all the Really San Francisco men wore homburgs and dawdled long over fine lunches, swishing the French Chablis around in their goblets, and all the ladies were swathed in chiffon, had sun-tanned legs of an impossible perfection, and danced the nights away in the Peacock Court.

It must have been a dream. How else account for that fact that a full moon seemed to be beaming down nightly on a Bay of lake-like placidity, while sparkling ferryboats sailed to and from the real (awful) world, out there somewhere beyond our enchanted hills?

★ ★ ★

The trouble with living long with a lady you love is that pretty soon you start seeing the pouches underneath the eyes instead of the merry twinkle still in them. Same with a city: it doesn't do to count the cracks in the picture window while ignoring the matchless view outside—the crazy panorama of pinnacles and pizza parlors, peaks and panhandlers, houses clinging to hills and hills clinging to clanging cable cars.

★ ★ ★

It is the very richness of the view, argues Artist Frank Ashley, that keeps those cracks in the picture window from being repaired. "The problems just never seem urgent in this city," he says. "When you can look outside at the marvelous scenery, nothing else seems as important. The view overwhelms everything, even when it's disappearing. Maybe if we didn't have it, we'd get a lot of other things done."

Perhaps so, but there is still plenty of it left — more per capita than any other city in the land (in New York they're paying $400,000, for penthouses that overlook a trickle called the East River, but of course there's a forest of skyscrapers to soothe your stony soul).

★　★　★

Sometimes it's nice to act young and wide-eyed again. To look at the majestic symmetry of City Hall, without thinking about the bumblers at work under that perfect dome (but there are some good men there, you know, some DAMN good men). To revel in the marble halls of the Opera House without looking at the patches on the great golden curtain or stewing about the criminal neglect. To gaze at Telegraph Hill at the golden clusters of the Bay Bridge, reflected on the black Bay, and push aside the thought that this wonder of the world, this short-term miracle, is approaching obsolescence.

The selective eye, that's the ticket, and if you can see "an upthrusting buoyancy" in the Hartford Building and "a carousel-like gaiety" about the Jack Tar (I quote), so much the better. In North Beach, ignore the honky-tonks and consider the pulsating life, turn your back on the unkempt and smile at the kempt, the true bohemians: Wing the artist, Macchiarini the jeweler, Ferlinghetti the poet, Henri Lenoir and his magic beret, Tommy and Terry running the parking lot next to Enrico's.

★　★　★

Even Market St. has its rewards. Lift your eyes from the filth and the flotsam and behold the blandishments: the young ladies with their coiffures pumped to 40 pounds pressure, the young men with 10 pounds of bangs, wearing pants so tight their eyeballs bulge. The self-anointed evangelists, standing on "Nut Island" (the concrete platform at the foot of Powell) exhorting the pagans to repent, while the pagans shake their heads and giggle at each other, meanwhile munching on their ice cream sandwiches from Woolworth's.

★　★　★

It's hard to stay angry at a city you love even when it does mean, stupid or foolish things. There is still so much laughter in the air, still so much beauty in the streets; if you look closely at even the dingiest, most ramshackle Victorian house, you find a touch of style, a dusty trace of something lovely. Certainly the "new" Hall of Justice is a warehouse, but inside you bump into an old-time Deputy Sheriff with a friendly red face who confides, "I sure miss the old Hall—it was so close to Tadich's, and man, how I loved to eat there."

It's still that kind of a city—a bit fat in the middle, a touch overfed, perhaps too fond of the good life, but still a joy. All

105

you have to do is look at it with love in your eyes, even if it means squinting a little. *February 6, 1966*

One of a kind: Like the Rolls-Royce Silver Cloud of which he was so enamored, they don't make them like that anymore. Lucius Beebe, who died Friday, was unique: a man of the past who, nevertheless, lived very much for the moment—to the hilt. Despite his published crotchets, he was gentle and courageous; despite his steady (and finally fatal) devotion to fine wines and cognacs, he was fantastically productive: books, articles, columns and reams of correspondence—all neatly typed on yellow paper—poured from his typewriter. His love for the past, as somebody once said, may have amounted to necrophilia, and, as he himself often said, "I am definitely an anachronism"—but even anachronisms can die too young. *February 7, 1966*

San Francisco is where: There are 10,000 friendly squirrels in Golden Gate Park—and not a single place within miles where you can buy a bag of peanuts to feed 'em . . . The only people up and about at dawn are the Scavengers and the stockbrokers . . . Everybody talks about the great restaurants, but the biggest seller on the biggest street is—hot dogs . . . People are parking lots in parking lots; either there, or under "No Parking at Any Time" signs . . . The United Nations flag has been barred by the War Memorial Bd. of Trustees, in whose Opera House the UN charter was signed . . . A socialite is somebody who gets her picture taken with a cigarette in one hand and a drink in the other . . . Architect Mario Gaidano, who designs some of the most far-out bldgs. in town, has his offices in a staid Victorian on Van Ness . . . The natives enjoy doing the same things that the tourists like to do (which may be the definition of a true World City) . . . The funny little hats aren't worn by women on Post but by men on Montgomery (those narrow-brimmed high crowned jobs) . . . The stop sign most frequently ignored (for good reason) is at the crest of the Taylor-California peak . . . The reason the grass looks greener at night in front of the Fairmont is—green spotlights . . . When a native says, "It's like a summer day," he means it's cold and foggy. And no wonder the visitors think it's always gloomy here. The sightseeing service is called The Gray Lines, isn't it? *February 20, 1966*

FROM HERE TO SENILITY

Frankly, I never thought it would get here so soon, but today is my 50th birthday. If that makes YOU feel older, think what it does to me. As for my doctor, he's a little disconsolate, too, since he once bet me 100 to 1 I'd never make it. Knowing him, I won't get the money, but the important thing is that I won—and it all evens out, anyway. If he'd won, he'd have had a hell of a time collecting.

* * *

Fifty. Over the hill and downhill all the way. "Congratulations, you're halfway there," as Richard Gonzalez put it, although I'm not sure what he meant by that (halfway I'd settle for). Old enough to know better, but not smart enough. Too young for Medicare, too old to die young—the latter being Nature's way of saving you from that fate worse than death, a Retirement Center. The funny thing is, I don't feel 50, but maybe that's because I haven't had much experience at it. I don't look 50, either, because I refuse to wear my glasses when I examine myself in the mirror. That way I merely look sort of blurry.

* * *

It's not easy to be light-hearted about achieving the Anxious Age (checking your own pulse, wondering whether it's your heart or dyspepsia, all that getting up in the middle of the night). When I was 40, I managed to dash off a pretty funny piece—I mean, it seems funny in retrospect—because even at 40, all your dreams and fantasies aren't quite dead. At 40, you think that by some miracle, your hair might start growing again. Or you might conceivably become the world's oldest baseball rookie, hitting the home run that wins a pennant for the Giants and dying dramatically on home plate. Or you might even have time to get out of the lousy newspaper business. But at 50, forget it, Charlie.

* * *

Fifty: a bleak and chilly word (what is a young, curly-haired boy from Sacramento doing in a cold place like that?). Seeking solace, I went to see my old mentor, Paul C. Smith. "Fifty isn't as old as you look," he said. I knew I could count on him. I consulted my friendly neighborhood psychoanalyst, the renowned Dr. B. "You're only as old as you feel," he observed (for this he gets $50 an hour?). "What you must keep in mind," he went on, "is that 50 is much younger than it was a generation ago. In your case, this is particularly true, since, while it must be conceded that you have passed adolescence, you still have a long way to go before you reach maturity." I asked for, but didn't get, a refund.

*   *   *

Of course, every minus has its plus (who says?). Having reached the Sad Plateau, I am now permitted to pontificate, ruminate and reminisce. When my peers say "Kids aren't what they used to be," I can nod agreement. What I mean by that is that the young ones are better than we used to be. I was one dumb kid, and so were my contemporaries. We put Stacomb on our hair and wore clean white shirts with filthy corduroys that had phallic symbols inked on them, and does that make more sense than what the kids wear today? Nooop. WE had our simple pleasures: crystal set radios with cat's whiskers, windup phonographs with breakable records, Model T Fords and ice boxes that used real chunks of ice we had to go to the ice house for. Today's kids have hi-fis, transistors and Mustangs, which is playing it smart. Besides, the youngsters now are politically oriented, which we never were, but who could get excited about a President like Calvin Coolidge? I still don't believe HIM.

*   *   *

The only way to fight a thing like 50 is to stay au courant if it kills you. When those electric guitars start to twang, I'm right out there on the dance floor with the rest of the idiots, doing a sort of offhand frug I call the shrug; it's not much, but it beats sitting around, waiting for the waltz. Sartorially, you've got to be with it, too. I wear pants so tight that every time I zip them up, my glasses fall off. Another sign of the encroaching years is to wear shoes with shoelaces. Out! In: pointy slip-ons or booties, even if you have to cut off your little toes to get into them. It's always important to watch your vocabulary like a hog. Nothing dates you faster than phrases like "Come up and see my etchings," "Sez you" and "Tain't funny, McGee." What you do is pepper your conversation with such all-purpose gems as "groovy," "swinger," "it's a gas" and an occasional "Would you believe—?"

*   *   *

Since old gentlemen of 50 are allowed a half-aphorism or two, let me say that there is no future in the past, wherefore I face my declining years with equanimity, equipose and Equanil. My birthday present to me is a plaque affixed to my forehead. It reads

"Established 1916," which makes me older than a lot of other institutions around town. Now my only worry is that they'll tear me down for a parking lot. Lord knows I'm square enough.

April 3, 1966

A palpable scandal: The 60th annvy. of San Francisco's moment of glory—the 1906 firequake—was celebrated last week by a touching ceremony, covered in excellent detail by the metropolitan press, all two of same.

Judges, Supervisors, church leaders, fire chieftains and dewy-eyed old-timers gathered at 20th and Church to pay homage to a simple fire hydrant. No! Not a simple fire hydrant. THE fire hydrant. "The Brave Hydrant" (headlines). "The little fire hydrant that could." In short, the hydrant that, on April 18, 1906 kept giving water when all the others around it had failed, "thereby saving much of the Mission District from destruction."

The hydrant (a Greenberg original, mfd. by our Cellini of fireplugs) was covered with praise and shining new gold paint. A bronze plaque was affixed, detailing its achievement. The Most Rev. Merlin Guilfoyle of Mission Dolores bestowed "the blessings of water." And Paul Belser, who discovered in 1906 that the hydrant was still delivering water, took a bow.

Oh, how it hurts to puncture this glittering balloon. But! The fire hydrant that received all this homage is a PHONY! It was installed not 60 or more years ago—but in 1960. In sad fact, it bore that very date until just a few days before the ceremony, when an emergency crew, under the cover of night, stealthily ground off the numbers.

A horrid story, but there you are. *April 28, 1966*

If there's anything a local columnist hates, it's being scooped on a local item by a faraway publication. So imagine my dismay to read in the London Style Weekly that the original Levi Strauss, the man who gave Levis to the world, named his pants "jeans" in honor of his wife, Jean, "back in the 1850 gold rush days." I put in an angry call to the Levi Strauss people and sat around in a funk for hours, wondering how I'd missed THIS fascinating piece of Early Californiana. Finally, blessed relief! The original Levi Strauss was a bachelor, and the term "jeans" is a corruption of

"Genoese," deriving from the blue pants worn by early Italian sailors. That London writer had made up the story out of whole cloth. Blue. *May 5, 1966*

Magic moment: The Bay was a lake of Mediterranean blue at dusk Wednesday night. The Coast Guard's shiny white cutter looked like an Onassisian yacht, waiting for a Princess. Behind the windows at Ondine in Sausalito—or was it Villefranche?—the crowd sat silent, watching a rotten orange of a full moon rise out of the Italian hills of—all RIGHT!—Oakland. The lights of San Francisco were reflected in a long dirigible of fog, turning it luminescent. The souffles and the moon rose together, the latter spilling a long white wake over the now black Bay, and a corny director insisted on sending a tiny sailboat across the cream. Vietnam seemed the thousands of miles away that it is, and reality was suspended—until 9:08, when a roar went up from a crowd in Ondine's corner. The ubiquitous transistor radio had reported Willie Mays' 512th home run. A spell and a record had been broken.

* * *

Bay City beat: After his shot heard 'round our little world, Willie went home with his friend and confidant, Banker Jake Shemano. No celebration. Dozens of wires arrived. Willie opened a couple, yawned, and said, "Well, guess I'll hit the sack. Read the rest of 'em in the morning. G'night, Jake." Ho-hum, sweet ho-hum . . . It was the end of a long vigil, too, for the 18 cameramen who had crowded Candlestick's press box for days and nights—some at $22.50 an hour—to record the historic blast. But why? Doesn't one Willie Mays home run swing look much like another? . . . At the Palace Hotel, meanwhile, Maid Rose Gallagher walked into a guest's room and noticed a man's jacket hanging there, one button attached by a safety pin. She sewed it on. Wasn't till later that Rose, a red-hot Giant fan, discovered that she had done a good turn for—Sandy Koufax. *May 6, 1966*

Still trying to catch up, I thought about Russ Wolden, the convicted Assessor (he spent the past weekend in Sequoia Hospital in Redwood City, collapsing of anxiety and exhaustion). The merits or demerits of the case to one side, his conviction marked the end of a San Francisco era—an era that began with Sunny Jim and lived on through Angelo Rossi, Roger, Elmer and even George. These were the years of tarnished gold, when it was the established San Francisco Thing to take care of your friends, to do favors for the inner circle, the power structure, The Establishment, call it what you will. For generations, the unwritten law prevailed and it worked reasonably well: take care of the people who take care of you. The jury was unanimous, but you'd have thought there would have been one member—perhaps an old-time San Franciscan— who'd have perceived that Russ Wolden was the inheritor, not the creator, of a San Francisco Way of Life. Well, that way of life is dead, as The Establishment is dying (of old age and decrepitude), and Russ Wolden has been selected as the sacrifice. But apparently the others who played the old San Francisco game—the bribers— are to go untouched. And in the wake will come a new establishment to play the game a different way, not necessarily better.

May 20, 1966

Nob Hill note: The next edition of the S.F. phone book will be minus one of its more endearing listings, now that the wonderful Mrs. James L. Flood is dead, at 90. For 24 years, she occupied a nine-room penthouse at the Fairmont, overlooking her former home (the Flood mansion, now the Pacific-Union Club), and for all those years she had herself listed simply as "Flood Mrs." When I asked her about that one time, she smiled: "Well, what would YOU do if you had a first name like Maude?" . . . The rumor around the Hill yesterday was that Ben Swig would now move into the Flood penthouse, thereby making him an across-the-roof neighbor of Atty. Philip Ehrlich, who occupies the other Fairmont penthouse. Can't you just see them trotting back and forth to borrow cups of money from each other? *June 30, 1966*

THE TROUBLED SUMMER

It should be, as always, the most fruitful and self-indulgent time of the year, and at first glance it is. The tourists smothering the cable cars and laughing-screaming down the hills. Freeways jammed with the chrome-hard bumper crop of the Affluent Society. Even the Giants are doing well and could win it all. Then why is there so little joy in this joyous season?

★ ★ ★

The answer is so obvious nobody wants to talk about it—yet it is always at the back of your mind and on the tip of your tongue. The answer is in the almost constant drone of planes heading Westward, the servicemen on the streetcorners, the gray carriers sliding past the Embarcadero toward the Gate, decks crowded with planes whose wings are folded as though in prayer. The answer is in caskets, casualty lists, napalm and inflation—in the war that is not a war in pursuit of a victory that has no name. The answer is in Presidential popularity polls that climb higher every time more bombs are dropped, and in bumper strips reading "Escalate! Get It Over With and Get Out!" (how appropriate that the popular American philosophers of the day are those who write for automobiles).

★ ★ ★

By unspoken assent, the big game at dinner parties these nights is to see how long you can converse without mentioning The Word. Anything else is an okay subject—especially religion (nothing controversial THERE any longer) and politics, as long as it is kept on the State level (God is alive and in the White House). Even LSD, that bore, is acceptable if you can think of something brighter to say than "I'd like to try it, but only under strict supervision, of course, as a scientific experiment." Travel is a safe topic ("I never fly tourist class because who wants to meet a lot of tourists?") and so are the redwoods and pollution, although conversation, like a lot of other worthy causes, seldom makes conversation. Civil rights is out—nothing left to say—and Berkeley buttons are in (the latest: "KCC——Kill a Commie for Christ").

★ ★ ★

But after the martinis, the wines, the coffee and cognacs, the pressure becomes too intense. At last, somebody snaps—the man who has been sitting grimly through the smalltalk ("Have you read 'The International Nomads'? Heaven!"). He pounds the table in agony: "Jesus, if we could only find a way out of that goddam—." Shocked silence. Reproving glances all around. But the delicate, artificial spell has been shattered. The game hostess begins falteringly: "How do you think the Brundage collection compares with—" and it is too late. Pandora's box is open. "Frankly," speaks up an advertising man, "I thought Steinbeck's reply to Yevtushenko was pitiful—hell, it sounded as though McNamara had dictated it." "McNamara—you mean that guy with Stacomb on his hair?" "You should be so smart." "How does he explain the Edsel? The

Edsel of wars, that's what we've got." The dinner table is roaring.

★ ★ ★

Amazing, the expertise that falls out once The Word has been spoken. Hans Morgenthau, Bernard Fall and Jean Lacouture are quoted. "The awful geography lesson," as H. V. Kaltenborn once called it, goes on: Da Nang, Hue, Mekong Delta, Annam, "did you know that the Chinese once occupied all of Vietnam?" A former Naval person speaks up: "We are the most powerful country in the world, so we have to use our power. What good is it otherwise? Crush 'em! We will impose a pax Americana on the world." A bespectacled psychiatrist murmurs: "The military mind is a pathological mind." A visiting European actress shrills: "The Americans are hypocrites. Why, if the Russians were doing what we were doing—." A stockbroker shrugs: "So it's good for business." "The hell it is," roars a prominent manufacturer. "I've got military orders I don't even want. Who needs this damn war? If I were young again, I'd grow a beard and demonstrate. I'm RABID on this subject." Magazine writer: "The first casualty of this was Humphrey—I wouldn't vote for him for dog catcher." The hostess, desperately: "What can we do? I mean, if you were the President, what would YOU do?" The psychiatrist again, again with his $50-an-hour murmur: "He is so Oriental about saving face—I wonder how he feels about hara-kari?" Naval person: "I agree with LeMay—bomb 'em back to the Stone Age." Psychiatrist: "You, sir, are a madman." Naval person: "I, sir, am an American" . . .

★ ★ ★

Midnight, the party dying in a flurry of wraps, hugs, pecks on cheeks, "marvelous dinner," apologies, "wonderful time," coldness, grunted apologies, growled acceptances. A last dying sentence down the stairs: "Can anybody remember why we went to Vietnam in the first place?" End of a summer night: a wet fog on the Bay and the misty lights of a ship heading toward—but we don't talk about that, do we?   *July 17, 1966*

THE WALKING CAEN

For an August day, you couldn't knock it, unless you happened to be a tourist feeling like a sheer sucker in seersucker. Out there by the Gate, the horns were fighting a losing battle with the fog. A crazy wind raced through the streets of the concrete jungle, playfully snatching men's hats and causing ladies to stand out in bras

113

relief. Fire engine and police sirens wailed at regular intervals, ambulances careened around corners, cars collided at various intersections, streetwalkers were calling out from darkened doorways, marijuana was being peddled in nearby alleys, the Black Maria was busy harvesting drunks—in short, a nice quiet day for a walk on the mild side.

* * *

Market opposite Fifth seemed like a good enough place to start. Or Market and Filth, as I sometimes think of it. Is there a dirtier, doggier, more trash-strewn (human and otherwise) stretch of retch in town? Probably, but let's not think about it. Even the sidewalk is an ill-fitting badly botched job. But at least there's action around there. At the moment, the action consisted of a bicycle messenger lying flat in the street after being belted by a car. I felt sorry for the kid as the ambulance came to sweep him up, but those bicycle messengers keep asking for it. The way they dart around, ignoring all known traffic laws, they're a menace. Crazy kids.

* * *

Turning into Powell, I leaped aboard an outgoing cable that seemed in danger of being torn to bits by a clutching mob of tourists (what a beating those gallant little cars take during The Season). I managed to get a toehold on the first outside step, where it still feels like Old San Francisco. Rattle of cable in ancient slot, whiff of wet fog in the face, and the gripman, king of all gongsters, belting out a counterpunch to the ship's bells marking time at Bernstein's Fish Grotto. Opposite Lefty's, he played the traditional five notes of "Shave and a hair cut," and the two cute miniskirted girls who shine shoes there clanged back the "Six-bits!" on the cable bell atop their stand. Beaucoup gemutlich. Tourist to gripman: "Does this car stop at every corner?" Gripman: "Sometimes even oftener." Laughter. LOL to gripman: "Do you go to the Top o' the Mark?" Gripman: "Can't afford it, lady." Chuckles. The gripman looked at me, rolled his eyes and said softly, as he had said so many times in the past: "Boy, do I get sick of being quaint and colorful!"

* * *

Feeling refreshed, jumped off the step at Post and walked through Union Square, which is now possible. The pigeon-trappers (M-Squab?) have been at work and the population has definitely been decimated. The people now outnumber the birds, which may or may not be an improvement, depending on how you feel about people and birds. However, there are still enough pigeons around to keep the Dewey Monument from relaxing, and the pavement could use a good scrubbing. The mosaics that immediately identify it as Guano Island are still there.

★ ★ ★

In I. Magnin, there was a Grover Magnin, who built the store and ran it for so many wonderful years until he retired. "When I hired Architect Tim Pflueger to build this store," he reminisced, "I told him to make it pigeon-proof. It was the first thing I thought of, because I live at the St. Francis and I could see what the birds had done to that building. So Magnin's has no ledges or cornices where a pigeon can get a toehold. Of course, the other kind of pigeons— the ones who buy the French originals on the third floor—have always been welcome!"

★ ★ ★

At 150 Powell, took an elevator to the third floor to visit the American Opinion Library, run by the John Birch Society. Very clean, neat and proper, with a fine American Flag in the window. A clean, neat and proper man called me "Sir" and invited me to browse. Two Little Old Ladies, not wearing tennis shoes (pearl chokers and trim suits), were chatting softly. The angry, baleful books, telling of impending doom from the Communist menace (unless, unless), contrasted oddly with this peaceful scene.

There was old Joe McCarthy, lashing out as in his heyday, pictured in his prime on a cover. The old right-wing hacks, like Ralph de Toledano, were heavily represented, as was the Rev. Billy James Hargis, attacking "The Communist Lee Harvey Oswald." Lots of Goldwater, and the recorded wisdom of Ronald Reagan. "Thank you, sir, call again," said the nice man as I left the quiet room with its violent wallpaper of print.

★ ★ ★

I walked out through the lobby, which contains a big, colorful newsstand filled with newspapers and magazines from around the world. Some were serious, some scurrilous, some silly, some trashy, some slightly pornographic, but they all seemed healthier than the neurotic notions being peddled upstairs under the American Flag. *August 14, 1966*

BECAUSE IT'S THERE

"I'd visit Angel Island one of these days if I could ever figure out how to get there," I wrote the other day, facetiously. It was a throw-away line that should have been thrown away, and it taught me a lesson I should have learned years ago: the facetious remark generally elicits a sincere response. In a trice, all sorts of warm, well-meaning people were on the phone, offering me transport, and there I was, hearst on my own petard. Charlie Bigmouth was on his way to Angel Island.

★   ★   ★

Early on a chilly morning, while you slug-a-beds were logging extra sack time, I found myself aboard a Harbor Tours water taxi, bouncing across a choppy bay. Capt. Jim Gill was at the controls, his clear eyes and firm jaw inspiring confidence. Ed Barrett, a 66-year-old veteran of the ferries, was the deckhand—a fine barrel-chested figure of a man, his hair as white and strong as his teeth. "Don't worry, mate," he hollered over the clatter of the engine, "We'll make it. We usually do."

I guess it was a beautiful morning on the bay, if you like that sort of thing. Fog shrouding the bridge, gray fingers creeping over the Marin hills, the city's towers lost in the mist—you know. Hundreds of sailboats were trooping off Belvedere, manned by people even crazier than I; they were out there because they WANTED to be.

As we passed Alcatraz—how odd to see people fishing so close to those once forbidden shores—I poked around in the picnic basket thoughtfully provided by the Fisherman's Wharf Association. They must have me figured for a trencherman: roast ham, fried chicken, smoked tongue, chicken livers, lobster, crab, shrimp, potato salad, French bread, olives, pickles, onions, toothpicks, even ashtrays . . .

"Would you care to split a stuffed egg with me?" I asked Ed. His reply was mercifully drowned out by the engine.

★   ★   ★

At last we rounded Angel Island and turned into the little harbor—warm, snug and enchanting. The natives, fishing at dockside, looked friendly and a few accepted my gift of stuffed eggs. Palm trees waved their fronds and I waved back. On a beautiful spread of green grass, American tourists were playing baseball and football. Nearby, picnic tables were filled with happy frolicking families, and Old Glory flew languidly from atop a 90-foot pole. An old Saturday Evening Post cover had come to life, and I felt at peace with the world, even if the world, sadly, feels otherwise.

★   ★   ★

I was welcomed officially by John Biggio, spruce and dapper in his forest green uniform, green tie with golden bear tie tack, and Smokey the Bear hat. Every man dreams of having his own island, and John has his. As the stalwart representative of the State Division of Parks, he is the boss of Angel Island, and a happy man. "Welcome to our beautiful island," he beamed. "I am delighted to be here," I said, pressing a stuffed egg into his hand.

*   *   *

The odd thing about Angel Island is that, despite its heavenly name and the peace-loving propensities of the American people, it is a very war-like place. Or was. Relics of every conflict, from the Indian Wars through the Cold War, are to be seen everywhere. At the western tip, where the view of the Gate and Bay is overwhelming, you find old gun emplacements, facing invaders who never came. In a quiet draw, a ghost encampment of wooden houses, Civil War vintage, where Indians were imprisoned.

On the other side of the island, a pre–World War I Army post, all stucco and tile roofs, alive with memories of campaign hats, Sam Browne belts and the sound of distant trumpets. In a leafy dell nearby, crumbling World War II barracks, the compound where German prisoners-of-war were held, and deserted streets where deer now walk daintily.

Strangest of all: the topmost point of Angel Island, where, not so long ago, Nike missiles bristled toward the sky. In the control bunkhouses, dead cables and dead switches, the residue of sudden obsolescence. All windows broken, an eerie feeling of futility—an authentic Space Age ruin.

*   *   *

Late in the afternoon, with the shadows lengthening over Snug Harbor, I clamored back onto the water taxi, waving good-bye to John Biggio and the other friendly natives. The State has elaborate long-range plans for hotels, restaurants and docks, but right now, Angel is still almost a virgin island. There isn't much there except unspoiled beauty, and when it is eventually "improved," it won't be half so pleasant. So you'd better see it now, so you can say, along with me, that we knew it when. Or almost when.

August 21, 1966

Herewith writer John Raymond with his annual up-to-the-second report on the Sept. '66 issue of the phone book: "Karl Marx lives!

117

(on page 402). Five listings for Goldfinger, only four for James Bond. The Doves outnumber the Hawks, 11 to 7, and who would have thought there'd be more Sparrows (3) than Pigeons (2). Only one Owl (first name Hamilton). But mighty is the Eagle—28 of them. Also 36 Hammers, four Nails, two Tacks, five Bolts and one Nutt . . . Love is very big in S.F. (73) but Lust (3) is losing and Passion (2) is petering out. Kiss (8) wins over Hug (3). The Little people (80) tower over the Large (one) and only two are Hip. There are more Popes (53) than Priests (11), far more Walkers (395) than Amblers (2), more Trotters (17) than Runners (6). A city with two Mountains, scads of Hills, three Peaks, two Valleys, 20 Lakes, 11 Pools and eight Flowers with a total of 70 Blooms . . . Then there are Otto Hertz and Pamela Avis. Avis presumably tries harder because she lives at 18 Pleasant St. Now I'm going to call up Carl Jung (also listed) for an appointment to straighten out my phone book syndrome. It's getting out of Hand (31). Best (59), John Raymond." *September 14, 1966*

These things I like: The noted Presidio Heights hostess who has her powder rooms bugged—so she can tape the remarks of her guests and play them later for fun and revenge . . . The ornate bronze doorknobs, inscribed "CS," in the Central Tower at Third and Market—the last and lasting reminder that this was once the beautiful Claus Spreckels Building . . . The dozens of electric guitars in the window of South o' Market pawnshops: solid evidence that not ALL rock 'n' roll groups make good, or bad . . . The Sept. issue of the L.A.-S.F. magazine, Artforum, devoted entirely to the wonders and horrors of surrealism, the "fad" that refused to die.

The fetching name of the bar in the 3000 block on Mission, catering to hospital nurses: Flo Nightingale's Intensive Care Unit . . . the beautifully-kept chocolate brown trucks of United Parcel Service (and the goodies they bring to your door) . . . The romantic name for vodka and soda: Crystal Chandelier (and if you remember when nobody drank vodka—because none was available—you belong in the first paragraph too).

Bobby Korter's sudden thought: "In a paternity case, it's always his child; in a divorce, it's her children" . . . Mark Twain's remark upon first hearing about the telephone: "The voice carries entirely too far as it is. Now if Bell had invented a muffler, he'd have performed a real service" . . . The tale of Oscar Wilde playing poker at the Cliff House, laying down four deuces, and raking in the pot with a languid "Two-two-two-TWO divine!" . . . Bob Quinn's short, pointy definition of Camp: "Corn revisited."   *September 18, 1966*

Babe at arms: Tosha, the snake dancer at Peppermint Tree, sent a batch of her pin-up photos to the warriors in Vietnam—and you know what happens when you cast a broad upon the waters. The other night, a group of wounded veterans who'd rec'd the pictures—several on crutches—arrived at the Tree to pay their respects. Tosha had to come out to the street to greet them, for, although they were old enough to get shot up, they were too young to be allowed inside the saloon.   *September 28, 1966*

Melodrama: Thurs. afternoon, a guy walked into Johnny Porter's 007-½ on Lombard in the Marina, downed a straight shot, wiped his lips and said to Bartender Gulley Foyle: "Well, so long, I'm jumping off the bridge." "I've heard that before," smiled Gulley. The guy handed him a letter. "For my wife," he said. "Do me a favor, mail it for me." After he walked out, Gulley ripped open the envelope, read the letter fast, as in a movie scene, and called the Highway Patrol. At 3:30 p.m., they got their man—with one leg over the railing.   *October 17, 1966*

Flash: The great sourdough French bread controversy—is our bread less sour than it used to be?—is raging on, and may even become a campaign issue. Thunders Assemblyman Willie Brown: "I will get to the bottom of this if I have to examine every mother in town!" ("Mother" is a baking term for the starter that gives the sourdough its distinctive flavor.) KSFO's authoritative Carter B. Smith joins the rising chorus: "Even whisky sours aren't sour anymore. In fact, the whole city has lost its sour smell." A baker who refuses to be identified, for obvious reasons, whispers: "We're making it sweeter because the newcomers to San Francisco just don't like the sour taste."

Now comes John Reddick of Stockton with further inside information: "I operated a gas station in San Francisco 25 years ago. On cold mornings I would go across the street to a French bakery to get warm by the ovens. The baker, a giant of a man, worked topless in the hot room, kneading a chunk of dough the size of a wash tub. After every few minutes of pounding and pushing at the dough on a table, he would lift it high above his head and, leaning back slightly, pound it against his sweaty bare chest. I always attributed that unique sourdough taste to this last operation."

This explains quite a bit. Somebody must have blabbed to the Health Dept. and spoiled everything. Bring Back Our Topless Bakers! *November 4, 1966*

REMEMBRANCE OF THINGS FUTURE

I've lived in this city, man and bore, for the better part of my wasted life, and I am now ready to concede that nothing is permanent here except change. The past decade has been dizzying: buildings built for the ages—veritable Parthenons—disappear overnight to be replaced by things that look like Lawrence Welk's accordian set on end. The mighty Hartford Building, a stupendous study in sterility, rises out of nowhere to lean on fragile Old St. Mary's. The Golden Gateway—pastel playing blocks arranged by a not particularly gifted child—replaces a Produce District notable for sweat, spinach leaves and rats bigger than cats. The 52-story Bank of America World Headquarters (at last, the world will have a place to call home) is soon to blossom out of the grave of the city's seamiest eyesores. Everywhere, the beat-beat-beat of the pile drivers, the sickening crunch of the steel ball slung by Davids in plastic helmets, the cranes hoisting girders out of a sea of mortgages. Money is tight, man, but somebody is hanging loose.

* * *

Seeking the city that was, or was it?—I walked through the downtown shopping area, mentally ticking off the changes: Robert Kirk Ltd., with a handsome facade by Wurster, Bernardi & Emmons, taking over the Post St. side of the old White House. The Nevada Bank, which survived Black Bart, already gone. The Crocker Building, which survived the earthquake, doomed. H. Liebes in the building once occupied by I. Magnin. Magnin's on the corner once occupied by Nathan-Dohrmann. Davis-Schonwasser gone, replaced by a bank. Owl Drugs out, Brooks Brothers in, Florsheim Shoes at the corner we thought Wurlitzer would own forever. The Post St. addition to the St. Francis, the one that throws it out of balance;

a church once reared its spire there. Around the corner on Geary stood, at one time, Union Square's only movie house, the St. Francis. Now it's Lefty O'Doul's. Even the people who used to say "Nothing ever changes in San Francisco" are gone.

★   ★   ★

The point about all this is that you have to stay contemporary, which is not the same thing as being With It. The trouble with being With It is that the "it" keeps changing, and there's nothing more embarrassing than being Not Quite With It. Staying contemporary is a different and much more difficult chore, requiring both self-discipline and self-delusion. It's not just agreeing that short skirts on women look fine and that the Rolling Stones have a great sound—that's With-Itism again. It's mainly a determination never to look back at a past that very well might have been as golden as we are told it was.

Woodrow Wilson or somebody once said that "The past makes the present livable," but in the case of a city with so special a past as San Francisco, I doubt it. It just makes the present seem tackier, and staying contemporary that much harder—unless you can convince yourself that Carol Doda is as authentic a character as Lotta Crabtree or Lillie Coit (we'll have to wait to find out whether Sterling Hayden becomes the contemporary Jack London).

Nostalgia is the house disease in San Francisco, and it's a tough habit to kick, even when the new buildings rise all around to symbolize the futility and fatuity. You can reminisce all you want about the six-bit dinners at Sanguinetti's and the baseball heroes of Old Butchertown, but it won't stop the Corinthian pillars from toppling in the financial district, nor will it solve any of the truly contemporary problems in the New Butchertown, out there by Hunters Point.

★   ★   ★

To stay contemporary, you must see beauty in the cunning curve of a freeway and the future in a high-rise whose walls are already beginning to crack. The view from the 25th floor is still great, if you can forget that the Bay is gradually filling with garbage. By straining your eyes a bit more than is comfortable, you can find artful counterpoints on all sides: the romantic French crown of 111 Sutter against the stark, vertical lines of the Wells-Fargo tower; the Gothic bulk of Grace Cathedral against the blazing glass facelessness of Mr. Tishman's apartments; the red Germanic brickpile of St. Mark's Lutheran surrounded by the concrete silos and blockhouses of Cathedral Hill. And surely the new pedestrian overpass

121

at Geary and Webster has a graceful fragility that comes as a pleasant surprise in this otherwise brutalized area.

★   ★   ★

Staying contemporary if it kills you: a hard role to play in a city with a magnificent past, a restless present and a future whose outlines—square and graceless—are already discernible on a hilltop earmarked for leveling. This could, of course, be a golden age: it's hard to know when you're living in one. But I'd say the odds are against it unless you're so damn contemporary you can find excitement in a traffic jam and poetry in the smog.

November 13, 1966

Believe-it-or-noddity: I met Comedian Woody Allen for the first time three years ago, when he played his first engagement at the hungry i. He was shy, unassuming, intelligent, a good listener and completely free of that egomania, bordering on megalomania, that makes so many show people unbearable. Since then he has scored a hit with his movie, "What's New Pussycat?", played a major role in "Casino Royale," written amusing pieces for the New Yorker, opened a successful play on Broadway, written and starred in another movie, "What's Up Tiger Lily?" and become a full-fledged member of the international In Group. Last week, with all fingers crossed, I had lunch with him at Bardelli's—and he is still shy, unassuming, intelligent, a good listener and apparently free of egomania. It's a miracle, folks.

★   ★   ★

Bagatelle: "Sorry, sir," said Marian Phillips, cashier at the Marina Chuck Wagon. "I can't cash your check because the boss isn't here." With a groan, the customer dug deep and came up with the cash for two dinners—less 55¢. "That's okay, sir," smiled Marian. "We'll trust you for the rest of it. You have an honest face." And so, with his pockets turned inside out, S.F.'s Gordon Peter Getty, son of the richest man in the world, escorted his wife inside for a prime rib dinner.

November 28, 1966

THE INDESCRIBABLE SOMETHING

Well, what is it anyway—that little touch of class (or style, if you will) that sets people and cities apart from the run of the mill millions? In the old days, it didn't seem so hard to define. "A classy guy," in the parlance of the Tenderloin, was a flashy dresser with a high gloss on his fingernails, a diamond pinky ring and, again in the patois, the ability "to go to his pocket pretty good." The pocket usually contained a roll of $100 bills obtained in some deliciously illicit manner, and if he peeled them off in full view, by means of a wetted thumb, he was a check-grabbing four-flusher. If he grabbed the check surreptitiously, and slipped $100 to the head waiter on the way out, with nobody noticing, he was a bona fide classy guy.

* * *

Today, the standards are more complex, and the manner in which a check is grabbed, if at all, is no longer a criterion. Now the individual with class is more likely to be the quiet one of firm resolve who will stand up and be counted, no matter how unpopular the cause (Joan Baez comes to mind). The subject, in fact, is such a knotty one that a national magazine has assigned a writer to tackle the subject monthly, and predictably, he is going around in circles. His best example of class and style to date has been the always classy and stylish Joe DiMaggio. Style: Joe DiMaggio, as a Yankee, loping after a long fly in center field, seeming hardly to move. Class: Joe DiMaggio, as a man, barring Peter Lawford from Marilyn Monroe's funeral.

* * *

San Francisco once had a great sense of style, which leads me to believe that the key is knowing who and what you are. In the golden era before World War II, there was a sense of belonging that permeated the entire city—all wrapped up in a mystical amalgam of ferry boats and fog, millionaires who weren't ashamed of it, longshoremen who were proud of it, and a vital, grassroots bohemianism that hadn't yet become estranged. The San Franciscans of that day seemed to have a strong sense of time and place, and there was an intermingling without self-consciousness. (The stresses and strains are more intense today; the groups that once mixed have retired to their various enclaves, whence they gaze upon each other with hostility.) I remember a party that Templeton Crocker once gave in his magnificent penthouse on Russian Hill. Among the guests was Henri Lenoir, who now owns the Vesuvio but was then poor and close to starving. As the hors d'oeuvres were passed, Henri stuffed them into his pockets, to stave off the hunger of the morrow. At one point, Crocker approached, took out a cigarette and asked "Do you have a light, Henri?" Flustered, Lenoir reached into his pocket and, to his horror, pulled out a sandwich. "You are priceless," laughed Crocker. "And also matchless."

★   ★   ★

Poise, wit, charm, chic—these things are part of style, but only part. And knowing who you are is increasingly difficult as the old standards evaporate, to be replaced by vague new ones. Doing the right thing at the right time in the right place used to be one of the yardsticks of class, but today it could even be square, and can a square have style? The Beatles have it, the New Christy Minstrels don't. Sinatra has it, Pat Boone doesn't. On the other hand, Lucius Beebe might have been a square, by today's viewpoint, but he had great style because he had an unwavering awareness of what was right for him. He wasn't out to impress anybody. He was also unfailingly polite without appearing condescending, class-conscious without being conscious of class (I will venture a flat statement: you can't have class without manners). He even got drunk—"taken by wine," as he put it—with a terrible and laudable dignity.

★   ★   ★

Well, in his own way, Lucius Beebe was courageous, and maybe you can't have class without courage. I'm a little tired, too, of Hemingway's "Grace under pressure" definition, but we've seen some stirring examples lately. Could anything have been classier than Pat Brown's graceful, pressure-packed speech of concession? The ability to smile and remain a whole man when your world has just crashed around you is a superhuman achievement; certain other politicians, in the same position, have proved all too human. Sandy Koufax, graceful in victory, was equally graceful in acknowledging defeat at the hands of fate. A lot of us, Pat Brown included, will be forever haunted by Caryl Chessman, who won in death what he fought for in prison: respect. No matter how he lived, he died with unbelievable courage and coolness. Minutes before he went, he consoled a distraught reporter. "Take care of yourself—don't worry about me, I'll be all right."

★   ★   ★

Class and style—you can have one without the other, and those who have both are the singularly blessed. Jack Shelley might be a fair example of a man who has class but no style, where a certain famous lawyer who shall be nameless has style but no class. Harry Bridges has both and so does Robert Watt Miller: neither has ever wavered from his particular, special view of life, and both have conducted their lives without phoniness. Thanks to an unquenchable jeu d'esprit, William Saroyan has class and style. While other

124

and lesser writers receive the acclaims and awards that once were his, he goes on doing what he does best, laughing at life and enjoying it hugely, never once denigrating the work of others.

★ ★ ★

Maybe, all I've proved is that class and style are hard to define, which is why I titled this piece "The Indescribable Something"—to get myself off the hook. No class, all the way down the line.

November 30, 1966

Wondering muse: I keep thinking about Post-Deb Melinda Moffett's statement last wk. that 17 out of 25 Cotillion debutantes (in her coming-out group) have used marijuana. It sounds like a radio commercial: "Seventeen out of 25 debs smoke pot!" And it was splendid of her to reveal that she has rec'd marijuana from escorts at the Burlingame Country Club, "but you can't buy it there," she added. Apparently the Club isn't as square as some people think, although Fran Martin admits to being naive: "I've been getting my grass from the gardeners and groundskeepers" . . . Anyway, maybe all this will stop subscribers from writing in to complain about society page photos of under-age debs with highball glasses in their hands. According to Melinda and her pals, drinking booze is nowhere, o-u-t, forGET it. I guess it's those kids who DON'T have a glass in their hand that you should wonder about . . . Actually, the pot puffers and LSD trippers are probably healthier than the rest of us. It has yet to be shown that marijuana, even without filters, causes lung cancer, and I doubt that you could take enough LSD on a sugar cube to cause diabetes. The only thing these kids have to worry about is bad prison food, and even that's getting better.

December 12, 1966

Add crises: There's sort of an unemployment problem out there in the Hip-Ashbury District, so a nice girl named Sharon Sweeney has opened "The Hip Job Co-op" employment agency. "You know," she says earnestly, "a lot of the hippies around here have college degrees, great ability and the desire to work. But the people in the square world just don't like to hire a young man who wears a beard and maybe doesn't bathe every week." (Every WEEK? Why, a guy could catch his death.) At the moment, she's trying to rent out "psychedelic hippies" to read poetry or otherwise entertain at square New Year's Eve parties—"most of which need this kind of color." Smellovision? *December 22, 1966*

1967

The last angry woman: That would be Geri Southworth, queen of the pigeon lovers. During the political campaign last fall, she was thrown out of the KGO-TV studios, whereupon she soaped this message on the station's front window: "Right plus left minus responsibility equals riots—write in Geraldine A. Southworth for Governor!" The station had her arrested for malicious mischief, but the D.A. declined to prosecute, so now she is suing KGO. Because: "I feel that grave damage was done to my political career by being thrown in jail with 400 prostitutes while running for Governor." *January 17, 1967*

Why I hate the theater: Rush home, change clothes, rush to a restaurant, rush through dinner ("Do I have time to go to the powder room?"), rush to the theater, stumble over four people ("Sorry, par-mee") to your seat, shift uncomfortably through the first act (stomach making embarrassing noises), squeeze into the lobby ("Hello there, good to see YOU!"), make small talk about the first act ("Interesting, isn't it"), reflect miserably that there's a second intermission, spend the third act fanning yourself to stay awake, wait forever for your car in a garage . . . Well, that's more or less the way I felt till the American Conservatory Theater came to town. That group—and we're so lucky to have them it makes my head spin—makes it all seem worthwhile. They've even made the tacky old Geary Theater look presentable, and for that alone, we should be grateful. *January 30, 1967*

. . . Another landmark gone: Johnny "Scooter" Leahey, the legless
mendicant who peddled his pencils outside the Palace Hotel for
the past 20 years, died last week—without ever having realized his
dream of walking. He saved enough money to buy artificial limbs,
but never could master their use. It was only two weeks ago that
he gave them to his friend, George Silliman, and said bitterly:
"Do me a favor, George—throw these things off the Golden
Gate Bridge." *January 31, 1967*

Among those who were surprised to find Don Sherwood off the
air yesterday morning was Don Sherwood. This was to have been
his final week on KSFO—after 14 years—but at the last minute,
his bosses told him NOT to mention the fact that he is leaving
soon for Hawaii. "You mean you want me to be on the air 15 hours
without saying good-by?" he exploded. "Forget it!" And so Jim
Lange stepped in yesterday morn and Old Donnie-Babe was
gone, fwhooosh, without so much as a farewell to his fans. We'll
miss him, too. He got us through many a painful early-morning
shave, with a hangover as bad as his worst, and for this we will
always be grateful. *February 7, 1967*

Gung hay and all that: Wednesday night in Chinatown, the eve of
the New Year's celebration. The markets overflowing with traditional oranges and tangerines and red azaleas. Lights tracing the
graceful outlines of the Family Association buildings, their romantic balconies overlooking the misty alleys where tongs once fought.
Year of the Sheep or Year of the Ram, depending on your translation ("I prefer sheep," said a cynical young Chinese. "They're
easier to shear. Year of the Sucker? Don't quote me on that—YOU
said it").

In the kitchen at Kan's, Venerable Ming, the premier chef of
Chinatown, hard at work on a feast for the aristocracy upstairs in
the backroom. Thousand-year eggs and ginger. Delicate Gold Coin
Chicken, a 24-hour chore. Succulent shreds of chicken and sprays
of coriander for the so see gai. Duck stuffed with lotus. Chicken
stuffed with glutinous rice. Steamed sea bass in a great silver fish.

As he works, Venerable Ming nibbles away at a box of See's candies given to him by a Pacific Heights admirer who had addressed the box "To the Greatest Chef in the World." He glances at the clock every now and then and finally his long night is over. As the firecrackers burst and fog settles over celebrating China-town, Ming pads through the streets to a little all-night counter on Jackson St., there to dine on HIS favorite of all dishes.

Apple pie a la mode. *February 10, 1967*

They say Jay Hoppe is back in North Beach. "They" would be those who remember the OLD North Beach of the Beat Generation of the 1950s, when the crossroads of the young world was the corner of Grant and Green, site of the Co-Existence Bagel Shop. Jay Hoppe owned it, and the fuzz (that was a new word then) co-existed there, especially in the person of Police Officer Bill Bigarani, the terror of the Beats. The Health Dept. co-existed there, too, because of the one co-existence toilet for co-existing boys and girls (in those days you could tell them apart).

The world and Allen Ginsberg were young and Francis Rigney, the Beat psychiatrist, hadn't yet become Dr. Francis Rigney, the society psychiatrist who wears velvet suits to museum openings. The bartender at the Co-Existence was Mark Green, a mordant observer who wrote a perceptive treatise titled "North Beach Sounds: Funky Scenes." Perhaps it was Mark who painted "Fuzz Is Our Friend" in red, white and blue letters on the police callbox at the corner. Fuzz-Buster Bigarani was not amused. He had the offending sentiment removed.

Now they say Jay Hoppe is back in North Beach, running, "of all things," an antique shop near Columbus and Broadway. Why "of all things"? He once ran an antique shop in Paris, didn't he? And he opened the Bagel Shop, which was to be "a nice quiet del-icatessen," to escape an ex-wife who followed him all around the world. Or so he said. Now they say he's married to a police cap-tain's daughter. Of all things.

* * *

La plus ca change? But it's never la meme chose, really. Mark Green has expatriated himself to Bernal Heights, where he works for civic betterment. Now and then he wanders down the hill to observe the Haight-Ashbury scene.

"I think what is happening there," he ventures, "had its

antecedents in the North Beach of the '50s. They are coming on the way they thought we were. Distorted. Ten years later. Like in the last days of the Bagel kids, when they were acting like characters out of Kerouac. Does a writer take from life or does life take from a writer?

"I have tremendous empathy with the young ones in the Haight-Ashbury but at the same time they anger me. Maybe because in them I see myself a little. Like them, we were searching for the truth and to find ourselves, but for most of us the ends became the means and very few of us found the freedom to be ourselves. I don't think anymore it's either be hip or be square. There's good in both worlds and the existential problem is to choose the good from both worlds and discard the bad.

"Granted life does look absurd, but I don't believe one creates meaning by becoming more absurd." Eric Berne, si, Tim Leary, no? It was Dr. Berne who said "To live in a world in which there is no Santa Claus, one must face the existential problems of necessity, freedom of choice and absurdity."

And what of Officer (now Inspector) Bill Bigarani, the Beat-buster? The other day he was quoted as saying, on the subject of repeatedly throwing drunks in jail: "Drunkenness is definitely a medical problem. It's not a police problem. Or at any rate, it shouldn't be. Many people don't realize that the police don't arrest the drunks on Skid Row just to be mean."

Maybe he learned something in the crazy Beat World he knew so well. Maybe we all did. *February 16, 1967*

The leader strikes again!: Bit of a flap over at Travis Air Force Base last Fri. night. Nancy Sinatra, pooped right down to the soles of her walkin' boots, returned from Vietnam, where she'd been entertaining the troops, and asked for a car to take her to S.F. Airport. "Sorry," said the protocol officer. "No car. But we can send you over there by bus." That did it! In tears, she phoned her father in L.A., and in a surprisingly short time, Frank Sinatra's personal jet was landing at Travis to whisk her home. So much for protocol. *February 21, 1967*

Herbert's sherbert: Well, the mystery of our "Mystery Lady"—she who parks almost daily by the Park's Portals of the Past in her chauffeured Rolls-Royce, to stare into space—has been solved from several sources. She's Lily Zellerbach Drake, who is pushing 80 in the most elegant manner, lives alone at the Palace, and prefers to be addressed as "Miss Drake." Although she's a sister of the late Isadore Zellerbach, the paper king, she sees little of the family these days. Gone past the Z's? . . .   *March 22, 1967*

Culture west: "Powerful passions crept in this fabled romance of forbidden love South of Bangalore!". . ."Hot blooded romance, illicit love and violent vengeance!" . . . "Earthy, passionate life in the raw!" . . . "To his fellow students, a poet related the story of his three strange loves" . . . Are the foregoing teaser ads for a Market St. porny house? Nope. They're from a brochure for the S.F. Spring Opera season, opening June 2, and the purple prose refers to "The Pearl Fishers," "Cavalleria Rusticana," "Pagliacci" and "Tales of Hoffman." The company is also doing "La Traviata," that pulsating expose of heartbreak and unbridled sex. I believe the police should look into this, since all these dirty shows were written by foreign agitators.   *March 27, 1967*

. . . Paul McCartney of the Beatles flew out to N.Y. yesterday after spending a couple of days at the Fairmont under an assumed name (Nathan Weiss???). Jane Asher of the Old Vic was his prime target, of course, but he also found time to work out with the Jeff Airplane at Fillmore Aud., performing so well on the guitar that Marty Balin said: "If you're ever out of a job . . . " Wearing his hair shorter and his moustache longer, he fired his camera around the Haight-Ashbury, where, of course, he looked positively square. He had a ready explanation for the fact that hardly anybody recognized him: "That's what is so great about this city—the straights don't stare at the hippies. They're accepted as part of the community." By some, by some . . .   *April 6, 1967*

I HAPPEN TO LIKE IT—

San Francisco, I mean—even though it seems to be losing some of its symmetry. But this could be all to the good, since the only

131

perfect symmetry is death ("Death," "symmetry"—there's a tiny pun there audible only to dogs and other caenines). In writing about the city, I used to be able to toss off such giblets as "Ah, San Francisco: the more it changes, the more it remains the same!" thereby demonstrating that it's easier to turn stomachs than phrases (and also that youth and truth have little in common except their rhyme). What we know now, for a fact, is that the more the city changes, the more it changes—it's as simple and complicated as that.

★　★　★

These clanking thoughts occurred to me the other night as I was driving aimfully around, trying to zero in on the city I once thought I knew so well. From time to time it all seemed blessedly familiar: the heavy overhead trolley and phone wires, redolent of the Naughty Oughties, and the block after block of wooden houses that escaped the Ought Sixquake. It's really quite amazing how many of those pre-fire houses have survived, and how balefully charming they look in the street lights of midnight; even those that are more tenemental than sentimental on the inside preserve a certain dignified facade—a cock-eyed extravagance that once was the warm face of a city. That face is now seen more clearly in profile, cold and angular.

★　★　★

Driving alone in the wakefully sleeping city, along freeways where spring flowers once grew, past row after row of stucco houses whose occupants I would never know but forever wonder about (who are they, what are they like, how do they feel about the city that has thrown us together and kept us apart?). Down Fillmore, with its immemorial Negro bars and the shadowy figures talking— about what?—on the corners. The big cars, the pretty girls, a vague smell of bar-b-qued ribs: the old pre-integration colored section. "Whitey Go Home" is chalked invisibly on every wall and I thank you for your hostility. Even when I don't anticipate it, I think I understand it.

★　★　★

The autumnal chill of springtime, tulips growing unseen in secret gardens. You can't see them as you drive around, but you know they are there—the hidden green belts behind the cold shoulders of Pacific Heights houses (from a low-flying helicopter, the sight of all these gardens comes as a surprise). Sacred Pacific Heights, where the movers and shakers live, and are they moving or shaking? Do they roll up their windows and lock the doors when they drive through the Fillmore? Have they ever even BEEN in the Crocker-Amazon, can they find Hayes Valley, have they visited Visitacion? Pacific Heights, a state of mindlessness, where happiness is just a thing called dough, and don't knock it, buddy; we all knead it, sour or otherwise.

★   ★   ★

San Francisco, the gorgeous mess—wooden yesterdays mocking steel tomorrows, or is it the other way around? Haight Street, that graight street, where the name Spreckels means nothing more than sugar cubes, and little care the hippies that some of the finest families of Old San Francisco used to live where now they dream their vagrant dreams. Past the sagging ricketies and along Skid Road—East Indian maidens in dirty saris, Tugboat Annies, the drunks sitting wine-sogged against walls, heads down between their knees (Skid Road always looks like a grainy documentary titled "The Shame of the Cities"—but here there is a hipless hopelessness, the last drag on the bummed cigarette).

★   ★   ★

In the Tenderloin, the bars closing, throwing more flotsam than jet-setters into the streets. Soon the cafeterias would be filling with people trying to sober up before it's time to go to work. I drove through the deserted financial district to the Golden Gateway— the new thing ("The NOW Thing!") in the city of too many pasts. Now I felt like a character in an Antonioni film, walking across clean-cobbled courtyards, through endless neat passageways and lobbies, rising in a sterilized elevator to the apartment of Night People whose door is always unlatched. Unhinged, I looked down from the balcony at the Gateway's planned mosaics, the gleaming tiles, the tiny trees just so, the bridgeways and breezeways. This, too, is San Francisco—and as I looked up and out, it was the Bay Bridge, the Ferry Building and cluttered old Telegraph Hill that suddenly looked out of place, distorted and dimly seen, as in a dream or nightmare. "Make that a double," I said to my host, a living person.

★   ★   ★

The City: all things to all people, or perhaps too much for some, not enough for others. Or is it just Too Much?   *April 9, 1967*

Speaking of the garbage problem (and the same to you), Ingle Shankel has a friend who lives in a glorious new high-rise overlooking the Gate Bridge, and a fine pad it is: air-conditioner, built-in hi-fi, color TV, balcony, wall-to-wall everything. Well, almost everything. The builder forgot a garbage chute. "Every few days," reports Ingle, "he used to put the garbage in an old suitcase and carry it out through the lobby, but he soon ran out of suitcases. Now he stuffs the garbage in I. Magnin, Saks or Roos-Atkins bags, puts 'em in his sportscar, drives downtown and parks. Then he lurks in a nearby doorway till somebody steals the packages. Downtown San Francisco being what it is, it's usually a short wait." I say!

April 12, 1967

OK, OK, all you writer-inners—I'm with you: Candlestick Park IS the place to dump our garbage. However, since it would hold 1,450,000 cubic yards of our swellest swill, and our output is 8,000 cubic yards daily, this would solve the problem only for 181 days—or, roughly, till the end of baseball season. However, I'm delighted to pass along your suggestion. Always at your disposal.

April 14, 1967

MR. NITELIFE STRIKES AGAIN!

I awoke late in the afternoon with the clock-radio playing that fine Duke Ellington tune, "Don't Get Around Much Any More" ("Missed the Saturday dance, hear they crowded the floor"), and it dawned on me, with a pain sharp and gassy as heartburn, that I HADN'T been getting around much lately. Peace marches, symphony concerts, museum openings and smuggling banana splits out of the Hashberry are all very well, but was I covering The Scene as of Yorick? Alas, no.

Well, no sooner said than undone. Leaping into the shower, I soaped myself thoroughly with Dial (that's Laid spelled backward—don't you wish everybody did?) and emerged feeling sticky and itchy. I leaped in again and turned on the water. Better, much better. Then, humming the peerless Anson Weeks arrangement of The Blue Pajama Song ("Why did I wear those blue pajamas before the big affair began?"—ah, Buddy Moreno), I put on my best tuckered bib, placed a carnation boutonniere in my teeth and set out for the fleshpots.

My wife had given me carte blanche and other credit cards for the evening and I felt postively jejune again. In the financial district, I stood at the corner of Dow and Jones, wondering where to begin. I smiled at the pretty girls and they laughed right back. I followed one transistorized model into a bar famed as a pickup (or After Ours) joint and bought her a deep-dish martini. After the first sip, she fished into her handbag and produced a photo of herself with no clothes on. I mean, starkers!

"Not so fast," I protested, thoroughly shocked. "Look, fella," she said coolly, "Time is money. Let's cut out the small talk and get down to the nitty gritty." Hastily throwing down my half of the check, I went away from there as fast as my wedgies would carry me.

★   ★   ★

Well, where WAS there to go in the New City? In the long nights of the old days, when I used to make the rounds till 3 a.m. (Imitate Walter Winchell—Earn Big Money!), the groove was a well-worn rut. First, John's Rendezvous, where Bill Gilmore was always at the bar, buying. Then to the Black Cat to argue with Bill Saroyan over whether Dong Kingman was a better artist than Matt Barnes. Out to Ocean Beach to slide down the slide into Topsy's Roost and listen to Ellis Kimball's band. Back to the Embassy on the Wharf to hear Ray Goman tell jokes that were old even then. Over to La Fiesta to watch Harry Bridges win the rumba contest. Down to the office to write those snappy three-dot items, and so to bed in broad daylight after playing tennis at dawn in Julius Kahn with Larry Fanning, Bob Ritchie and Grant Mathews. Well, they're mostly dead now, give or take a couple.

★   ★   ★

But it was only 9 p.m. Swallowing a yawn, I checked in at Ernie's, but nobody was there except the Maharajah of Baroda, Noel Coward and a man who looked like Gertrude Stein. At the Blue Fox a woman who looked like Hubert Humphrey was in deep conversation with a fat man who was either Orson Welles or Curtis LeMay, perhaps both or neither. I took a few notes—not for the column, but to make things tax-deductible. On Old Broadway, a busload of hippies rolled past, all of them staring in disbelief at the tourists going in and out of the topless joints (to a hippie, a topless joint is a marijuana cigarette without a filter).

In the Condor, the music was so loud you could see it, psychedelic lights were whirling and topless dancers gyrating. "You gotta have everything going at once," explained Gino del Prete. "You give the customers time to think and they're liable to say 'What the hell am I doing here?' and out they go." I said "What the hell am I doing here?" and cleared out.

135

I peered in at the Peppermint Tree, a steam bath filled with naked ladies. All the customers were men—it looked like an old-fashioned burlycue, Bald Head Row and all. More acres of flesh at the Gay 60s, where Bee Goman kept rolling her eyes and saying "Isn't it just awful—but golly the business we're doing" (I wish she'd stop saying that). Again, mostly men, staring joylessly at the joyless nudies. Basin Street West was packed for the post–2 a.m. breakfast show. Coffee was a buck and a half a shot and cheap at half the price. Where do all these people come from? "May I take you home?" "Mine or yours?"

★ ★ ★

At 4 a.m., there I was in an unlikely Geary St. cellar called Guys and Dolls, not unattractive. A terrific rock 'n' roll band called The Straight Men (an inside joke, judging from some of the customers) was whanging away and off-duty topless dancers were trying to top each other in exhibition performances. Truly a remarkable place. As the dawn thundered up over David's Delicatessen, I tottered out onto gray old Geary, thoroughly convinced that night life is not dead. I wish I could say the same for me.   *May 14, 1967*

For instant painless nostalgia, it's hard to beat the re-re-reruns of "Lineup" on Channel 5 (now called "San Francisco Beat"). You get flashes of Portsmouth Square before the garage, the Embarcadero before the freeway, the Aquatic Park area before the Fontana, the old Hall of Justice in full swing. Or don't you feel nostalgic about any of those? . . .   *May 21, 1967*

Yesterdays: The death of Dorothy Parker this week recalls her first visit to S.F., in the late Thirties, when Editor Paul C. Smith entertained her in his Telegraph Hill apartment. Among the guests was Harry Bridges, and Miss Parker, who was turned on by left-wing causes, said earnestly to him as he was leaving: "Oh, Mr. Bridges, I do so admire what you stand for. I'm going from here to Hollywood, and if there is anything I can do there for you—ANYthing—just say the word." "Well," shrugged Bridges, "could you get an autographed picture of Shirley Temple for my daughter?". . . In due time, the picture arrived and later figured in a totally incredible headline-grabbing charge by Martin Dies, then head of the

House Un-American Activities Committee, that Shirley and other stars were supporters of left-wing causes (one of her autographed pictures had also popped up in a French radical newspaper). Shirley was about seven at the time, and never autographed a photo to anyone—the job was done by the studio. It's all a matter of fond memory now, like the bittersweet humor of Dorothy Parker.

June 10, 1967

Hello there: Barnaby Conrad dropped in at Roland's Bar in the Marina the other night and gazed longingly at a magnificent photo of the late matador, Carlos Arruza. "I'd like to use that in a new book I'm doing," he said to Owner Frank Perez, who shook his head, explaining "That picture has great sentimental value for me." Barnaby: "Well, could I borrow it and have a copy made?" Frank: "Nope, I'm afraid I might not get it back." Barnaby: "Why does it mean so much to you? Did you know Arruza?" Frank: "No, but 13 years ago I stole it from the wall of YOUR bar, the Matador, and I wouldn't want it to happen again."

July 10, 1967

Sutter St. salient: The hippies made their deepest penetration of the current campaign on Monday night (but eventually were thrown back without loss of faith on either side). By the hundreds, they poured into the heart of Straightville—by foot, via bus, on hogs, in psychedelically painted VWs, in buses so ancient they might have seen service in the First Battle of the Marne. Bells tinkled, beads jangled, beards bristled, plumes waved in the salubrious evening overcast. In all, a brave sight, and no fuzz around to tighten up the scene (San Francisco, I Love You).

Their target: The Moore Gallery, an Establishment institution on Sutter between Mason and Powell. The reason: a preview of a show by the leaders of the Hippie Academy of Applied Art—Wes Wilson, Mighty Mouse, Mascoso, Griffin, Kelley. Between 6 and 10, some 3,500 people, largely wild, jammed into the place, dressed in fantastic costumes—old uniforms covered with medals, American Flags worn as headdresses, pirate outfits, cavaliers and miniskirts so short that Carl Larson described them as "a pride of loins."

Champagne corks popped to the tune of 25 cases. Country Joe & The Fish played. Perfume, sweat, pot and incense blended into a mixture smoggy enough to make the eyes water. A social type swept out, snorting "I didn't know hippies drank champagne." "Only when it's free, lady," said one happily. A pale girl drinking her first glass ever said, "It tastes like soda pop." "It's not the best champagne in the world," I offered. A young fellow wearing bangs and a Boer War uniform said rather loftily, "The champagne at the Legion of Honor is much drier" (Oh God, they're getting in EVERYwhere).

★　★　★

A man who said he was a fire inspector stood on the sidewalk and muttered nervously: "I believe they're exceeding the limit in there." "What's the limit?" I inquired. He shrugged hopelessly: "Whatever it is, they're exceeding it." On the big patio behind the gallery enough pot filled the air to turn on the entire neighborhood, whose residents were falling out of their windows to stare at the bizarre scene. In the fading sunlight, you could look beneath the beards and through the lank hair and see that most of these young people look rather ill. Malnutrition, perhaps? "Do you ever eat?" I asked a wan child mother holding a baby not much younger than she. "Doughnuts," she said at last. "Lots of doughnuts."

The art, what you could see of it through the packed bodies, looked promising. The posters, at $2.50 each, are of course magnificent. The other works by The Big Five will bear closer scrutiny, being Establishment-priced at $150 to $2,500. The man who owns Moore Gallery—Dr. Norman Moore of Woodside, physicist, former Vice-Pres. of Litton Industries, board chairman of Reed College in Portland—is delighted with the whole scene: "These are real artists with a wide range."

That could well be true. What is definitely true is that there has never been an art preview quite like this one; for once, the two dozen duck-billed platitudes who kept saying "It could only happen in San Francisco" were right.　　　　*July 19, 1967*

ONE FINE DAY

I was standing at the bar in the House of Shields on New Montgomery, shaking dice with Hard Hat McCabe and feeling reasonably at peace with the world, even though I was losing (no sweat, since no skill is involved in the game). Shields, of course, is the kind of place that inspires feelings of bonhomie and good will, especially at the lunch hour: friendly-tough bartenders, a handsome round-the-Horn back bar, a heavily ornate ceiling that couldn't be duplicated today—the whole scene very masculine without latent overtones. We sat down to some kind of steak smothered in onions, and I reflected that if it weren't for that goddam war in Vietnam, life wouldn't be half bad, considering that all of us Shields types were uptight, well over 30 (hence not to be trusted) and probably guilty of playing the Establishment ball.

★　★　★

Anyway, the Establishment isn't all bad, I mused euphorically. If you hang around the fringes of it, at least you eat and drink well, and there are all those parties with the hired butlers passing creamed Ken-L-Ration, or whatever it is. Everybody is clean and smells good, even the bores, and so what if the conversation seldom reaches a Noel Coward pitch? Who listens? Most of the Establishment people have decent feelings, all in all, and would have voted for McAteer, a bigger airport and a better Opera House. They sense that the Negroes deserve a break and that the hippies represent something disquieting, hence important—even when the more acid Hashburies refer to THEM as "heppies." That's fairly funny, and the Establishment prides itself on an unflagging sense of humor.

★　★　★

I walked out into the sunshine, still feeling pleased (except for that g.d. war, Lyndon's lead balloon). What makes the whole scene tolerable is the never-ending joy of San Francisco, of being a San Franciscan, one of the few remaining titles a man can take pride in. A miracle: how can the city retain its special flavor in a world going stock staring square? As the late Frank Lloyd Wright said not so lately: "Only San Francisco could survive what you people are doing to it." Peter Berg of the Diggers calls it, this very minute, "a holy city." An intelligent observer from the L.A. Free Press, an underground paper, scrutinized us minutely for weeks and reported "Compared to L.A., the S.F. media and officials are turned on." Interviewed in Los Angeles, Rudolf Nureyev says flatly: "San Francisco is a marvelous city." And Los Angeles? "A little bit square—not courageous enough."

★　★　★

What is this mysterious amalgam that keeps on working? There is no plan, certainly, and never was. It is almost in the realm of the metaphysical: a brew of gold rushes and silver bonanzas, sailing ships and shrouded dawns, overnight fortunes and brilliant disasters, bootleg gin, champagne suppers, minestrone and Peking Duck, new-old, beautiful-ugly—a city like no other, sea-girt, Bay-blocked and wide open to the winds and the wildest ideas, none so wild that an audience can't be found. Sometimes tacky, sometimes tawdry, often dirty and too often heedless—and yet, even in the current explosion of Plastic Inevitable, strong enough in personality to anthropomorphize: San Francisco lives!

*　*　*

As the glass boxes rise out of the Carpenter Gothic and the traffic writhes in horse-and-buggy streets (and the junk threatens to choke off the glitter), the magic lives on, and to whom do we offer thanks? To an enlightened Establishment, to be sure. Even when it is most blind to reality and feels most threatened, its leaders react (sooner or later) to the surge of San Francisco—a century-old thread of humanism, a bond that comes of being thrown together with all kinds of people on a tiny spit of land at the western edge of a continent. Maybe whatever form of non-government we have in City Hall is to the good, by and large; San Franciscans have always liked to fend for themselves, and undue authority is looked upon with a foggy coolness. Also by and large, the police are okay; at best, it's a miserable job, and a few of them are miserable about it—but, according to a man whose record attests to his credentials, there are more good cops here than you'll find among their counterparts anywhere else. I believe it.

*　*　*

I rose in my mythical helicopter and looked down on the hippies and the heppies, the brokers and the broken, the champs and the charlatans, the Mime Troupe performing on the Marina Square, the fog chasing the boats off the Bay, the old geezers lounging in the sun at Powell and Market, the kids playing in the alleys of the Mission, and I knew I was still in love with the whole beautiful mess. And I knew I was not alone. *July 23, 1967*

Rebuttal: Hippie David Simpson, the Mime Troupe actor charged with being a public nuisance, chose to defend himself before a jury and won—but that's not the item, since it has already been printed. This hasn't: In summing up her case against Simpson, Asst. D.A. Jean Wright warned the jurors not to put their faith "in his sincerity—after all, he's an actor and is trained to be dramatic." At which point Mime Trouper Lynn Brown piped up: "Hey, what about Ronnie, George and Shirley???" (Laughter).

August 3, 1967

Out of the mouths of babes dept. (royalty div.): While Princess Grace was being driven through Lincoln Park she looked at Rodin's statue of "The Thinker" at the Legion of Honor and smiled: "You know, when my son, Prince Albert, first saw that statue, he asked me what the man was thinking about. 'Well,' I said, 'I think he's trying to remember where he left his clothes.'"

Grace and Rainier loved San Francisco, and San Francisco found them pleasant, gracious and relaxed. The Prince: "I had no idea it was so beautiful. We must come back. I wish we'd arranged to spend more time here." (And less in Los Angeles?) When the Prince heard that Mayor Sam Yorty of L.A. was arranging a civic reception, he said: "No-no-no, this is supposed to be a pleasure trip—a holiday." (What's a Yorty, daddy?) Actually, the royal couple didn't say too much that was quotable, for a good reason. Confided a member of the entourage: "They're much too intelligent to say anything astounding."

Funny scene, though, in a Chinatown shop. Here's Princess Grace looking at three tassels on a wall and asking the woman owner: "Do they have any religious or cultural significance? What do you call them?" Woman: "Tassels." Press Rep. Russell MacMasters, valiantly interjecting: "What the Princess means, ma'am, is do you use them for any special purpose?" Woman: "Tassels." Russell, turning to a Chinese sage acting as guide: "What do you call those in Chinese?" Sage: "Kow sui." Russell: "Ah, and what does that mean, exactly?" Sage: "Tassels."

Late Sunday evening, the Prince and Princess sneaked away from everybody and had a quiet dinner with two old friends at the Empress of China, where the fortune cookies rang the bell twice. The Prince opened his to read: "You will discover the top is a very lonesome place." Princess Grace's: "You will be happy socially and in your work."

August 3, 1967

Scent: People have trouble with rats? Rats have trouble with people. One noon last wk., reports Spencer Van Gelder, this big fat rat wearing a ratty coat shows up in the middle of Fourth and Market, having been flushed by the BARTmen. For a few minutes, it tried frantically to find another hole to crawl into, but every crack a dud. The traffic made it so nervous it began running around in circles. Then it darted into the pedestrian lane, causing women to scream and strong men to pale. It was last seen rat-tailing it up Ellis, presumably in search of a drink (where are all those cats when we really need them?).

That lovable landmark on not-always-lovable Market St.—the handsome 60-year-old clock outside Albert Samuels—was removed yesterday, and that brings to mind a souvenir of San Franciscaena: the role of that clock in the trial of Tom Mooney and Warren K. Billings for the 1916 Preparedness Day bombing.

As an alibi, the defense produced a photo showing Mooney and his wife Rena on a Market St. rooftop at the time of the bombing—many blocks away from the scene. The time was established by the Samuels clock, clearly visible across the street. The prosecution, however, countered that the clock was one hour off, and made the point stick.

Undeterred by this, Rena's lawyer, the late great Ed McKenzie, took a photo of the clock every day for a year, to prove its unvarying accuracy. After he'd taken a final picture, exactly one year after the bombing—when the shadows were in precisely the same position—he went into court and won freedom for Rena. And, at the same time, exonerated the clock of the vile charge that it didn't tell the correct time.

Now watch some spoilsport like Author Curt Gentry come along and insist it was a different clock. *August 24, 1967*

HERE AND NOW

The most interesting thing about the hippies is not whether they are dead or alive—but, as always, the reaction they elicit (or provoke) from so-called established society. It may well be the twilight of this peculiar manifestation (one hesitates to call it a movement) of quiet outrage and noisy estrangement. But if it needed a raison d'etre—and even its most articulate champions seem unable to give it a point—it has been provided, ironically, by its unbelievably foamy-mouthed critics. In the face of the hippies' implied disdain, a truly well-established society would not have lost its poise, would not have blown its cool, would not have cried its outrage in such lamentable fashion.

*   *   *

It is quite true that society has inflated their importance grotesquely beyond their weight and numbers, and it would take a psychoanalyst to unravel the reasons (a love-hate syndrome, or just plain old-fashioned guilt?). Whoever wrote the "official" funeral notice for the Death of Hippie observance a few days ago knew what he was about when he described the deceased as "Hippie, devoted son of Mass Media," for indeed the hippies used the media for all it is worth, and media seemed pathetically eager to be used.

*   *   *

All this razzle-dazzle aside, the hippies, even if they're dying, have made a tremendous impact on this city—and, for that matter, the world. They constitute a frontal assault on everything that our frayed society holds dear, and, to make it more unnerving, they do it only by indirection. Writers who report, to this day, that "the hippies sneer at the straights" are guilty of wishful thinking: a sneer can easily be cancelled by a counter-sneer. The general hippie attitude is more one of pity (now that hurts). The more important facets of their criticism are merely implied; a guilty society makes the interpretations. The celebrated dirtiness of the hippies is one of the best examples. This is such an outrage in our world of "What, you left your family defenseless? Get off my sand dune!" that even reasonably intelligent people have been reduced to saying, in frustration, "Don't they know that cleanliness is next to godliness?" (Who wrote that, anyway—a soap salesman?)

*   *   *

By just standing there (or sitting, sleeping, turning on, shacking up), the hippie is an affront to all segments of The Establishment, even Joan Baez, who also seems to have a thing about soap. It's not just the conservatives and reactionaries who feel threatened. Old Bohemians, once frowned on themselves, frown on them as "going too far"; the Old Bohemians know they themselves never went far enough? One self-styled "liberal" commentator in this city has gone absolutely crackers over what he calls the "creepies," boiling them in the kind of invective once reserved for witches; if this were 1692, he would be setting torches to hippies—and so much for liberals. The Puritans among us are, of course, haunted as always by the dark suspicion that somewhere, somebody might be having a good time. And, as always, without them. As for those dear souls

143

who hope to "understand" the hippies, they're wasting their time. They'll have to find their absolution elsewhere.

★   ★   ★

For all their dirt, disease, slovenliness, laziness; for all their hedonism, clannishness, and undoubted egomania; for all the possibility that they might be in their death throes, the hippies have a message, even if few can be bothered to articulate it. As a wise old doctor once observed, rather sadly, "They are our consciences, walking around in bare feet." It simply is not enough to flog them, as Establishment critics do, for dropping out, "for refusing to integrate themselves into a meaningful protest movement" (the old liberals heard from again), for using drugs, "for creating an unnecessary burden on the taxpayer" (there's a hollow phrase for you), for leading "lewd and immoral" lives, for not flushing the john, or whatever they do that bugs the critics; anyway, most of the foregoing applies equally to Brooks Brothers types living at Good addresses.

★   ★   ★

No, what really bugs the critics is what the hippies are saying without saying a word: "What are YOU doing, brother, that's so damn important?" And this is the question—with its ghostly overtones of Vietnam, taxes, bigotry, hypocrisy, corruption, cancer and all the other ills of established society—this is the question that has no answer except fury.

★   ★   ★

As Voltaire might have said, if the hippies hadn't existed, it would have been necessary to invent them.   *October 15, 1967*

San Francisco joys: After a hot spell, being awakened one 6 a.m. by the Fugue for Five Foghorns, rattling the windows. Having your umbrella repaired at the good old S.F. Umbrella Works on Sutter and getting it back just as the rain begins. Rating a salute from the traffic cop at Sixth and Market—the one who always wears white gloves, a trim uniform and the supercool look of a supercop who never panics. Giving your small change to a hippie who says "Gee—wow." Riding on the outside step of a cable car with a girl in a miniskirt, a Marine, and a guy playing a harmonica with one hand. Going into a bar for a quiet nightcap and discovering that the bartender doesn't feel like talking, either. Riding in a cab with a driver who knows all the shortcuts and uses them. Without preamble, driving a tourist into Lincoln Park and drawing a satisfactory gasp from him as you pass the Legion of Honor and turn toward that sudden, unbelievable expanse of the bridged Gate. Dreaming that Candlestick Park, the Dumbarcadero Freeway and the Hartford Bldg. disappeared overnight. Discovering that the "new" Tadich's looks every bit as ancient as the old one. At Schroeder's, being with a girl on a diet when the waiter tells you they have only one left of those unbelievably caloric cream-and-blueberry desserts. Giving a justified horn-blast at a Yellow cabbie drowsing at a green light. *November 12, 1967*

NIGHTS OF OLD

I came home late from a dull party the other night, flipped on the TV, and there was Sam Spade (Humphrey Bogart) standing on a Bush St. corner, the tic working in his upper lip as he stared down at the bullet-riddled body of his partner, Miles Archer. His face hardened, the eyes turned cold and vengeful. Like Sam, I set fire to a cigarette. Then I settled back to watch "The Maltese Falcon" for the 40th time, and for the 40th time, it worked its peculiar spell. Once again, I was back in the movie's setting—San Francisco of 1940–41, the last years of an era that seems rather special now (during and after World War II, the city, like Hollywood movies, changed considerably for the worse).

★ ★ ★

Bogart as Sam Spade was the first and greatest of the private eyes—and the last. He didn't drive a big car, his secretary was plain and his office was a dump, probably on Kearny. He was mean and sallow and he worked for peanuts. "We didn't believe your story," he says thinly to a client, "we believed your $200." A loner living on the ragged edge, but not to be shoved around. "Either charge me and arrest me or stop leaning on me," he barks at the District Attorney, exiting with a slam of the door. Paul Newman tried to do the job as "Harper" and failed. "Frank Sinatra IS Tony Rome!" cry the current ads. Frank Sinatra is always Frank Sinatra and Tony Rome is a name as phony as the film. Spade's lip would curl, the tic would start working . . .

★ ★ ★

The '40–'41 San Francisco was a Sam Spade city. The Hall of Justice was dirty and reeked of evil. The criminal lawyers were young and hungry and used every shyster trick in the law books they never read. The City Hall, the D.A. and the cops ran the town as though they owned it and they did. Hookers worked upstairs, not on the street; there were hundreds, maybe thousands, most of them named Sally. The two biggest abortion mills—one on Market, the other in the Fillmore—were so well-known they might as well have had neon signs. You could play roulette in the Marina, roll craps on O'Farrell, play poker on Mason, get rolled at 4 a.m. in a bar on Eddy, and wake up at noon in a Turk St. hotel with a girl whose name you never knew or cared to know. Sam Spade went through all this and his face showed it. You'd see him alone at 1 p.m. at a Taylor St. lunch counter, drinking coffee, chain smoking, the tic worse than usual.

★　★　★

Peter Lorre as Joel Cairo is a fascinating character in "The Maltese Falcon." He is living at the Belvedere (probably the Bellevue—Author Dashiell Hammett always changed the names slightly). He goes to a play at the Geary, wearing a dinner jacket and batwing collar: people dressed up more in those days. Sam sniffs at the perfume on Joel's handkerchief and pegs him immediately for a fag. The other great character in the story is The Fat Man, Gutman, played by Sidney Greenstreet, and they don't make them like HIM anymore. Gutman is living at the St. Mark. "I combined St. Francis and Mark Hopkins," explained Hammett one time; he knew San Francisco well, having worked here in the '20s as a Pinkerton private op. But in the film, the lobby of the St. Mark is obviously the Fairmont. It looked imposing. That was before Dorothy Draper turned it into High Camp.

★　★　★

Enter Mary Astor, who has a string of phony names. She and Cairo and Gutman are on the trail of the Maltese Falcon, a fabulously valuable gem-encrusted bird, covered with black lacquer, dating back to the Crusades, or something. Miss Astor is living in an apartment on "California Avenue": I'll never know why Hammett thought he had to turn street into avenue. "You've got to trust me, I'm so alone," she says to Spade. "You don't need help," he says with that chilly grin. "You're GOOD." She breaks down, "Everything I told you was a lie," she sobs. "I lie all the time. I've led a terrible life. Oh, trust me, Sam, trust me." His face turns bleak. "Now you're dangerous," he growls. Then, shaking her: "I need your loyalty, all you've given me is money." She gives him more but he doesn't save her from the cops anyway. "I'm turning you over," he says as she stares at him in disbelief (most movies had

146

happy endings in those days and Miss Astor wasn't counting on going to jail).

★ ★ ★

Night falls over the old, rotten city. Sam props his feet on his scarred desk, pours three fingers of whisky, and looks out the window. His face is sad, the tic working overtime. Maybe he'd fallen in love with Miss Astor—a little. But a guy can't let a dame get away with gunning down his partner. He shivers and heads out into the cold San Francisco night. You know he'll wake up late the next day with a terrible hangover, getting old before his time, like a lot of San Franciscans in the peculiar years of 1940–41. . .

November 26, 1967

1968

Man on the Move

At 12:45 p.m. on Wednesday, Senator Robert F. Kennedy was standing curbside on Sacramento St. near Montgomery, dripping charisma all over the place. He was chatting with two of his henchmen (Democrats have henchmen, Republicans have aides) and his mere presence had an electrifying effect. Motorists slowed down to gape at him. A chubby, giggling Japanese waitress emerged from a coffee shop to wait, shivering, for an autograph. An elderly Japanese in a black overcoat asked for one, too (you know how these Easterners stick together). Four men emerging from the Red Knight suddenly stopped, transfixed, to stare at him as they picked their teeth with toothpicks. The Senator glanced at them with a tentative smile. They moved on, still picking their teeth.

* * *

"Lunch," he said, jaywalking toward Jack's with a young henchman, Peter Edelman. We went upstairs to Private Dining Room One, a one-windowed cubicle barely big enough for three. The Senator—it's hard to refrain from calling him "Bobby" although his friends call him "Bob"—stared at the buzzer on the wall. "To summon the girls," I said. He looked nervous till I explained that it USED to be possible to take girls upstairs at Jack's. "Now then," I went on, "let's light up cigars and nominate a Vice-President" (I forgot to tell you, I'm great fun at parties). He smiled a tiny one. The waiter whispered nervously in my ear: "How do I address him?" "Senator," I whispered back. "Sir," said the waiter, clearing his throat, "would you like a drink?" The Senator ordered a beer—"Coors."

Kennedy was dressed conservatively: dark blue suit, white shirt, round gold cufflinks, striped tie, black shoes, white handkerchief in breast pocket. He is taller and slimmer than he photographs. With his Sun Valley suntan and that great shock of copperish hair, he looks more like the Spanish bullfighter, El Cordobes, than like "The Fifth Beatle," a favorite needle among his detractors. It's not a bad way to look. He speaks softly and shyly, stumbling over words at times. In casual conversation, the celebrated toughness isn't apparent. In 90 minutes, he made only one bitter remark—while talking about an Air Force decision (made over McNamara's objections) that cost us nine planes in Vietnam. He went on to the "futility" of bombing North Vietnam, and recalled how, during World War II, German production had actually increased under heavy bombing. "The Air Force," he snapped, "is never right."

★ ★ ★

We ordered fresh cracked crab. "This is wonderful," he enthused. With a glance out the window: "What a beautiful city." Helping himself to more mayonnaise: "I could sit here all afternoon, eating cracked crab." He asked about Joe Alioto and (a note of concern here) how Eugene McCarthy is doing in California, but he wouldn't be drawn out on the subject. Hunters Point came up and I mentioned that Eastern newsmen were always saying that our slums are garden spots compared to theirs. He nodded: "It's better to be poor in San Francisco than rich in New York." Yes, he had followed Proposition P closely: "And those 80,000 'Yes' votes were an amazing response. It's hard to call that a defeat." But in his new book, "To Seek a Newer World," he states that "withdrawal is impossible," and I asked: "Do you think withdrawal is any crazier than continuing escalation?" "Not crazier at all," he replied.

★ ★ ★

"If the war is still on when your oldest son reaches the draft age," I said, "what will you tell him?" He took evasive action. "Well, we'd talk about it, all about it, and then I guess it would be his decision." Then he told, with apparent approval, an anecdote about a friend of his who had been "a terrific hawk" before he went to Vietnam and who is now "a terrific dove." "He has an 18-year-old son," Kennedy went on, "and he told me 'If that kid doesn't burn his draft card, I'll do it for him!'" I told him about a young San Franciscan—the son of a friend of his—who was ready to go to Canada rather than be drafted. "I don't think I could do that," the Senator said slowly. "I couldn't stand the thought of being a man without a country. I'd rather go to jail—that way, I'd feel I was paying my debt."

* * *

He had some more cracked crab, murmuring "Wonderful" again. He looked up with a grin: "I was interviewed by five reporters this morning about my book. I could tell that none of them had read it." On his mail: "It's heavy, but most of it is from the already committed, one way or the other. Then there are all those people who just want to 'win' it. How? There are no parallels in our history for this war. This stuff about 'Munich' is utterly ridiculous. Are we there to fight Communism? We weren't ready to go to war to save Indonesia from Communism, and that's 10 times as important as Vietnam. The reporters this morning wanted to know what I thought about all those North Vietnamese killed at Da Nang. What I want to know is how did they get that close to Da Nang? Can you imagine what it's like to be a North Vietnamese that far South in enemy country? Frightening. What courage."

* * *

We stepped outside and he was immediately engulfed by autograph-seekers. "Senator," somebody called out, "your helicopter is waiting"—just like in the movies, and he drove away with a wave and that shy smile. Would I vote for him for President? Well, a man who likes our cracked crab and thinks it's better to be poor in San Francisco than rich in New York . . .   *January 5, 1968*

FIRST SUNDAY AFTER

I'll let you in on a secret of no importance: newspapermen are just as neurotic as the next misanthrope, who may be you, for all I know. If so, greetings, amigo—and what I mean is that during the recent strike, we fell prey to all sorts of ignoble thoughts directly related to the ego. As follows: did anybody REALLY miss us? COULD the city get along without our services, such as they are? Is there such a thing as "news" without newspapers? And so on.

* * *

During the Seven-Week War, I got pretty nutty. Okay, nuttier. Just this side of crackers. I took to checking Union Square Garage every day around noon. If there was no line of cars waiting to get in—and there seldom was—I felt reassured: the downtown advertisers were suffering. Why should I have derived a sickly pleasure from the misfortune of the merchants? I leave that to you, doc. When I heard that a night club opening was crowded, despite the news blackout, I fell into deep depression. I attended the first S.F. Symphony concert after THAT strike, and my heart took a guilty leap upward to find the Opera House only half-full—or half-empty, depending on how you look at these things. Even the long-faced musicians conceded that "If the papers had been publishing, we would have had a full house." I had to agree. To do otherwise would have been to imply that nobody cared about the orchestra.

★　★　★

For seven weeks, our spirits rose and fell. There were these awful people who would say airily: "I find I can get along without the morning paper very well. Besides, it's healthier. One less cigarette and one less cup of coffee at breakfast." I've done a little checking around, and I find they're back on the team. Good morning, sir or madam; may your coffee and your cigarette both be safely filtered. The people I felt sorriest for are those who are hooked on horoscopes—they felt cast adrift in uncharted seas. "But aren't there horoscope magazines?" I asked one hookee. Gloomy response: "Yes, but they don't count. They're stale. It's only the one you read fresh every morning that means anything." I didn't know that.

★　★　★

On the other hand, to employ a libertarian phrase, it wouldn't be accurate to say that the city fell apart without us. Life went on, though temporarily undocumented by the recording devils. As Frances Moffat pointed out classically: "It was a good time to get divorced and a bad time to get married." ("Isn't it always?" retorted a cynical bachelor I know.) Even the print-out couldn't conceal the fact that our new Mayor, Mr. Alioto, was making waves in all directions. His now familiar face seemed to be on the telly every hour on the hour, and a deft performer he is. He created confusion only once—when he referred to the Fairmont demonstrators (protesting against Dean Rusk) as "neo-Fascists." This was confusing because the demonstrators, mainly New Left, probably think of Dean Rusk as a "neo-Fascist," if they use such dated terms; they did respond mildly by calling Mr. Alioto a "neo-Mayor" (will he get the buses to run on time?). Parenthetical note: The hippies aren't as non-violent as they used to be. I warned a long time ago that only a saint can return love for hate indefinitely, and the hippies aren't saints.

★　★　★

Seven weeks out of the lives of all of us San Franciscans, their outlines imprinted only vaguely on videotape that may never be seen again, or lost forever in the airwaves. Seven weeks of babies being born, people dying and so on (the proper San Franciscan, like the proper Bostonian, gets his name in the papers only three times—when he is born, when he marries, when he dies—but for seven weeks, no one could be completely proper); seven weeks of books being published unread, speechmakers speaking into a void, plays opening and folding unwept. Good jokes vanishing, like the one about the East Indian gentleman telling a hippie: "What would you say if I told you that Ravi Shankar is our Lawrence Welk?" Happy events unrecorded, like Seiji Ozawa's triumphal concert with the S.F. Symphony, which ended with a football-like roar and a mad rush stageward; tiny, skinny Ozawa from Japan, of whom someone said: "He must be transistorized—if he had ordinary tubes, he'd be nine feet tall!"

★ ★ ★

Well, the continuity gap is now closed, happily, and can we fit the missing tiles back into the broken mosaic? Only time will tell. Time and The Chronicle.   *March 2, 1968*

CITY AT HALF-MAST

We are the survivors: we lived through last week, a seven-day fugue of joy and despair, hope and tragedy. One man who did not survive, the Nobel Peace Prize winner, may not have died in vain—it is still difficult to tell. As is too often the case, the true stature of the man emerged when it was too late, in the outpouring of feeling that followed the blast in the Memphis night.

Thanks to the quick intelligence of Mayor Alioto, there was no doubt about San Francisco's response—in general. He set the tone and set it well. Again in general, the police here reacted with tact and restraint, but over in Marin, an officer was not afraid to say with venomous satisfaction "One down, two to go" (again, bitter memories of JFK). The flags were at mourning on Friday, but the owner of one important building refused to fly the flag at all, rather than lower it to half-staff for "that man."

Many were magnificent on television—none more so than Senator Muskie of Maine, who delivered an emotional plea for understanding from the Negro people, "though we have no right to ask it"—but on CBS, a Southern Senator said incredibly, "I'm just surprised it didn't happen sooner. That man was poking his nose into other people's business, he was going places he had no right to go . . . "

Tom Braden, listening to this, said in utter despair: "We are destroying ourselves, destroying ourselves."

★   ★   ★

No week in recent years had begun so auspiciously. After the President's unexpected and magnificent speech, you could feel the lift everywhere. The long fight for sanity seemed to be nearing victory: "Peace" was no longer a dirty word—it was in the headlines nine feet high, it was on the air without quotes or apologies. A cabbie said, "Man, I feel like I'm breathing again." The waiter captain at the St. Francis said, "People are even smiling when I ask them to wait for a table."

Was it too much too soon? All you could do was hope, and what in hell were those planes doing North of the 20th parallel? Still, the stock market was soaring (Karl Marx would never have believed a "dove" market), the daffodils were thick in Maiden Lane, the Giants were coming home to win a pennant, and it would soon be Over There as the long winter drew to a close . . .

And then the shot rang out in Memphis. Suddenly it was cold and dark again on Montgomery St., where an icy wind was blowing and a lone newsboy was standing on the corner of Sutter, shouting a cry not heard for years: "Extra . . . Extra . . . read all about it . . ."

★   ★   ★

There were parties amid the gloom on Thursday night, and at Earthquake McGoon's where the music of Memphis is played, the same request came over and over—for "Beale St. Blues," Beale St. in Memphis. That one line in the lyric burned in your mind: "And business never closes till somebody gets killed." And business did close that night in Los Gatos, where Cal Tjader was to give a concert before a packed house. "I can't play tonight," he said. "It wouldn't be right." On the 41st floor of the Wells Fargo Bldg., Stockbroker Bill Hutchinson was unveiling his lush new offices. Champagne but little laughter. His partner, Red Fay, looked down at his glass and began "Just when you think everything is going to be all right—." He stopped, having said it all.

★   ★   ★

The Hilton Hotel was jammed for Senator Eugene McCarthy that night of forced gaiety. Before the banquet, the Senator entertained a few dozen of his suddenly intimate friends in the Impe-

153

rial Suite, with its rooftop view of the shining city. "The hors d'oeuvres are Oysters Rockefeller," reported Jack Vietor helpfully. Bishop James Pike was wearing around his neck an inexpensive brass peace symbol surmounted by a cross. "I bought it in the Haight-Ashbury," he said, "and it has been properly blessed by the 100th Archbishop of Canterbury." The Senator moving through the crowded suite, troubled but trying. A beautiful red-haired Southern girl blew him a kiss across the room and he hurried to her side to return the kiss on her lips . . . "Senator," she said archly, dimpling, "ah can hardly WAIT to vote for YEWWWWW."

★   ★   ★

A huge and successful banquet, "the biggest political banquet in San Francisco history," but who counts. "We are serving 7,000 dinners tonight," said Hilton's Henri Lewin. "I guess it's some kind of record but who counts? Remind me to count the silverware." The new look in politics: the master of ceremonies was the man who plays Mr. Spock on TV's "Star Trek," minus his pointy ears. He was good, and spoke eloquently of the slain man in Memphis as the waiters played double concertos with trays and dishes.

The Senator was good, too, in his rather cool, disengaged way, but somehow the little jokes rang false this night. Still, he's in a campaign, and certain customs must be observed. The constant refrain—"I like him and I'll certainly vote for him even if he can't win"—is simply a wearying example of the cynicism that seemed on the point of dissolving early last week . . .

And then the shot rang out in Memphis, and the Beale St. Blues swept the land, drowning out the laughter.   *April 8, 1968*

THE FADING VIEW

They're going fast now—those old-timers who remember the Great Fire (and lowercase earthquake) of April 18, 1906. Next Thursday marks the 62nd anniversary, and only a dwindling few will be able to look back over the years to the beautiful April dawn that was shattered by a catastrophe that changed Old San Francisco forevermore into The City That Was. Catastrophic in many ways, for San Franciscans ever since have been schizophrenically plagued by doubts: did the true, the only, the legendary San Francisco perish in those flames?

★   ★   ★

They seem to have been a special lot living in a special place, those True San Franciscans of '06. (Or perhaps the TRULY true San Franciscans are those who were born nine months after April 18, 1906, to parents who lived in tents in Golden Gate Park). Today you look at their pictures and find it hard to identify with them—those severe-looking women, those hairy young men whose beards made them look old; beards today are the badge of youth. In the face of destruction and privation, they were proud, brave and humorous: it was then, in the burning city of 1906, that the San Francisco spirit was born, to become famous around the world.

★　★　★

If it still exists—and may it never be put to so grueling a test—it is thanks to these people, of whom Maj. Gen. A. W. Greeley, the martial law administrator, was able to write: "It is safe to say that 200,000 people were brought to a state of complete destitution. Yet I never saw a woman in tears, nor heard a man whine over his losses." Maybe cocky is the word for those forebears, who immediately posted signs all over the ruined city reading "Eat, drink and be merry—tomorrow you may have to go to Oakland." Cocky was certainly the word for the then young Larry Harris, who lost no time writing his defiant poem about "The damndest finest ruins ever gazed on anywhere!"

★　★　★

As the pall still hung over the hills, these people vowed to build a bigger, finer city, and perhaps they did. The phoenix bird, rising out of the ashes, became the symbol, and the buildings began to grow again, with remarkable speed (only nine years later, San Francisco charmed the world afresh with a glittering International Exposition). But even then the doubts were growing: had something irretrievable been lost to the flames? Will Irwin was foremost among those who thought so. As the buildings were still toppling, he lamented the death of "the most pleasure-loving and carefree city of the Western continent." It would be rebuilt, he said, "but it would never be the same."

★　★　★

For those who love San Francisco, there is an irresistible and neurotic fascination about that era of a city "whose Golden Age," wrote Poet Michael Grieg, "was an earthquake." You go through photo after photo of the '06 city, trying (in vain) to recapture the special charm that must have been there. The surviving landmarks are so few: the Flood Building, the Ferry Tower, the Flood mansion, the rows of Carpenter Gothic houses that are going so fast—

going before you had time to soak up their stories of The City That Was. The Palace Hotel is still there, but not in its pre-quake elegance. The Fairmont was just a shell. And the ornately European City Hall had collapsed, dome and all, fittingly symbolizing the wide-open graft that prevailed.

*   *   *

What was it that died on April 18, 1906? What was this quality that, in a few decades, had transformed a Gold Rush village into a world-renowned city? What outlandish dreams and ambitions enabled these early San Franciscans to build so grandly and so well? Even the old-timers who knew the magic are no longer sure what it was. "Well"—much rubbing of chin and watery eyes—"it was smaller, friendlier. Everybody knew everybody else. Goats on Telegraph Hill, cobblestone streets, cable lines everywhere, that sort of thing. Lots of wonderful saloons, cheap food, cheap wine. I don't know— it was like a party was going on all the time." Trying to make amends: "Of course the city is better today. Much bigger and richer"—and then the voice falters, the eyes look into the distance to whatever it was in The City That Was . . .

*   *   *

Next Thursday, the 62nd year after. Somebody will place a black wreath at Lotta's Fountain ("Lottie's Pump," then) and that will be that. In a few more years, the last man who knew the glory will be gone, leaving the rest of us haunted to our dying day with questions nobody can answer. *April 14, 1968*

An industrious shoplifter (male) who scavenged his way through the downtown stores one day last wk. was finally nailed by police in the Post-Powell Roos-Atkins. An inspector took the shoplifter's big paper bag, dumped the contents on the floor and identified a pair of pants from Pauson's, two shirts from Hasting's, a tie from Bullock & Jones—and finally an alpaca sweater from Roos-Atkins. "Thank God!" exploded R-A's Dave Falk. "For a minute there I didn't think you liked our merchandise."

*   *   *

Keeping up with the complicated world of hip: First we had—and still have—the bearded young men and their ladies, peddling underground papers to the straights of Montgomery Street. Then we had Tony Kent and his merry men going out to the Hashbury to sell the Wall Street Journal and Daily Commercial News to the

156

hippies—"because to them THESE are underground papers."
Meanwhile, there are the plastic hippies—the sons and daughters
of the rich who spend their weekends among the true hippies.
And finally, the latest phenomenon: the weekend straights. These
are true hippies who find out when their well-to-do parents are
leaving town for the weekend. They they go back to the old home-
stead in Pacific Heights, to shave, shower, load up on food and
drink and watch TV in comfort. On Sunday afternoon, having had
their fill of middle-class goodies, they go back to the Haight-
Ashbury to rejoin the hip world.   *May 6, 1968*

Swinging septuagenarians: Two wonderful old dames—and I use
the latter word in the grandest sense—join forces at the Fairmont
Sunday afternoon from 2:30 to 4:30 for a cookies-and-punch party
that will be open to the public, free, come one, come all . . . Pouring and passing will be Mrs. Rose Kennedy, mother of the candidate, who says: "I want to meet everybody in San Francisco." And
the hostess for all this will be Mrs. Henry F. Grady, who says, "I
want to stretch my purse strings to the breaking point!" . . . Mrs.
Kennedy is 78, Mrs. Grady 76—adding up to 154 years of
unquenchable enthusiasm.   *May 16, 1968*

NIGHTMARE ALLEY

"I reject the diagnosis that there is a fatal sickness in our society"—
Lyndon B. Johnson in New York, May 20, 1968.

★   ★   ★

The United States, where assassination has become the American
way of death. We are all walking in the crosshairs of somebody's
telescopic sight. Assassin: The word still makes you think of
the Balkans and Mittel European terrorists in bulky overcoats,
throwing the cartoonists' version of a sputtering bomb into the
Archduke's open carriage. Today, it's only in America—except
for the West German who shot Red Rudi Dutschke. His inspira-
tion, he said, had been the assassination of Martin Luther King.
The FBI, even with Efrem Zimbalist Jr. in service, still can't find
that killer . . .

★   ★   ★

Weird, wild unbelievable. Only a few hours earlier on Tuesday

night, I had scribbled a note on my pad, a squib from Corre-
spondent Charles Michelmore of Fairchild Publications. Out at
Hunters Point, a Negro had told him: "No, I didn't vote for
Kennedy. I don't want him to win. If he gets elected he'll be killed,
just like his brother and Dr. King" . . . Earlier at Enrico's, Kennedy
Aide Dick Tuck had been saying to a group of us: "Senator
Kennedy is the No. 1 assassination target in this country." Howard
Gossage retorted: "Then why does he expose himself to crowds so
recklessly?" Tuck: "Ever since Dallas, I don't think he cares any
longer about his safety."

★   ★   ★

Up until the newsflash at 12:15 a.m. yesterday, it had been a pleasant evening as Election Nights go. The Kennedy workers gathered
at California Hall, where the drinks were free and plentiful, the
bartenders hard-working and heavy-handed. When the big blackboard showed Kennedy running slightly behind McCarthy, a girl
chalked above the figures, "Still Better Than Oregon!" Pandemo-
nium as Ted Kennedy arrived. "A great night," he said. "California is coming through for us" . . . At a party in an old house on a
hill, the pro-Kennedys and the pro-McCarthys were getting along
well. There were even drunken vows to switch support to the winner. But the main topic was the archaic law that closes the bars on
Election Day. "The only day you can see guys shaking bull dice for
Calso," grinned Glenn Dorenbush. . . . And then came the newsflash. Time stood still and everybody froze except one girl who
ran to the bathroom to throw up . . .

★   ★   ★

It was an eerie replay of November, 1963. Wandering lost in the
electronic maze—radios crackling, TV sets ghost-lighting dark
rooms through the long night. The confused and conflicting
reports, the incoherent eye-witnesses, the strained voices of newsmen. As is always the case in times of paramount tragedy, the electronic forces were magnificent—especially the team at KNX, the
CBS station in Los Angeles. Its men seemed to be everywhere in
that wasted vastland. Good Samaritan merged inescapably with
Parkland in Dallas, the bullet in the neck seemed an overpowering
coincidence. The words of almost five years ago were heard again:
"I thought it was firecrackers" . . . "I'm not sure how many shots
there were. The echoes, the ricochets—" . . . "Yeah, we got him out
of there in one piece and we got him locked up where nobody can
get at him—there won't be a Jack Ruby in Los Angeles . . ."

★   ★   ★

The city of San Francisco, quiet, so quiet under the wintry fog of early summer—quiet in spite of all the sets going, the coffee pots perking, the rooms full of sleepless people sitting in the various attitudes of despair: backs bent, heads down, drawn faces in hands. A very real smell of guilt, frustration and shame. Cigarettes piling up in the ashtray, the occasional strangled "What's the USE?", the sudden groan aloud from people who had to break the choking silence somehow . . .

★   ★   ★

At 5 a.m., there was NBC's Sandor Vanocur in what they call Election Central in Burbank, his face puffy with fatigue as he struggled to recount—this time for the morning watchers in the East—what he had seen that night at the Ambassador Hotel, which now goes into history with Dealey Plaza, the Book Depository, the grassy knoll and the other landmarks of insanity and disgrace. In his tired voice, Vanocur said "And now back to the 'Today' show," for time does march on, but there was no switchover. He kept sitting there, facing the world hopelessly, and then the camera drew back for a shot of the entire huge studio. Empty, except for Sandor Vanocur and the debris, the desks and the typewriters, the figures on the wall that showed Robert F. Kennedy was winning in California . . .

★   ★   ★

And let's hear it for the print newsman who elicited this quote from a sad young GI in Vietnam: "I'm glad I'm over here where it's safe." And let's hear it for the gun lobby, with its out-of-date Americanism, its phony portrayal of The Rugged Individual armed with a gun, defending his inalienable right to shoot. Let's hear it for Dr. Max Rafferty, too, who is forever complaining that education in California is not what it should be, and whose victory proves it. And let's hear it for the good citizens of Dallas, who complained in November, 1963, "It could have happened anywhere." They were right.   *June 6, 1968*

Friend of mine wandered into an after-hours joint in the Tenderloin at 3 a.m., ordered coffee and was asked by the waitress for his ID. "For coffee?" he complained. "Well," she said, "you could be a cop, after all." After displaying his various identifications to her satisfaction, she said briskly: "OK, now what kinda coffee do you want—Scotch or bourbon?"   *October 17, 1968*

Now that the Olympic Games and the S.F. Film Festival have ended, what is there left to make the blood course through our arteriosclerotic veins? Why, San Francisco's OWN Olympic Games! We hereby challenge the world to come here and compete in the activities, indoor and out, that have made our city a synonym for "Howzat again?", wherever Sanskrit is spoken . . . Tentative list of events: Standing Broad Jump off the Golden Gate Bridge (individual or team effort), Name-Dropping (extra points for names nobody heard of), Last Man on Cable Car (scores only after 100 people have already boarded), Grabbing Bus Seat Before Pregnant Woman (elapsed time and length of pregnancy count here), Blindfold Martini Drinking (winner is participant who doesn't know blindfold has been removed), Hill-Climbing (backward on California St.), Muni Bus Drag Race Through Yellow Signals, Drag Queen Contest (all participants must pass chromosome test), Russian Roulette Crab-Eating Contest (one crab is four days old), Expectoration Decathlon on Market St. (direction to be chosen by judges, depending on wind), Kite-Flying in Candlestick Park, Pigeon Kicking in Union Square (object must clear Dewey Monument, not under own power) and Gate-Crashing Pacific Union Club (length of time inside club before ejection is determining factor; minorities not eligible).

★ ★ ★

Footnote: San Franciscans, with their superior experience, figure to win gold medals in all these events, but I stress that plans are only in the formative stage, like most San Francisco plans. They may never get off the ground. Like BART, they may not even get INTO the ground. If City Hall will hand us about $55,000, we'll undertake another great S.F. specialty—a Feasibility Study (winning team gets a computer that proves it wouldn't have worked in the first place but let's go ahead anyway).   *November 3, 1968*

JUST FOOLIN' AROUND

Why do they call it "background music" when it's so intrusive? . . . Shocking discovery: There are bartenders in this cosmopolitan city who don't know how to make an Americano. Deport 'em to the mainland . . . Don't tell my editor, but I've gotten quite fond of the Embarcadero Freeway—especially on those clear days when you can see forever, if not the Farallones, from the top deck. To the right, all those see-worthy ships. To the left, the new skyline

as wrought by God and overwrought by Warnecke and Nat Owings
. . . Sodden thought: "The Silent Majority" seems too kind a name
for those who are really Dead Center . . . Suburbia: the DMZ for
urban dropouts . . . Even more sodden thought, while watching a
swinging steel ball demolish a fine old building: Will San Francisco someday be known as the Cleveland Wrecking Co.? . . . Perhaps it's significant that Cleveland Wrecking has branches in every
principal city except Cleveland. It's too late for Cleveland?

*　*　*

Every time I see a big joint of beef in a restaurant window, suspended from heavy chains and cooking over a slow fire, I figure
the chef's name is Torquemada . . . Natives who live in the Deep
Mission think they know more about Old San Francisco than anybody else, and are usually nasty about it . . . If the CIA really cared
about its image, it would assign an agent to hijack a Cuban airliner
to Miami; don't tell me Cuban security is better than ours . . .
Those bank robbers in Bank of America's big ad the other day,
photographed by hidden cameras, looked pretty grim. I suggest
signs in all branches reading "Smile! You're on Bandit Camera" . . .
If credit cards were called by their right name—debit cards—how
many people would use them?

*　*　*

Losers weepers: Winning football teams never complain about
"lousy officiating," best-selling authors don't cry over critical
reviews; people with chauffeurs aren't aware of the parking problem; winning candidates couldn't care less about the "bugs" in
computerized vote-counting; successful businessmen are never
heard to say: "The unions are killing me." As Joe E. Lewis philos-
ophized, "I've been rich and I've been poor and rich is better." So
is Winning.

*　*　*

Among the sights I never hope to see while driving up the Powell
St. hill: a cable car with a "Student Driver" sign on the rear . . .
Our winters have to be different from anybody else's. Where else
do you find people driving around with their tops down and
heaters on, wearing sunglasses with their overcoats, and shivering
in line to buy ice cream cones at Swensen's? Where else, in fact,
can you get a hot buttered martini? . . . Maturity is when you don't
feel you HAVE to go to "The Nutcracker," listen to the Modern
Jazz Quartet, or take your kid to the Ice Follies . . . Frank Sinatra
has joined the growing list of singers who think "The Star-Spangled Banner" should be replaced by "America the Beautiful." Years

ago, I campaigned assiduously for the latter, but a lot of readers complained the song wasn't stirring enough and some felt that the ending ("And crowned thy good with brotherhood," etc.) was a little too—you know—democratic?

★ ★ ★

With all our know-how, why hasn't somebody invented a way to get gum off your shoe? . . . The best articles always appear in the current issue of the magazine you canceled as of the previous issue . . . The recent opera season confirmed it all over again: there wasn't, isn't and probably never will be another tenor like the late Jussi Bjoerling. My idea of a great evening is a stack of Bjoerling records on the turntable, a bottle of J&B at hand, and another Bjoerling fan in the room to gasp along with . . . A pox on people who dial your number by mistake and hang up without so much as a "Sorry" . . . The Era of Schlock officially began when they stopped making those elegant squirt-type seltzer water bottles . . . Agnes Albert's definition of the ultimate luxury: "Being able to leave your front door unlocked at night without worrying about it."

★ ★ ★

Memo, a little late, to the State Supreme Court: Every assassination in the U.S. has occurred in a state that has the death penalty . . . Whatever happened to florist shops that used to place a bowl of bachelor buttons outside the front door, free for the taking? Back then, San Francisco was known as "The City With a Flower in Its Buttonhole"—and that was real flower power . . . Add small bores: "Of course I never watch TV but last night I happened to see—"; putting phonograph records back into their jackets; "We're out of stock on that at the moment, try next week"; people who seem to expect an answer to "What's new?"; all variations on "An hour later you're hungry again" . . . Whenever my kid says "Tell me a story, Daddy," I begin "Once there were three bears—papa bear, mama bear and camembert." He doesn't get it, but it's my way of remembering George S. Kaufman, who made it up.

December 8, 1968

Of human interest: Yesterday morning, Mrs. Maude Phillips, a widow who lives at 446 Moscow St., went down to her basement, picked up a white-sprayed Christmas tree, and carried it to her living room—a ritual that is now 28 years old . . . Back in December, 1940, her son Robert, then 22, bought that tree, the last one he enjoyed. The day after Pearl Harbor, he enlisted in the Navy, and in November, 1942, he was killed in a Japanese attack on his destroyer, the USS Cushing . . . Mrs. Phillips, mother of eight children and grandmother of 11, says with a smile and a sigh: "Well, the tree doesn't look too bad, really. Amazing how it has held up all these years. When they were little, the children kept pestering me to get a new one. But now, they wouldn't part with it for the world." *December 20, 1968*

1969

THE LOST CITY

It's out there somewhere—buried beneath the Golden Gateway, gone (and perhaps forgotten) under the assorted lookalikes of the "new" financial district, hidden behind glass and aluminum curtains, lurking in the odd shadows cast by cylindrical objects, claptrapezoids and the high-rise tombstones of Cathedral Hill . . .

On foggy nights, when memories grow suddenly sharp in the gloom, you know the old city is still around you, just below the surface—an Atlantis on the Pacific. Maybe it's the foghorns calling mournfully to each other, the only voices still around that evoke the swish of paddlewheels on ghostly ferries. Or, barely visible in the mist, a cable car disappearing over a hill on its plunge into yesterday.

Halos on streetlamps over empty sidewalks that knew the tread of feet long gone . . . On a long January night in the quiet city (just before it stops being late and starts to get early), the ghosts begin dancing again, atop the creaking ferry slips, through the venal parking lots where lovely buildings once stood, across the steel bones of cable car lines that were buried without funerals. Bits and pieces remain, the leftover pieces of a jigsaw puzzle we could never quite fit together.

★   ★   ★

The mysteriousness of cities like San Francisco. For a long time, it seemed to stand still, in a golden glow, unreal and provocative. Its familiar outlines were as fixed as a bee in amber: gentle skyscrapers (not one out of proportion to the surroundings), Coit Tower a white exclamation mark over a tumble of wooden shacks, North

Beach an Italian village (accordians and arias, but without self-consciousness), rickety stairways to hidden leafy streets on Russian Hill, the Sunset a desert of sand dunes where movie companies filmed Foreign Legion epics . . . It would all be there forever, this enchanted little city at the end of the world, and suddenly it was gone, one cold morning. We had no idea that wrecking crews could be so efficient, or that sentiment had so little sentimental value.

★   ★   ★

It was a Scott Fitzgerald–Saroyan kind of place, not a Hemingway–Steinbeck one—a city that lived on dreams (Maxfield Parrish's, not Picasso's). The distant sound of dance bands in hotel lobbies, fringed lamps on tables for two at Tait's-at-the-Beach, muffled laughter behind drawn shades upstairs in French restaurants like the St. Germain, a melange of mirrored walls and frescoed cherubs. The artists starved well at the Black Cat and slept well for little on the Hill until Gardner Dailey and Whitney Warren built the mansions that ended an era . . . But it was all unplanned. The city was a hodge-podge that grew in clumps of accidental beauty. Now we have the planners, arranging trees forever spindly around buildings with the character of packing cases.

★   ★   ★

The eternal verities—how perishable they turned out to be. Of course there would always be a St. Mary's–Santa Clara football game at Kezar on a certain Sunday in the fall. We would never be without the Seals, the finest and most appropriate name for any baseball team anywhere (San Francisco Giants still doesn't ring true). Technically there was nothing major league about the city and yet everything was—from the teeming, brawling, lettuce-strewn Produce District (look, there's A.P. Giannini eating at the Oregon Cafe!) to Fred Solari's club-like restaurant in Maiden Lane to the saloons where the clam broth was free and you got a tumbler full of tiny Bay shrimp for a dime (nobody had shrimp like ours and now we don't either) . . . You were in danger only on Big Game Night, when gangs of campus toughs would stop you to snarl "Okay, who you for—Stanford or Cal?" If you didn't guess right, you were beaten up, and felt you deserved it.

★   ★   ★

How could they all go so soon: the pools and slides at Sutro Baths, White Hat McCarthy and Foghorn Murphy, Jack Johnson drinking fizzes at the Waldorf bar on Market, Helen Wills and Helen Jacobs trading forehands at the California Tennis Club, and those laugh-

165

ing boys—Hal Bruntsch, Murray Benton, Hitch King, Maxie Baer and George Lewis—boarding a ferry for Ma Schmidt's Cottage Baths in Alameda. What quality the city had (you can still feel a little of it in the Flood Building lobby and the Merchants Exchange): the most ornately beautiful streetlamps in the world, and proud old streetcars with real leather seats and brass scratchers for the kitchen matches the men carried . . . Now we have paper matches, sleazy buses and the same ugly streetlamps they have in Peoria and Oshkosh. What kind of trade is that?

★ ★ ★

"I never look back," said an old-time San Franciscan the other day. "I live in the present for the future." Brave words: it's almost too painful now to think about the city that was, to root around in the plastic junkyard for the evidence that it truly existed. But on a foggy January night, with the foghorns calling to each other . . .

January 12, 1969

"Why doesn't he ever print any NICE stories?" Okay, okay. In 1960, when he was Attorney General, State Supreme Justice Stanley Mosk went after the Professional Golfers' Association: stop discriminating against "non-Caucasian" golfers, or be denied the use of California public courses for PGA tournaments. After a long hassle, Stanley won his point—and last weekend, Charlie Sifford became the first black to win the $100,000 Los Angeles Open. He didn't forget the man who made it possible: Monday, Stanley received a telegram reading "Thank you for opening the doors of golf to the Charlie Siffords of this world."

★ ★ ★

Lost & found: Harold Nash of Oakland wishes you'd be on the lookout for his poodle, Charlie, who disappeared from his house Sunday. Charlie is no ordinary poodle: he weighs 120 pounds and wears prescription glasses, being nearsighted. "He left home without the glasses," laments Harold, "and I hate to think of him out there, bumping into things." If Charlie bumps into you, give a holler.

January 15, 1969

Charles Linder, a 21-year-old student, had a leg amputated at UC Hosp. last week, and was feeling appropriately depressed when in danced Trader Vic, who'd heard of his plight. "Look, kid, it's not so bad," barked Vic, taking down his pants to show off HIS wooden leg. "I've had a helluva good life on one meat leg, and you will, too." A little later, in walked Vic's son, Lynn Bergeron, with a seven-course dinner. "I do feel a little better," admits Charlie . . .

February 5, 1969

September Song in February: All we seem to be doing these days is saying good-by to old friends. I was driving along Great Highway last Sunday and noticed with a twist in the ticker that Roberts-at-the-Beach is being razed. Ah, if those walls could only talk, they'd be sued for libel, so maybe it's just as well. Every Sunday night for decades, the place was jammed with politicians, judges, lawyers, police and assorted toadies, trading favors and making deals over the mustard steaks (great!) and sparkling Burgundy. A venal arrangement, perhaps, but it seemed to work, and it was educational. At Roberts-at-the-Beach, I first discovered that "Sober as a judge" is the most ridiculous simile of them all.

February 7, 1969

Judith Shay, director of community services at Cathedral Hill Medical Center, is back from her first trip to Cuba. She stayed there only 12 hours—hardly long enough to mail any "Having wonderful time" postcards—but all in all, the experience was not unpleasant. You might want to know this in case YOU'RE ever skyjacked.

"Our plane (National) was near Houston," she recalled yesterday, "when we heard the pilot say over the loudspeaker, 'Have we enough fuel to get to Havana?' Then we knew. The skyjacker was a young fellow, about 30, blonde, looked like a bank teller. He wasn't nervous and neither were the passengers. The stewardesses immediately began pouring drinks for everybody—all you wanted, no charge.

"The Cubans who met us at Havana airport were grim but cordial. The food we were served there I won't discuss. Then we were loaded into two rickety buses and driven 90 miles to Veradero Airport. That was the only scarey part. The drivers raced each other all the way, passing on hairpin curves—very hairy. But at Veradero, the steaks were terrific, and the Cubans brought in a five-piece band to entertain us. Quite gay.

"At the beach nearby, there were about 30 Russians—doctors, engineers, other technicians. All I can say about them is that they were getting blistered in the sun. We were given hotel rooms to wash up in, and then a prop job from Eastern arrived to fly us to Miami. Well, I guess that's about it."

She means it beats watching in-flight movies, but just barely.

February 14, 1969

San Francisco, February, 1969: Famed Guitarist Gabor Szabo, the one-time Hungarian Freedom Fighter now headlining at the Matador, left that club about 3 a.m. the other day and was strolling down Kearny toward his digs when three hoods jumped him. One grabbed his money (about $60) and belted him in the eye. The second shoved a knife into his ribs (fortunately it struck a bone) and hurled him to the sidewalk. And the third pulled a gun, cocked it and said "I'm gonna kill you." Gabor, a survivor of Budapest '56, pleaded for his life: "Look, I'm just a musician. I have nothing against you. I came here because the Russians were going to kill me—I don't want to die in America." The thug slowly uncocked the gun and the three hoods left. Next night, taped, bandaged and wearing a patch over his eye, Gabor was back on the stand at the Matador. "Good evening," he said to his questioning listeners. "I am now a San Francisco Freedom Fighter . . . "

February 17, 1969

We San Franciscans are urbane, right? Check. Therefore, despite dire predictions from seers, roebucks and other nuts, we are not worried about a catastrophic earthquake here next month, true? Indubitably.

Nevertheless, everybody elsewhere seems concerned that we will all slide into the sea during April, Mr. Eliot's cruelest month. In the past couple of days I have received queries from the august New York Times (it also publishes the other 11 months), two newsmags, a London Sunday Times stringer and one underground paper (the Express-Times) all wanting to know "what San Franciscans are DOING about it."

They don't seem to believe me when I say we're not doing anything about it. The subject never even comes up, at least in my set. I don't know about yours. We just go on doing what we've always been doing: drinking too much, eating too well, getting everything but enough sleep, looking for fireplugs to park alongside and so on. We're like the kid in Mad magazine: "What, ME worry?"

The only floating rumor that seemed to have possibilities—that an "unusually high" percentage of local workers were requesting vacations in April—turned out to have no substance. I set The Admirable Bundsen to checking our 10 largest corporations, and it isn't so. No tremors of doubt there. "As usual," said one personnel mgr., "everybody wants off in July."

★   ★   ★

Anyway, why April '69? Apparently it was started by one seeress, whose name escapes me since I've never been a seersucker. Curt Gentry, author of "The Last Days of the Late Great State," etc., isn't leaving town. The late Edgar Cayce, pronounced "Casey," who made some memorable prophesies, predicted San Francisco would be "destroyed" around 1968–69, but he picked no month and he already blew '68. I'm betting he blows '69, too.

(If you are even a tiny bit nervous, you may be relieved to learn that Cayce's son, Hugh Lynn Cayce, will deliver a speech at College of San Mateo on April 15. On the other hand, maybe he wants to be here when It happens. I guess you can read that either way.)

Anyway, let's not put the knock on earthquakes. The one we had in April Ought Six was our Golden Age, was it not? The citizens rallied 'round in a show of spirit unequaled until the London Blitz of World War II. To hear the tales, there never was such a feeling of oneness before or since, and the jokes flew as the chimneys fell: "Eat, Drink and Be Merry, For Tomorrow We May Have to Move to Oakland!" Those who lived through it still have a special aura, almost a nimbus. San Franciscans born nine months after the quake, to parents who camped out in Golden Gate Park, are the True Nobility.

Besides, how else are we going to find out if our new "earthquake-proof" buildings really are? And if you still feel queasy at the thought of approaching April, ask your doctor for earth control pills.   *March 14, 1969*

At the Opera House Sunday afternoon, Artur Rubinstein had standees, a full house and three rows of people seated onstage behind his Steinway. As the house lights darkened, a late-arriving lady emerged from the wings and walked across the length of the stage to find a seat, whereupon the audience burst into ritual applause. "Wouldn't it have been a groove," said the man next to me, "if she'd played 'Chopsticks'?" Another golden opportunity blown.

It's hard not to cry a little when Rubinstein plays. It must be his great age plus his irrepressible gaiety. His face radiates humor; you wouldn't be surprised if he stopped in the middle of Chopin to tell a joke. His publicity says he's 80, he says he's 82, his intimates say he's 85 but it doesn't matter. He's always the youngest member of the group.

Later, at the St. Francis, he nodded at a compliment: "Yes, I played well today. It's because I have this terrible cold. Like Maestro Avis, I tried a little harder." He had once explained in a classic phrase why he didn't play Mozart—"It's too simple for children and too difficult for artists"—but he is now playing Mozart again. "I stopped," he said, "because I had lost my innocence. But now I am so old I have regained my purity—call it retroactive virginity."

Bundled up in a greatcoat, with a thick scarf around his neck, he strode through the St. Francis lobby, spry as a teen-ager. I remembered the time he was riding in a cab to Fisherman's Wharf, and the cabbie had said, "You look familiar, what's your name?" When he replied "Artur Rubinstein," I said "Why didn't you let him guess?" "Because," smiled Rubinstein, "when I let people guess they always say I'm Leopold Stokowski." Now passersby were turning to stare at him in the lobby. They knew his face was familiar but they weren't sure. "Isn't that Leopold Stokowski?"

March 18, 1969

A death in the family . . . All the words so dear to San Franciscans—urbane, worldly, cultured—applied to Grover Magnin, who died Monday at 83. It was he, all by himself, who made I. Magnin synonymous with high fashion around the world, and he leaves a lasting monument: the marble block at Geary and Stockton that is still one of the handsomest buildings in town. When he and the late architect, Tom Pflueger, completed the plans, he phoned to say: "You're going to love this building. Absolutely NO place on it for a pigeon to roost!" Grover had his pride, too: when the men with the minds of accountants decided his insistence on elegance was costing too much, he walked out—and stayed out of his own building for years. Cries of "Mr. Grover is back!" rang out all over the place when he finally relented. Now he is gone, but he left an indelible trademark of quality on this city.   *March 19, 1969*

THE WALKING CAEN

The tourist season may be off to a sluggish start, but there is still more action in San Francisco on a Wednesday night than you'll find in New York or Paris on a Saturday (I'll exclude London—for an ancient scene, that swings pretty hard, too). On Powell, there was Joel Grey signing autographs and parrying hecklers on a cable car. At Trader Vic's, Bing Crosby, teeth clenched on pipe, sat between Claude Jarman and Barnaby Conrad, who were trying to talk him into an afternoon appearance at the Film Festival. "Duck season, duck season," Bing kept murmuring, teeth still clenched. "We'll fly ducks across the stage and you can pop at 'em," offered Jarman. "That might do it," nodded Crosby, making a note of the date. In the St. Francis, hotbed of the Establishment, Tom Smothers sat propped up in his cool bed, inveighing happily against the Establishment (with room service). Model Pat Mahan relaxed at Enrico's, showing off her new bra, made of gold coins: "I have to warm them in the oven before going out at night." At the parking lot next door, Terrible Terry—always with a cigarette between her lips, like Mike Nomad—was back on the job, shuffling Ferraris, Maseratis, Aston-Martins and even an occasional Fiat. And so on . . .

★   ★   ★

We kicked off the evening at Claude Berhouet's Restaurant (formerly Hotel) de France on Broadway near Powell. If I had to pick the most underrated eating place in town, this would be it, going away. To start, a silver tureen of pea soup, laced with almost invisible vermicelli. "What, no croutons?" I said in mock dismay. The waiter, a charming young Frenchman who turned out to be a Yugoslav, raced into the kitchen and reappeared with a platter of peasant-sized French bread croutons, made on the spot, hot, crusty, buttery. Then a creamy light crepe of chicken livers, followed by veal and artichoke hearts cooked with delicate precision. A perfect souffle to finish off, with two sauces, vanilla and chocolate, and of course cafe filtre. All this—mirabile dictu! for 11 bucks and a few odd cents, wine and drinks extra. The chef, Louis Marticorena, late of La Bourgogne, is the master who works these miracles. The Restaurant de France has yet to win a Holiday magazine award, and that's only ONE of the good things about it . . .

★   ★   ★

Outside, the usual bumper-to-bumper crop of cars was inching along (for better or worse, there's no street in the world like

Broadway at night). We walked a few steps down the street to the Montmartre, the authentically French bar that has resisted the urge to "improve" itself, for which we should all be grateful. Jacques Brel and Mireille Mathieu on the jukebox, acrid smell of Gauloises in the air. Roger, the trilingual bartender, was playing liar's dice in French with a cognac drinker. Enter, the Italian navy, with a smashing blonde in tow! Roger switched to fluent Italian. One of the sailors had a noisy Italian fight with the blonde, slammed his hat against the wall, and told her to get lost. She headed for the door, head held high. As he bent over the jukebox, she delivered the greatest goose since last Christmas. "Yiiiii!" cried the Italian navy, scuttled again . . .

★   ★   ★

Broadway, Bawdway, Fraudway—call it what you will, it's a terrible, wonderful scene and I confess I find it endlessly fascinating. All that shlock rock music—good on the outside, bad on the inside—pouring through the open doors. The cold-eyed young hoods in their silk threads, trying to look like Mafioso and succeeding. The cops prowling past in their skunk cars, adding another note of tension. Hordes of shiftless kids, too many of them obviously stoned, and all those pretty young girls wandering about, some literally asking for trouble . . . Well, if it's relevance you're looking for, buddy, it's all right there, a smorgasbord of tidbits, bare and otherwise.

★   ★   ★

At hot and smoky Fillmore West, the usual 2,500-odd kids were strewn about the floor. Maybe they're the same 2,500-odd you always see there, maybe they never go home. Costumes wilder than ever, hair shaggier, smell more pungent. On the walls, the light show was displaying rustic scenes, the California countryside, perhaps a social comment. Everything's a social comment here.

Old Woody Herman was on the bandstand with his Fifth, Ninth or 31st Herd. I've lost count. Old Woody stays young by hiring 25-year-old musicians, and these were wailing "Caledonia" at a furious pace that called for incredible musicianship. The 25 year olds were equal to it. "Cal'donia, Cal'donia, what makes yo' big head so HARD????" hollered Woody for the 9,000th time. Shrieks from the mighty brass section, shrieks from the kids, some of whom were hearing a big band for the first time.

"I really dug it," said a hairy and bearded young head, scratching himself as he spoke, "Woody made me feel good. The band is so—uh—well—ENTERTAINING! Yeah, I really felt GOOD, man."

On came The Who, from Britain, to do selections from their remarkable rock opera, "Tommy," and we split, out through the sprawling kids and the spilled drinks, past the lost youngsters sitting on the Market St. sidewalk, out in the cool 1 a.m. air of the city that still knows—the "how" endlessly changing in patterns of bizarre intricacy.   *June 20, 1969*

NATIONAL DAY OF MOONING

Back in 1962, when he was managing the Giants, Alvin Dark turned to Sportswriter Harry Jupiter during batting practice, watched Pitcher Gaylord Perry taking his cuts and sighed: "There'll be a man on the moon before Perry hits a home run." Thirty-four minutes after Neil Armstrong set down on the lunar surface, Gaylord Perry hit his first major league home run.

*   *   *

The man with the typewriter—or the hoe or the shovel or any other pre-electronic device—had to feel pretty much out of it the last couple of days. This was technology's finest hour, not only in the performance of the "hardware" (that faintly ridiculous term) but in the way television worked, on the moon and on the ground. There was a sudden renewal of pride in that much-derided phrase, "Yankee know-how." Detroit may be recalling thousands of cars, we may be polluting sky, field and stream, our tanks may be duds, our swinging plane may be a flop, some of our combat rifles may jam—but for once, this time, everything worked, with the whole world watching and applauding. (There will always be a local angle: The Ets-Hokin Corp. wired Houston's mission control center, Jeremy having submitted the winning bid of $7,777,777.77.)

*   *   *

For most of us, it was the longest vigil at a TV set since that bleak 1963 weekend in Dallas, and how ironic that the man who was killed there inspired the drive to put life on the moon. Uncle Walter Cronkite and Astronaut Wally Schirra were magnificent. They supplied the one ingredient otherwise missing during the tense hours: humor. Walter, an old print man himself, tried to make us typewriter jockeys feel better by showing the front pages of the N.Y. Times and Daily News ("the largest type the Times has ever used," he noted). As a former United Press reporter, he also gave a plug to a wire service reporter for what he called "a great lead": "They kept the whole world waiting for two hours

173

while they dressed to go out."

★ ★ ★

Further solace for ink-stained wretches: If you saved anything to show the grandchildren, it was probably a copy of yesterday's newspaper. It may have been television's day but you can't fold its pictures and put them in the bottom drawer.

★ ★ ★

Cronkite after Neil Armstrong, the bona fide All-American Boy, planted that oddly touching plastic Flag: "Somehow you expect to hear music." Schirra as the long night wore on: "This is the longest late-late show I've ever seen without a commercial. I'm impressed." Schirra during those throat-constricting moments after the moonwalk, when all was frightening silence from the lunar module: "I wish one of them would go over to a window and wave." But CBS doesn't win all the plaudits. ABC did the best in the pre-moonwalk period, especially with its film of previous space flights to a musical accompaniment of "Yellow Submarine" and the theme from "2001"—an inspired idea ("2001" is the movie that won one Oscar while something called "Oliver!" was winning seven).

★ ★ ★

Terrestial life goes on: NASA at Moffett Field was closed yesterday; a recorded voice advised callers it would reopen at 8 a.m. today . . . Some downtown stores have resurrected their New Year's noisemakers, funny hats and confetti for Thursday's splashdown celebration . . . After Pres. Nixon talked by phone to the moon, Bob Scott of KKHI placed a person-to-person call to Neil Armstrong at NASA in Houston, where the operator deadpanned: "Mr. Armstrong is not taking calls today, he is on the moon" . . . Anthony Ricci, Pres. of Wollak Co., the big cheese importers, held his breath until Armstrong reported the surface as "almost a dust." Cheeseman Ricci: "Thank God, now I won't have to bid on it" . . . Esther Plottel figures the old Sinatra movie, "Oceans Eleven," may have to be shelved (it was shown here a few hours before the moon vigil began). After Sinatra outlines the plot to rob all the Vegas casinos, Dean Martin asks: "How come it's never been tried before?" Sinatra: "For the same reason we haven't sent a man to the moon. No equipment."

★ ★ ★

Mel Torme used to sing a fine song called "No Moon At All," and in most parts of overcast San Francisco Sunday night, that's the way it was. But who cared: we were seeing it as no man before had ever seen it—although I was a bit taken aback when the TV screen

174

suddenly showed a crescent moon with the announcement: "There is the moon as seen over Los Angeles." Los Angeles clear? Truly it was a day of miracles. Inevitably, the remark of the Little Old Lady came back to mind: "Oh, before they send our boys up there, I do hope they wait for a FULL moon." They didn't.

★ ★ ★

No green cheese, no lunatic monsters hopping around, no grotesque caves—only a bleak and brooding expanse. As a print man, I have to feel sorry for the writers of fantasy, although I imagine that at this very moment, one has thrown a piece of paper into his typewriter and begun: "Kringeloyde the Awful, absolute ruler of the planet Aardvaark, summoned the council of war in the great hall. His seven eyes flashing with anger, he roared: 'Two earthlings have landed on our faroff sister, Moon. It is only a beginning but we must stop it now . . . '" *July 22, 1969*

Cutting the entire epic moonburst down to size, Tom Flippen of Oakland flips: "It was a typical American vacation: three days to get there, eight hours deciding where to stop, a day walking around, three days to get home and 21 days to rest up after all the rushing, only to discover that those new pieces for the rock garden could have been purchased from a mail order company that has mineral rights to a crater site in New Mexico . . ." *July 29, 1969*

Not the least of the late Jim Pike's attributes was his humor. In 1966, shortly after a group of illiberal Bishops wanted to try him for heresy, Bishop Pike gave a Sunday sermon at a smallish church here. As he was speaking, the lights went out, and a row of candles was hurriedly placed in a circle around the pulpit. Gazing out over the flames, Bishop Pike smiled: "I thought I'd at least get a trial first!" . . . Jim Pike will be missed, even by his detractors. In a world largely gone gray, he was colorful and unafraid. The faceless men who feared his individuality attacked his ideas as heresy. Yet he, not they, will be remembered. As another individual, Oscar Wilde, once said: "An idea that is not dangerous is not worthy of being called an idea at all." Jim Pike never had a safe idea in his life.

September 10, 1969

A Long Day's Night

"This," said Field Marshal Erwin Rommel, contemplating the Allied invasion of Normandy, "will be the longest day." While I do not wish to besmirch the memory of the courageous men who fought and died on 6 June 1944, the second longest day took place in San Francisco 16 September 1969. With the sun still high in the heavens, strong men buckled themselves into their starched white armor, making horrible faces as they struggled with their itty-bitty bow ties. Women screamed like shrews and harpies at their hairdressers. Limousines raced to and fro, filled with reinforcements. With studs popping to the left and zippers sticking to the right, they at last made their mad assault on the farthest shores of culture—the seemingly impregnable Opera House—and, after a brisk battle with traffic cops and press, established beachheads at all bars. However, since the opening night opera was Mr. Verdi's "La Traviata," under the general direction of Field Marshal Kurt Herbert Adler, perhaps this must be viewed in the end as a German-Italian triumph.

★   ★   ★

In San Francisco, the opera opening is taken with commendable seriousness, as befits an excursion into High Camp (in fact, it seems to be getting campier every year). Everybody gets into the act with great good nature; it is an annual exercise in creating a San Francisco that never was, except in the dreams of children and journalists, a possible redundancy. Playing their roles to the hilt, the peasants cluster around the carriage entrance, pressing noses to glass and tugging respectfully at their forelocks. The chauffeurs, even those hired for the evening, open the car doors with a salute. The members of the haute bourgeoisie, cheeks flushed with conspicuous consumption, can barely suppress their giggles as they swish around the lobbies, chatting like dress extras. It is our finest hour, our Academy Awards and Miss America Pageant, and all so innocent that there wasn't a single picket line around the Opera House. It isn't even worth a protest.

★   ★   ★

Not that the evening was without tension. Like the Montagus and the Capulets, the Aliotos and Reagans made a career of not looking at each other. Mrs. Reagan, who has a smile that could unhorse a dragoon at 20 paces, was wearing her hair in a stunning shade of brown, matching the Governor's almost exactly. "Well," someone said ungraciously, "at least we know what the Bobbsey Twins looked like after they grew up." Later, at the party in the S.F. Museum following the opera, the Mayor confided: "I wanted to make a little speech, welcoming the Governor—after all, as a former actor I'm sure he is well acquainted with the Alexandre Dumas story that inspired 'Traviata'—but a Museum official asked me not to. Well, it's not MY party. By the way, I'm going through the BART tunnel under the Bay Friday, meeting the mayor of Oakland halfway. Will this be construed as an underworld meeting?"

★   ★   ★

Back in the Opera House—has any other local house, including those of ill-repute, afforded so much pleasure through the years?—Harold Zellerbach was in his usual seat, directly behind Rose Goldstein, the opera's brilliant costumer. Rose usually drenches herself with Joy perfume, which Harold can't stand, to the point where he said "I'll buy you a bucket of any other perfume if you'll just give up on Joy on opening night." She was drenched in Bal de Versailles, to Harold's relief . . . "What a beautiful dress," Tony Kent said to Lucia Anderson Halsey. "Thank you," preened Lucia, "it's an Oscar de la Renta." Tony, feigning deafness: "Eh, what's that—you RENTED it?" Joan Hitchcock was done up to the teeth, and if you know her teeth, you know she was really done up. "I feel like getting married again," she beamed. "Phone me in the morning." Melvin Belli, his white locks in Julius Caesarean ringlets, was with a smashing looking girl young enough to be his daughter, which she isn't. In the mezzanine bar, Decorator Val Arnold looked balefully at the paper champagne buckets and the plastic water pitchers decorated with green leaves. "What is this, the Sheraton-Opera House?" he asked . . . The hot news flashed through The In Group: On Oct. 16 in Vienna, Maestro Josef Krips is marrying his late wife's constant companion, Baroness Harrietta von Prochazka.

★   ★   ★

Unlike the other gland opera in town, nobody disrobes in "Traviata," but it's a pretty sexy piece of business anyway. I only had time for a quick look at the libretto before the lights dimmed, and it seemed to read as follows: "At a party in the salon of Violetta's house in Paris, Alfredo, who has come with friends, is introduced to the hostess who, suffering from consumption, retires to a small country house where she has to sell her jewelry until Alfredo's father, Germont, finds his son in despair, at which point Violetta takes up with a new companion, Baron Douphol, whom Alfredo may or may not challenge to a duel for reasons known only to Germont, who won't reveal them even when Violetta is sick in bed and dies in Alfredo's arms as Germont arrives with the doctor." The moral is simple. If you send your lover's father for the doctor, he'll be late every time. Ingvar Wixell, singing Germont, stole the evening, and as for the lyrics, I consoled myself with Voltaire's remark: "Anything too stupid to be spoken is sung."

September 18, 1969

Ready? Go: Five Husbands, nine Grooms and three Brides. Two Cops and 11 Crooks, 72 Jews and 12 Gentiles, two Races and seven Creeds. Twenty Friends, 30 Romans and 3 Countryman. Fourteen Bachs, one Brahms, four Vivaldis, 15 Schuberts, dozens of Wagners, five Verdis, 10 Puccinis. Forty Francos, 11 Nassers, two Hitlers, one Stalin, one Despot. Fourteen Harps, three Clarets, five Ports, 12 Sherrys and four Beers . . . So much for our annual report on the new S.F. phone book. Most fetching name therein; Mr. Bambang Wiwoho.

October 12, 1969

Add infinitems: Poor, embittered Jack Kerouac, dead at 47, almost forgotten in the North Beach byways he frequented—and helped make famous—more than a decade ago. In his last years, he turned on the young people, sometimes viciously, and they in turn turned their backs on him. Yet a small literary niche will forever be his: "On the Road" remains the finest chronicle of the Beatnik era . . .

October 22, 1969

THE CRUST OF SOME PEOPLE

The timing was exquisite. At about 6:30 Wednesday evening, two Film Festival officials were complaining over a drink at L'Etoile: "We just haven't had enough publicity for the Festival. What we need is another Shirley Temple walkout story—something to get us some headlines." Less than an hour later, the Grand Central Station filmmakers of Sausalito, alias Soupy Sales Fan Club, were filling the Nob Hill air with badly aimed pies, followed by screams, curses, sirens, the Tac Squad, lights, cameras, action and headlines, from coast-to-coast. As a mess, it was a masterpiece.

★ ★ ★

Police Capt. Don Scott of Central Station, who bore the brunt of the stunt by mistake, took it all with a remarkable cool. A Lieutenant observed mildly: "It's nice to have something soft thrown at us for a change." The traditional Little Old Lady said fiercely: "The Mayor is responsible for all this. He is soft on hippies! Oh, how I'd like to see somebody shove a pie in HIS face!" Charlotte "Tex" Mailliard tasted a bit of the ammunition and decided: "Not bad. Banana cream?"

★   ★   ★

A beribboned Green Beret, Sgt. George Bradley, had pie all over his Class A uniform. "Oh, you poor soldier," sympathized several formally dressed first-nighters, stuffing paper money into his pocket. "Here, use this to get your uniform cleaned. Imagine anybody throwing a pie at a Green Beret!" Sgt. Bradley found himself $15 to the good—the joke being that he was part of the pie-throwing contingent. His assignment was to throw a pie at a naked, tattooed girl who had split in panic when she saw all the police.

★   ★   ★

Publicity aside, the incident was a bummer. Although the Grand Central Station group had rehearsed the action for three weeks, it didn't come off as planned: the actors were supposed to throw pies only at each other—bystanders, innocent or otherwise, were not to have been spattered. (Quick, go tell Capt. Scott!) There was ugliness, too: Fred Berk, a member of the troupe, was shoved through a plate glass door by an irate but unidentified man and had to have 15 stitches taken in his face. "He was mad because he had some pie on his suit and I was handing him a towel," says Berk. "I was trying to get away from him when he shoved me through the door. But I feel okay." Culinary note: News reports that the 300 pies were "inedible" are incorrect. "They were meringue and fruit coloring," reports Peter Adair. "We experimented with them for a long time. We wanted something that wouldn't leave a stain— it should wash right off." (Quick, go tell Capt. Scott!)

★   ★   ★

Claude Jarman, executive director of the Film Festival and another San Franciscan who never loses his cool: "We had a tip the day before that something was going to happen, but we didn't know what. I took the precaution of having a few police on hand, but we were still taken by surprise. Actually, it was quite well planned. This truck drove up and a man got out the back with a tray of pies—as though he were delivering them. So nobody moved at first. He walked up the red carpet and stumbled—very realistically—and the pies went all over the place. Then the others

179

jumped out and began throwing them. Their aim was not all it might have been," winning Mr. Jarman the prize for understatement of the week.

★   ★   ★

Inside Masonic Auditorium, there WAS a Film Festival opening, albeit anticlimactic. Mayor Joe, who may need a new gagwriter, rattled off what is becoming known as The Joke: "Don't cancel your subscriptions to Look—I plan to own it soon." Perhaps it's time to drop The Subject. Anthony Quinn, star of "The Secret of Santa Vittoria," made an odd little speech that sounded like a cop-out: "Y'know, nobody ever starts out to make a bad picture. We all go into it with love in our hearts. So when you see it, have a little love in YOUR heart." Well, "Secret" is neither the worst nor the best picture ever filmed, but a pie-throwing sequence might have souped it up a little. After viewing the mess outside, Victor Borge made the most acute observation: "As I've been saying for years, we should get violence off the screen and back into the streets, where it belongs."

★   ★   ★

Postscript at 1 a.m. from a police officer who'd rather I didn't quote him by name: "I'll admit I was pretty sore when those pies were flying around, but now that I look back on it, I guess it was pretty funny." Of course, his uniform was spotless. That helps the old perspective.

★   ★   ★

Other voices, other rumors: Tomorrow night's Festival film will be a French job, "Z," starring Yves Montand, which is so revolutionary (apparently) that the Black Panthers showed it here recently at a benefit. Donald Rugoff of N.Y., who imported the film and loaned it to the Panthers, couldn't get the print back until he gave Bobby Seale round-trip first class air fare to New York! . . . As for the other Hottest Topic, an eight-year-old boy named Buck who attends Green Gables School in Palo Alto was asked by his mother: "How do you like your teacher?" "I think she's Zodiac's wife," grumbled Buck . . . And Wed. morning, Mal Segal was watching Melvin Belli talking to "Zodiac" (or Sam the Sham) on the Dunbar Show when Mal's nine-year-old, Dan, popped into the bedroom. Peering at a closeup of Belli, Dan remarked, "Dad, aren't you a little old to be watching Captain Kangaroo?"

October 24, 1969

Farewell to a champ: Lefty O'Doul was the kind of a guy who would have been embarrassed at the glowing phrases being written about him, now that he's dead. In the terms he preferred, he was a helluva guy—"all heart," as a Powell Streeter said yesterday (incidentally, he did not die of a coronary, as reported, but of a clot in his lungs; nothing wrong with his heart, ever) . . . Lefty O'Doul: what a marvelous name. It rings and rolls with the rhythm of sport, pure Butchertown Irish, and yet he was as much French and German as Irish. His Irish grandmother married a Frenchman named Odoul—but not until he promised to insert an apostrophe and change it legally to O'Doul . . . Twenty years ago, Collie Small wrote a fine piece on Lefty for the old Saturday Evening Post, all about his $40,000 a year salary for managing the minor league Seals in the jewel box called Seals Stadium. Collie's title summed him up: "Too Big For the Majors." Also for the Hall of Fame, which never saw fit to honor him, to its everlasting disgrace . . . As for my favorite paper, the Old Chron did it again the morning after he died, running a front page picture of Lefty wearing a SAN DIEGO cap! I can hear him now: "Hey, what're you bums over there tryin' to do to old Lefty?" I wish I could hear him now.

December 10, 1969

Francis Ford Coppola, the brilliant young movie director, may be ready for San Francisco (he now lives among us), but is San Francisco ready for Francis Ford Coppola? . . . Jerry Paris, who directed "Viva Max," invited him for dinner at La Bourgogne, our best French restaurant, where Owner Jean Lapuyade took one look at Francis and declaimed: "But you are dressed for the JUNGLE! Are you a HUNTER? I'm terribly sorry, but—." "Gee, and I really dressed UP to eat here," lamented Francis, who was wearing a bush jacket, fatigues, boots, a striped silk shirt and a flowered tie to go with his long hair and beard. (He and Paris retreated to Oreste's) . . . "However, I understand," adds Coppola. "La Bourgogne is very elegant. But a few nights earlier, I was kicked out of La Pantera because of my beard. Imagine being kicked out of an ITALIAN restaurant in NORTH BEACH. I, Francis Ford Coppola, whose grandfather was one of Garibaldi's One Thousand and whose father was solo flautist under Toscanini!" *December 19, 1969*

THERE GOES WHATEVER IT WAS

There may come a time when we will look back on the Sixties with nostalgic affection, but I'm inclined to doubt it. The decade wasn't all bad but not for lack for trying: the three graceful men who might have embellished it fell to the assassins, and as we went on trying to save Vietnam by destroying it, we discovered we were destroying ourselves; a country that has a Pentagon doesn't need enemies, it turned out, and the graffito of the decade may well have been "Pragmatism doesn't work."

★　★　★

In San Francisco, the tall buildings rose to blot out the views of a Bay that is disappearing. Hair grew longer, skirts shorter; sniffed Cecil Beaton: "Never in the history of fashion has too little material been raised so high to reveal so much that needs to be covered so badly." Caryl Chessman died at San Quentin in what they call the fireless cooker as Gov. Pat Brown agonized; "The difference between Pat Brown and Caryl Chessman," went the black joke after the execution, "is that Caryl Chessman is still alive." Wrong. Mr. Brown, the Tower of Jello, master of instant indecision, went on to defeat the man who had been beaten for President at the beginning of the decade and would be President at its end.

★　★　★

The Beatniks faded out and the hippies flowered in, one of the early ones explaining "I'm just overcompensating for a tendency to be a compulsive worker." The Chronicle launched a fearless crusade against bad restaurant coffee after Pat Buttram drank a cupful that tasted "like something you sit in to remove a tattoo." Alcatraz lost its reputation as the world's most celebrated leakproof pen; three prisoners dug their way out with spoons as TWA's Bob Brady sighed: "Too bad—if they'd taken 22 prisoners with them they'd have qualified for a group fare to Europe." So many demonstrators were arrested at the massive sit-ins at the Palace and on Auto Row that Inspector Bob Quinn looked up from a mountain of paper work to gripe: "What this department needs is an Arrest-a-Plate." And LBJ refused to send Hubert Humphrey to Winston Churchill's funeral because he was afraid Hubert wouldn't be able to stop smiling.

★　★　★

"If you like him you pronounce it Ray-gun," explained Bob Finch, "and if you don't, you call him Reegan. As I was saying to Governor Reegan just the other day—." The historic White House

182

department store folded; a Little Old Lady who worked there collected her last check, went to Don Silverthorne's S.F. National Bank to deposit it in her account, found THAT had folded, and smiled wanly: "Well, at least I'm not pregnant." "WHAT Pill?" read the bumper stickers on the Dy-dee Wash trucks, and the Surgeon-General's report made cigarettes the Topic of Cancer. At the Cow Palace, Barry Goldwater ("He's as American as apfel strudel") was nominated for President and said "I'm optimistic." "Naturally," added Stan Freberg. "He looks at the world through rose-colored bombsights."

★ ★ ★

As Chiang Kai-shek collected yet another $50 million from Washington, Ed Sachs mordantly described Nationalist China as "A cause advocated by people who wouldn't rent to Orientals." "The problems of this age are infinitesimal," noted Prof. John Bunzel. "The atom, the ovum and a touch of pigment." Asked Bishop Pike: "Why do most people want the front of the bus, the back of the church and the middle of the road?" Walt Kraemer summed up the difference between capitalism and communism: "They can't give THEIR astronauts a ticker tape parade." Still, the market slumped so sharply that when a man said "I'm going downtown to see my broker," his wife asked: "Stock or pawn?"

★ ★ ★

The Bay Bridge humped, San Franciscans twisted, jerked and frugged, and Dr. Schwarz brought his Christian Anti-Communism Crusade here to warn that "When Krushchev takes over he will use the Mark Hopkins as his headquarters"; Al Adolph ruined him by inquiring "will he take the cable Karl to the Top o' the Marx?" At the height of the anti-war fever, Hubert Humphrey insisted in a burst of floratory: "No sane person likes the war in Vietnam and neither does President Johnson." Speed reading became such a fad that Prof. Mark Schorer asked a student "Felt any good books lately?" and as for books, Christine Keeler's was to have been titled "Tories I Have Served Under." Movies grew longer and cars shorter. "Ben-Hur," said Dave Falk, "is too long even if you're Jewish," and George Lemont accurately summed up the American compacts: "They will be longer, lower and wider than any other small cars in the world."

★ ★ ★

The Sixties: "Would you believe?" and "Sorry about that." Carole Tregoff was tried and found wanton. Happiness is the third martini on an empty stomach, "Santa Claus is North Polish" and

183

"Mother Goose Is a Honky." In Santa Barbara there was trouble on oiled waters and bumper strips reading "Union Oil Is a Slick Organization." The decade that went like sixty, and will the Seventies be an improvement? Well, as Hemingway's Jake said in "The Sun Also Rises," "Isn't it pretty to think so?" *December 28, 1969*

1970

★ ★ ★

Guided tour: White walls slashed with bright stripes. Transparent plastic furniture. An antique inlaid pool table in the lobby, alongside a huge Tom Cara espresso machine topped by a golden eagle. Blownup photos of Kurosawa, Eisenstein, D. W. Griffith, Antonioni. Fantastic $13,000 German editing machines, marvels of tooled steel. In a cubbyhole, a 19th century toy called a zoetrope, a forerunner of the movie camera: whirl it and the painted figures inside seem to be in motion . . .

This is American Zoetrope, one of the most exciting new ventures in town. A few months ago, it was just another empty warehouse on Folsom Street. Now it is a scene of mad activity, the center of big-time moviemaking in San Francisco, presided over by the talented 30-year-old director, Francis Ford Coppola, pronounced "Cop-POLE-a."

Coppola is roly-poly, requisitely gentle and cool, wearing the requisite shaggy hair and beard. "We're already running out of space," he says, rambling around the three big floors. "We may have to take a building in the center of town and go vertical." He has gathered under his wing a group of equally young directors: John Korty and George Lucas, among others. Lucas has just completed American Zoetrope's first feature movie, a sci-fi titled "THX 1138," filmed in BART tunnels, Marin Civic Center and other locales here.

"We brought it in for $700,000," Coppola is saying calmly. "Would have cost twice that in Hollywood, and we have better equipment here than they have there. No Hollywood studio has editing equipment to compare with ours. They'll be coming up here to use it." The measure of American Zoetrope's promise may be found in a note pinned to the bulletin board. It is from the celebrated Stanley Kubrick of "2001" renown, offering to film his next movie in San Francisco—at Zoetrope. "It is very exciting."

As the scene fades, Coppola draws himself a cup of espresso from the gleaming machine, picks up his cue and resumes his game of eight-ball on the antique pool table. Behind the eight-ball? Not he. *January 8, 1970*

What goes up: Ten years ago, Lee Tyler (that's a girl) wrote an article titled "How to See San Francisco on a Dollar"—a price based on Muni fares, glass of draught beer at the BeeVee, a walkaway seafood cocktail at the Wharf and so on. Now the piece will be included in a Doubleday book titled "Around the World With the Experts"—so Lee decided she'd better double-check the route. New title of her article in the book: "How to See San Francisco on Two Dollars." *January 19, 1970*

If there were a Michelin Guide for the Bay Area, it would have to award three stars ("Worth a special journey") to the new Oakland Museum, where works of art are housed in a building that is itself a work of art. "Fun" is a word that rarely applies to a museum, but the Oakland is just that: spacious, relaxed and decidedly ungloomy—maybe because it has so many slightly oddball items seldom seen in museums. Somebody's old "junk" has become today's treasures, thanks to loving care and tender display, and what a joy to see so many examples of the artful corn of Arthur F. Mathews. Charles Rollo Peters, Samuel Marsden Brooks and Xavier Martinez . . . In the history section, neat signs, hanging from the ceiling, comment ironically on the tragic story of California's Indians. "At sunrise the Indians came welcoming us, one behind the other, singing and dancing"—Father Pedro Font, 1776. "We rejoice to find so many pagans upon whom the light of our holy faith is about to dawn"—Father Francisco Palou, 1782. "When Red Cane comes, we Wintu forget our songs"—The Coming of the White Man. *February 1, 1970*

Onward: Grace Cathedral, begun in 1910, is now one step closer to completion. Newly installed: the 12 stained-glass windows in the clerestory, made by Gabriel Loire in Chartres, France, and showing the likeness of Franklin D. Roosevelt, John L. Lewis, Albert Einstein, Col. John Glenn, Luther Burbank, Thurgood Marshall, Frank Lloyd Wright, Robert Frost, Dr. William Welch, John Dewey, Jane Addams and Henry Ford as the outstanding figures in their fields. The expensive windows were paid for by a San Franciscan who wishes to remain anonymous—but his lavish gift was not without controversy. For a while there, it appeared that two of the windows would remain blank as conservative members of the hierarchy argued strenuously, but eventually futilely, against the inclusion of Roosevelt and Lewis. *February 13, 1970*

In memoriam: San Francisco was diminished by two deaths last week . . . Police Sgt. Brian McDonnell, who died after the maniacal bombing of Park Station, epitomized what they used to call "the good cop": decent, kindly, sensitive, dedicated. When you hear the kids loosely toss around the term "pig," you cringe when you think of men like Brian McDonnell. In the afterblast of that dark and senseless deed, something more had vanished than this good guy. What also went up in smoke was the picture of San Francisco as a city of good feelings, where assorted beliefs and passions could exist in delicate balance. No earthquake has shattered us but the city is atilt all the same . . . His life and his death were an entirely different matter, but San Francisco is less without Robert Watt Miller, too. He had the grand style, the kind we don't see much around here any more: courteous without being a bore about it, cultured without affectation, aware of great changes without being afraid of them, generous with time and money. If this Grand Duchy of a city ever had an Ambassador who commanded respect wherever he went, it was he. The gap he leaves in the skyline is his monument. *February 23, 1970*

. . . EDDIE ELKINS, the fabled steward on SP's Del Monte Unlimited, is retiring Sat. after 41 years in the service, and the old rattler will never be the same. Or maybe you never heard Eddie announce, in his rich baritone, "Watsonville," "Castroville," "San Jose," etc., and then, as the train approaches Third and Townsend, "This is—The City!" The SP should tape that. And the former

Friendlies better do right by old Eddie, a giant in a white jacket.

March 19, 1970

I love a parade: But I must say that the one last Saturday, commemorating the 100th birthday of Golden Gate Park, had very little to do with those thousand acres of verdant loveliness. It was so MILITARY: soldiers, sailors, Marines, airmen, but, as a parade official explained: "Where would YOU go to organize a parade? You think we could get the Jefferson Airplane to march?" He had a point.

If you're worrying about a shortage of drum majorettes, forget it. There were hundreds, of all sizes, shapes and colors, demonstrating various degrees of ineptitude. One curly-haired, dimpled and lipsticked darling dropped her baton in front of the judging stand: her mother trailing alongside looked about to slug her. High school bands and ROTC units marched past by the hundreds, all out of step—and a good thing. If they were IN step, the Park might have collapsed. Anway, totalitarianism seems a long way off.

Mayor Alioto and Angelina emerged from an air-conditioned Cadillac with tinted glass, took a bow, and disappeared. Sheriff Matt Carberry rolled past, teetering in the back seat of an open car. "Fasten your seat belt, Matt!" came the cry. "Don't fall out!" Matt has been known to take a drink. Some aged oaf grabbed the mike away from Carter B. Smith and delivered a re-election speech for Matt to a chorus of boos. The baby elephant—"Awwww"—trundled past just in time to save him.

* * *

Pot-bellied veterans of ancient wars shuffled past, carrying flags. "Why do they look so grim?" asked a hippie girl. "They won, didn't they?" Somehow. Down the road came two handsome Filipino women, dressed in long silk gowns and carrying a flag-draped picture of Douglas MacArthur. They were followed by a car whose ribbons proclaimed eerily "Survivors of the Bataan Death March Association—Sponsored by the U.S. Army Recruiting Service." Appropriately, the car was empty except for the gaunt driver, and can't the Recruiting Service find something to sponsor that has a more pleasant association? How about the Survivors of V-J Day?

It was a peculiar way to start the Park's Centennial Year. Nobody so much as mentioned William Hammond Hall and John McLaren, the dedicated men who made the sand dunes blossom into magnificence. Still, there was a large and happy crowd. The Berkeley Barb estimated it at 1,100, Ramparts at 2,700, the Recreation & Park Commission at 100,000 and the streetsweepers, who followed the horses and elephants, at 983,765.   *April 7, 1970*

Action city: Koni Goeldlin, boss of Freight Forwarders, was driving out Third St. on his way to Candlestick when all sorts of odd things happened. Cigarette between his lips, he punched the cigarette lighter on the dash, extracted same and dropped it, whereupon it rolled under the front seat and set it ablaze (hey—I'll bet even Ralph Nader doesn't know THAT!). Smoke rising about him, Koni raced to the nearby Bluxome St. Fire station, where the crew put out the flames. "Sorry to have caused so much trouble," apologized Koni. "Forget it," grinned a fireman. "If everybody delivered their fires to us, this job'd be a cinch!"   *April 10, 1970*

This column has saved another life! If you've been paying attention, you remember our story about the brave frog that escaped from the cleaver-wielding chef at Oakland's Mirabeau, and was reprieved to enter the Jumping Frog Contest last wkend at Angel's Camp. (Of course you remember it—nothing else has been going on lately.) Anyway, the frog, Fifi, performed miserably. Having been fed too much steak, she jumped only three feet, when the record is around 19 feet. This so embarrassed the chef, Jacques Boiroux, who accompanied Fifi to Angel's Camp, that he leaped 19 feet 8 inches for a new record, but the judges decided he was the wrong kind of frog and disqualified him . . . For losing, Fifi was about to become an entree again but little Janet Greenstreet, of Modesto, who read our original item, phoned the Mirabeau and pleaded for Fifi as a pet. She picked her up Friday night and have a nice day.   *May 22, 1970*

The annual Bohemian Grove encampment on the (White) Russian River ended on an anticlimactic note, as far as most of the brethren were concerned. The final speaker, following Secty. of State William Rogers, was Neil Armstrong, the first man on the moon, who spoke for an hour about population control. And divisions in our society. And food shortages, plus various esoteric ways to produce substitutes. And the application of nuclear energy to combat diseases. And—well, the point is, he never mentioned the moon ONCE, to the mystified disappointment of most of his listeners. Nor did he offer any explanation, although there is something to be said for an astronaut who is now completely concerned with the problems of his own planet. *August 4, 1970*

THE TANGLED WEB

Beniamino Benvenuto "Benny" Bufano will be buried today with all the pomp and panoply that a democratic city can provide—but his story will not end at graveside. He led too long and varied a life for that. His past continues to haunt him. And us.

At the funeral today will be the only woman he was married to, Virginia Bufano Lewin of Mill Valley. With her will be Erskine Bufano, her son by Benny. And accompanying them will be the eminent lawyer, Hilary Crawford. When Benny and Virginia were divorced in 1932, Crawford represented her—and his presence at her side today indicates the story is not over.

For when the mourning ends, Crawford will sue to break Bufano's will, which makes no mention of Erskine. "After all," says Virginia, "he is Beniamino's only legitimate heir. I named him after Colonel Charles Erskine Scott Wood" (author of the once-celebrated book, "Heavenly Discourse"). "Without Colonel Wood, I never could have survived Benny. Not that we fought on personal grounds—only things. He only cared about his statues. He was not much of a father to Erskine, but to ignore him in his will is a disgrace."

Erskine Bufano, now an X-ray technician at Ross General Hospital, was 42 on August 16—two days before Benny's death. And Virginia and Benny were married August 18, 1925. Students of the stars may be able to make something of that. Bufano's age? "He always made himself out to be ten years younger than he really was," says Virginia. "When he died, he must have been 80-odd. And sometimes very odd."

*   *   *

The moving finger: Albert Bender, the late great S.F. art patron, was one of Bufano's early benefactors, paying the rent on

190

his studio and buying many of his works which he later presented to museums. A more recent patron was Trader Vic Bergeron, the restaurateur who is also an accomplished painter and sculptor. Vic started paying Bufano's studio rent in 1961, but was appalled at the condition of the place. It was he who moved Benny to his last studio—on Minna—in 1964, paying the $200-a-month rent throughout the intervening years.

In gratitude, Bufano gave Vic the huge lead bear that now stands at the entrance to Senor Pico in Ghirardelli Square (it had to be covered with wire mesh "to keep idiots from carving their initials in it," adds the Trader). At Vic's insistence, the bear will now go to the S.F. Museum of Art. "It's too good," he says, "to be standing in front of a saloon."

Although Vic continued to pay the studio rent, he and Bufano had a falling out recently over the sculptor's eating habits. "I told him he could eat anytime he wanted at Trader Vic's," he says. "Meat and potatoes was okay, but when he started going for nothing but caviar, pate and champagne, it was too much. Still, he was a magnificent artist, a giant, the finest sculptor of the age, and the biggest pain in the neck I ever met."

* * *

The gesture: Bufano was a political naif, impulsive in his gestures, generous with his treasures. One of his last acts of involvement was to give a handsome 31-inch sculpture of St. Francis Assisi—the model of his most famous one—to the Soledad Brothers Defense Committee in San Jose. Raffle tickets were sold for $1 each, raising $900, and the statue was won by a San Jose businessman and his wife. "It should have brought $10,000," said Benny.

* * *

The letter: Thousands of words have been written about Bufano, but his own are the best at defining his lovely, poetic spirit. He wrote me this letter in 1955, about the very same celebrated statue:

"Well, here I am in Paris working like a beaver on my statue of Saint Francis that I made here in 1928, '29 and '30, and, as you know, gave to San Francisco. They financed my trip here so I could get it ready for shipment. But the money they allowed me is so small that I have been living for the past two months on black bread, figs and milk while working in this damp and cold warehouse where Saint Francis has been in prison so long.

"But the Saint is still smiling. So I keep on polishing, rubbing and warming his face and find myself singing a half-sad and half-joyful song, 'Brother Francis, we will be out of here, we will be out of here in a week or so, and then out in the sun, the sun of California, California, California . . . There we will dry our tears and share our song with the people, all the people, peace and good will!'

"In a little while his years of imprisonment will be ended and he will have a beautiful place on the steps of The Church of Saint Francis of Assisi. There in all his humility and grandness Saint Francis will call upon the people of all nations to live in peace with one another. Now I pray this time his message will be heard.

"Herb, our greeting comes to you from 6,000 miles away and God Bless you and all our friends, including our enemies. Beniamino."

★ ★ ★

The footnote: The great statue that Bufano labored so long over didn't last long on the steps of the Church of St. Francis of Assisi here. People complained "It gets in our way," and it was moved, first to Oakland, then to Longshoreman's Hall—as restless and sad-eyed as the man who created it.   *August 21, 1970*

THE ROCK SCENE

Alcatraz today: An icy wind whistles in from the Gate, rustling the dry grass and the tough wildflowers that cling to outcropping and crevice. Broken glass, dented Coke cans, shattered windows, burned-out building looking like the relics of a World War II bombing raid. Cats chasing mice, ragamuffin children whooping after each other in cold stone corridors, gaunt dogs snarling and snapping . . . Once they were city dogs, but here on The Rock, they have reverted to nature—lean and wolflike, hungry eyes burning, fangs bared. An Indian landing on Alcatraz for the first time looked at the dogs fighting and nodded in satisfaction: "This is Indian country."

★ ★ ★

"Red Power," symbolized by a huge clenched fist painted in red on a wall near the landing dock. Over the useless water tower—water is still the big problem—flaps the flag of the Indian Nation: a tepee and a broken arrow, symbolizing peace. Stickers read: "Impeach Hickel." The main yard, where the Federal prisoners once played baseball, is dotted with maybe 30 garbage cans, stuffed with gasoline-soaked rags. If the Feds ever try to recapture the island by helicopter invasion, the rags will be set afire . . . If the Feds ever try, however, they will probably be successful, for the Indians are unarmed, despite the rumors of "armed patrols." There were two guns on The Rock, both toys, and last week, they were thrown into the Bay "to relieve the paranoia of the Coast Guard."

★   ★   ★

It is nine months now since the Indians took Alcatraz—without force. "But we were ready to lay down our lives if we had to," says La Nada Means, who talks like a young woman who means what she says. "We are ready to lay down our lives to stay here." La Nada is 23, a Shoshone Bannock born on an Idaho reservation and recently a student at Berkeley. She is good-looking (blue-black hair, strong white teeth), intense, intelligent, the mother of two young sons—and militant. "They call us Indian hippies, red Commies, red niggers, but it doesn't matter. We're Indians, all of us, and we belong on Alcatraz. Indians never had prisons—yet here, in this white man's prison, we have found freedom for the first time."

★   ★   ★

La Nada, a member of the Council of Seven that runs Alcatraz, is one of the three original invaders still there. The others are Charles Dana (Choctaw) and John Trudell (Sioux): it was Mrs. Trudell who, four weeks ago, gave birth to the first child born on Alcatraz during the occupation, "the first Indian child born in freedom in almost a hundred years" (the boy is doing fine) . . . Once there were as many as 800 Indians living on The Rock. The number has dwindled to "between 60 and 75, including a couple of dozen children—it's hard to keep accurate records, there is so much coming and going," all on the cockleshell boat run from Fisherman's Wharf by a pleasant white man named Jim McCormick.

★   ★   ★

Alcatraz is an eerie, ghost-ridden place. In the chill, empty main cell block, names have been inscribed over a row of cells—Nixon and Agnew, Alioto and Reagan, Julius Hoffman, Andrew Jackson. The last one in the row is named for America's young sweethearts, David & Julie. "Sometimes at night," said La Nada, "we play hide-and-seek in the dungeons down below. No lights—so dark and silent it makes your hair stand on end. It's a real mind-blower." Up above, the burned-out houses stand out starkly against the misty

193

sky: the warden's house (handsome fireplace), the doctor's house, the recreation hall. The Indians claim they were set afire by landing parties of vigilantes. "They try to come ashore all the time," reports La Nada. "Sometimes they succeed. Sometimes we drive them off with rocks. The other damage you see was caused by our children. We call them the wrecking crew. If the Coast Guard ever tries to land, we'll put the kids out front—they'd scare the hell out of anybody."

★ ★ ★

It's a hard life. Morale and health are high (most of the occupants are young) but everything else is low. Breakfast is mush and bacon, lunch is canned soup, dinner is meat, if and when available. Tap water is brought over from the mainland by Skipper McCormick, in big bottles. There are only two generators, one to run the lighthouse, one to light the administration building–mess hall. For the rest, it's candles and flashlights. "People keep asking what they can do for us," said La Nada. "Well, we need meat, fresh fruit and vegetables, warm clothes—please, no ball gowns or gold slippers, which some people sent." (The address is Alcatraz Relief Fund, Pier 40.) But if we have to, we can make it on our own. If people REALLY want to do something, tell them to read, tell them to find out what has been happening to all our oppressed people, tell them to look around and stop being so goddam dumb!"

★ ★ ★

On the boat back to the mainland, La Nada mused: "Alcatraz is a symbol to us. You know, the first prisoners on Alcatraz were Indians—in the old days—put there without light or water. Just like us! And it is written in the prophecies that the Indian Nation will be reborn on an island at the mouth of the Sacramento river. We will never leave. We are home." *August 25, 1970*

The letter that will never be read: Fillmore Bill Graham was a happy man Friday. A star he had been after for weeks had just agreed to appear at Fillmore West and East on two weekends in December, so he dashed off a note to her at her Larkspur address: "It'll be just great to have you in the family again. Thanks for coming back to us" . . . The letter, of course, was to Janis Joplin, dead at 27 (her body was found Sunday night in a Los Angeles hotel room). She had been making an album for Columbia, whose officials haven't decided yet whether she had completed enough songs for a release. But the tunes she had recorded at the time of her death add up to some kind of epitaph for this talented, tempestuous and troubled girl: "Get It While You Can," "Trust in Me," "A Woman Left Lonely"—and "Cry."   *October 6, 1970*

Caenfetti: Kezar Stadium was jammed Sunday, of course, except for two seats in Section M, 48th row. A Little Old Lady, more confused than most, left the tickets for those seats Sunday morning at "Will Call" in—the Opera House! Joe Allen, boss of the Opera House, struggling for a solution to the mystery: "All I can figure is that she also left two tickets for 'Otello' in 'Will Call' at Kezar" . . .   *December 1, 1970*

Now then: Why do the Salvation Army belles ring their bells over black kettles? The reason that's a good question is that I just discovered the answer. Back in 1894, there was a shipwreck off the Gate, and the survivors were sheltered and fed by the Salvation Army. When the food supply was exhausted, an Army lass grabbed the empty kettle and walked through the Barbary Coast, calling out "Keep the kettle boiling—help the shipwreck survivors!" That's such a nice story I hope nobody tells me it's untrue.
                    December 14, 1970

OF TRUMAN INTEREST

It may have been my finest hour, there under the lights of Civic Auditorium at the opening of the Women's Pro Tennis Championships Wed. night. Even though saddled with Billie Jean King as partner, I slashed and smashed my way to victory over Hoppe and Casals (Willie Hoppe, the late billiards player, and Cellist Pablo Casals, who's 94) in a match so exciting that the half-vast crowd was constantly on its feet, moving toward the exits. Afterward, flushed with pride and Scotch, I headed toward the stands, where my old friend had been sitting. His seat was empty. The explanation came in the form of a note handed to me by Carol Brown Severin, an Assoc. Prof. at S.F. State. It read: "Not everyone can claim the honor of having Truman Capote walk out on them while WINNING their tennis match" . . . It was true. Overcome by the sheer brutality of my game, Mr. Capote had departed to walk around the Civic Center until he regained his composure. "Not since the Vidal-Buckley debates," he explained, "have I been moved to such ennui."

★　★　★

Later, over Bongo-Bongo soup at Trader Vic's, he talked of many things. Of his friend Johnny Carson's annoyance because Capote appears so often on the Dick Cavett show ("I've known Cavett longer than I've known Carson. Perfectly true. Cavett is beating him in the big cities but I guess Johnny still has Middle America"). Of then Gov. Lester Maddox of Georgia walking out of the Cavett show last month after a remark about "bigots." Backstage, Capote said to him: "That was a ridiculous performance"—at which Maddox worked up a mouthful of spit and deposited it one inch from Capote's foot. "THAT," spat Truman, "is undistinguished even for a Governor of Georgia."

★ ★ ★

We talked about the illustrious freeloaders (the Duke and Duchess d'Uzes, Der Prinz Tassilo van Furstenberg, Col. Serge Obolensky, and so on) who are here to pay homage, but nothing else, to Rudolf Nureyev, their plane fare and hotel bills being on the house. "You're not surprised, are you?" said Truman languidly. "The really really rich never pick up a check." About Nureyev:

"Princess Lee Radziwill, Nureyev and I shared a penthouse at the Ambassador East in Chicago—and one day I walked in unexpectedly to find Rudi standing in front of a full-length mirror, staring at himself with the oddest expression. After a few minutes of this, I walked over and asked 'What are you LOOKING at?' Without moving or changing that strange look on his face, he said 'Him.' "

★ ★ ★

The charmed life: From here, Capote goes back to Palm Springs to close up his house and then to New York, where he will board the William Paleys' yacht for a cruise to the Bahamas. There, the Guinnesses will pick him up in their plane to take him to their house on the West coast of Mexico. After a respite there, he will fly to London and Paris on the Gulfstream II jet owned by another old friend, Financier Bob Anderson, who owns everything worth owning in New Mexico. It's one way to live. It may be the only way.

★ ★ ★

During the past Christmas season, a mutual acquaintance went shopping in New York with his close friend, Jackie Kennedy Onassis. In a rare-book store, she picked up an 18th century book, very large and grand, containing illustrations of seashells.

"How beautiful!" explained Jackie. "I think I'll frame each picture and hang them in the 'Christina' (the Onassis yacht). Then turning to the salesman, she asked "How much?" When he replied "$40,000," she gasped "Oh, but that's too much. Sorry."

Later, they strolled past a bookstore whose window was filled with copies of the recent Fred Sparks book about Jackie and Onassis' first year of marriage, titled "The $20,000,000 Honeymoon." This inspired the friend to suggest: "Why don't you go back and buy that seashell book? It's expensive, but what difference does that make?"

Pointing at the Sparks book, Jackie said hotly, "But those are

197

lies, all lies! I don't have any money. When I married Ari, my income from the Kennedy estate stopped. I didn't make any pre-marital financial arrangements with Ari. I know it's an old Greek custom, but I couldn't. I didn't want to barter myself. Except for my personal possessions, I have exactly $5,200 in a bank account."

"But then how do you LIVE?" wondered the friend.

"I just charge everything to Olympic Airways," she explained. And now you know. *January 8, 1971*

Yesterday's saddest news: the unexpected death of Artist Jean "Yanko" Varda, at 77, of a heart attack at the Mexico City airport (he had been vacationing at La Paz, and, in his own words of a week ago, "Never feeling better"). The irony of it all: for the first time in his long career, a major S.F. museum, the de Young, had been laying plans for a big retrospective of Varda's works, later in the year. Director Ian White, enthusing about it, said only a few days ago that "it would be more than just a show. We want to capture Varda's life style, his liveliness, his warmth, his love of beauty—yes, and of beautiful girls. We may bring his boat into the museum, and his girls and his music" . . . The show will go on, but now it will be more than a retrospective. It will be a memorial to one of the gayest and most pleasure-giving people the Bay world has ever known; yet, without his life-enhancing presence, it will be inescapably sad. Varda was unique, hence irreplaceable. *January 12, 1971*

After Many a Deadline

If you live long enough in this racket, you could spend half your time writing the obituaries of fallen comrades. The invisible sniper, firing at random, picks them off one by one—not that old newspaper guys are a difficult target. They're a dying breed even in the best of health, burning themselves out between editions. Some die in the gutter, others are found face down at their typewriters, still others suddenly pitch forward at their desks . . .

★　★　★

The other night, I stood on the Powell St. curb, across from the Sir Francis Drake, and lagged a penny toward the cable car slot. It hit metal with a tiny "chinnng" and disappeared, to join whatever pennies might still be down there, under the tracks. A ridiculous gesture but it was the only tribute I could think of to Larry Fanning, dead at 56 up there in Anchorage. If our roles had been reversed, he might have done the same for me, for the hell of it, for Auld Lang Syne, for bittersweet memories. Larry went the way we all go if we stay in this racket, down and out, at the desk and the deadline he had faced that once too often. The presses keep rolling but the ticker gives out—a heart that gets old in a hurry, hurry, hurry.

★　★　★

Before World War II, when the city was still young (a time that now appears to have been enchanted), Larry Fanning, a genius of a copyreader named Bob Ritchie, and I would close up The Chronicle at 3 a.m. We'd take final editions, the ink still wet, over to Tiny's, an all-night coffee shop on Powell (Sears occupies that spot now, an entirely different matter). There, we'd pick up a rival Examiner and sit till dawn, comparing, arguing, criticizing. We loved The Chron, we hated The Ex, we were excited about the business. And as the sun started to come out of the East Bay, we'd stand on the Powell curb and lag pennies at the cable car slot. I no longer remember how the game started or why, or even what the point was, since the "winner" was the one who lost his penny down the slot. It simply appealed to the child in us, the child that lives in every newspaperman of whatever age.

★　★　★

It was a great time to be young, in a city that hadn't quite grown up yet, in a world on the brink of disaster, but still poised for the plunge. We were living in the twilight of a golden age of journalism: four dailies at each other's throats, and great newspapermen on all of them. Paul Smith, the boy editor of The Chronicle, Lindner and Wren at The Ex, with Hyder, Hyman and McQuade at the front typewriters, Benny Horne, who coined "Cow Palace," tough Tom Laird and Art Caylor at The News. A mob of tabloid terrors on The Call-Bulletin and Larry Fanning, the kid managing editor of The Chronicle—lean, mean, talented and giving the paper the kind of devotion money can't buy. We were all like that, living and breathing the newspaper business. At the old Press Club at Powell and Sutter—open all night, with slot machines in the bar— we'd take on anybody who'd dare denigrate The Chron. It was Jim Kieldson of The Ex who called our staff "a bunch of young punks." And it was Larry Fanning who smashed him to the floor, where his head lolled between the cuspidors.

*   *   *

My God we were young and indestructible. We'd work all afternoon and run up to the Mark's Lower Bar for a drink (it was The Palace, then) and down to the old Bay City Grill on Turk for dinner and then back to work till the final edition was off the presses and then on to the coffee and coin-lagging at Tiny's and sometimes instead of going to bed we'd drive straight out to Julius Kahn Playground to play tennis by the dawn's early light. Sometimes we'd go without sleep two days, without fatigue. We worked too hard, drank too much, married and divorced too often, blew our health and our home lives, loved our newspaper, dug each other and, in most cases, died too young. It never occurred to us to put in for overtime. We were having too good a time all the time.

*   *   *

Sunday was brunch day at Paul Smith's. It wasn't enough that we worked together six days a week, almost 24 hours a day, we had to be together on Sunday, too, there on the deck of Smith's Telegraph Hill digs, looking out over a city that was still softly pleasant, out toward Treasure Island where there was still time for World's Fairs, out toward the bridges that were more than big enough to handle the traffic (we even worried that the Golden Gate Bridge might never make it, business was so slow). We'd drink and eat and sneer at The Ex and glow over The Chron. Paul called us "The Clan" and we were, closer than most families. There on Telegraph Hill, with the lights of Treasure Island coming on at dusk, we felt on top of the world, in the glow of youth and good Scotch.

*   *   *

Now Paul Smith, after a series of strokes, languishes in a rest home down the Peninsula. Larry Fanning is dead. So are Horne and Caylor, Rob Ritchie, Kieldsen, Lindner, Wren, McQuade, Laird, the News, the Call, the old Press Club and Tiny's. Sometimes I feel like the survivor of a Last Man Club. Throw another penny at the slot and remember the good times. Oh hell.   *February 21, 1971*

Shortsnort: It's a rainy night in Carmel Valley, and along comes Rudolph Fromm, wearing jeans and an old jacket, at the wheel of his MG. He sees a hippie hitchhiker, jams on the brakes, and picks him up. Since the hippie is shaking with cold, Fromm takes him home, gives him dry clothes and a bed—and next morning pre-

200

pares a big, warm breakfast for him. Excusing himself, Fromm then goes to his room and reappears in his U.S. Army Major's uniform. En route to the Monterey Presidio, where he is stationed, Major Fromm stops to drop off the hippie, who has only one thing to say as he gets out of the car: "The whole thing is incredible, just incredible." *March 2, 1971*

Flashing on the Fight of the Century (at Winterland): Souvenir programs were two bucks a copy. Sneered an old-timer: "Man, I used to pay less than that to see live fights in this place." Advice from a cop: "If Frazier wins, get out of here fast—there'll be a riot." There wasn't, but Joe was thought to be The Man's favorite (The Man being Whitey); when he won, his black supporters came to life. Overpowering smell of booze, patchouli, sweat, smoke—and the animal odors of fear and excitement. When the sixth round ended—the round Ali predicted would be the last for Frazier—you knew Muhammad had had it. Some faces in the crowd: Lee Mendelson, Blair Fuller, Enrico, the North Beach Mafia, David Pleydell-Bouverie with his cook and butler, Barnaby Conrad, Howard Nemerovski. Hippies in the aisle, beautiful black chicks in HotPants with handsome dudes in white flarebottoms. Whitey never looked whiter or more out of place. A religious fanatic at the end: "Ali has been humbled, now he must return to Jesus, the Lord has spoken!" On the way out: "Was it a fix?" "When's the rematch?" And a beautiful black girl to her guy: "I'm not goin' to the party, I'm goin' home to cry all night." *March 10, 1971*

It figures that a fancy town like Burlingame would have a Fire Chief named Reginald Moorby—but that's not the item. Maybe this is: Monday night, there was a garage fire behind a house on B'lingame Ave., and Chief Reggie, at the head of his gallant smokeaters, gracefully vaulted the garden fence and disappeared without a trace—eight feet down in the swimming pool on the other side. It will not be necessary to send Reg a "Get Well" card. He and the garage were saved. *April 7, 1971*

Life in the city: He looked like just any other shaggy-haired nondescript hitchhiker, standing there on Van Ness, except that he was carrying an expensive Mark Cross attache case—and inside the case was $55,000 cash, mainly in $100 bills.

How would anybody know this? Well, a few minutes earlier, he had gone into a nearby bank to change three of the $100 bills into smaller denominations, carelessly allowing the teller to see what the case contained. Bug-eyed, the teller immediately called the police. The police called in the Feds. The kid was detained on some vague charge like "under investigation for possible possession of counterfeit money."

The $55,000 may have originated in narcotics sales, because the young man immediately summoned Atty. Michael Stepanian, one of the famous "Dope Lawyers." "There is no way you can hold this boy OR the money," argued Stepanian, and shortly after, the kid was released. A few minutes later, he was back on Van Ness, again hitchhiking—but this time the load in his Mark Cross attache was considerably lighter.

The Feds had taken out $16,000 for income tax. And of course there was Stepanian's fee.   *April 9, 1971*

Last man: With the death of Russ Hodges, the New York Giants have finally lost their voice. I say New York because Russ was New York to the end, the New York of the Polo Grounds. Third Ave. bars, Muggsy McGraw and Mel Ott kicking his foot just before he swung, Russ never seemed quite at home at Candlestick (who could?) and "San Francisco Giants" always sounded odd when he said it. He had that New York voice, a little tired, sometimes bored, the voice of a man who was used to living with defeat. When he got excited, the manner suggested that you shouldn't take it too seriously; coming in second every season isn't all that bad. A lot of fans, this one included, sometimes made fun of his garbled sentences, his talking while munching on something, but he took it like a pro. To him it was part of the game that won't be the same without him. For better or worse, the team is now the San Francisco Giants.   *April 21, 1971*

THE LAST PEACE MARCH

"WHAT DO we want?" . . . "PEACE!" . . . "When?" . . . "Now!" . . .

"What do we want?" . . . "PEACE!" . . . "When?" . . . "NOW!" . . .

Over and over, the familiar catechism, ringing out over the shuffle of thousands of marching feet on a clear and beautiful morning in San Francisco. On Saturday, there we all were again, for the third time—or was it the fourth?—demonstrating easily and glibly for the cause, enjoying the thrill of solidarity, feeling even a little silly at joining in the schoolboy chanting of simple words.

By nature, Americans aren't demonstrative: only a war as long and miserable as this one could have drawn so many shy people out of their protective shells—and even then it took years. In 1965, only a few hundred were willing to lay it on the line (to be photographed, filed in a memory bank, sometimes busted). By 1967, there were tens of thousands: in '69, hundreds of thousands, and now maybe half a million, here and in Washington.

Still, in a country of 200 million, only a drop in the bucket. The President gives no signal (was he occupied again by a game on TV?). His Administration ignores it. If you can believe Dr. Gallup and his ten-foot polls, a majority of Americans are now against the war, but it's still a minority that marches.

* * *

One more time, trying to get the message through, trying to reclaim the American dream here in the loveliest of American cities. But all those red flags flapping in the morning breeze—do they mean the revolution is really here or are they merely young defiance? All those Viet Cong banners. "I don't know why," says a somber young woman who has walked in every march, "but I hate to see those. I know the VC are fighting for their country, but we're fighting to save ours." Her American flag bore the peace symbol instead of stars, but red flags dominated the last peace march.

* * *

The cadres formed downtown, gathering momentum and people as they swept into Geary Boulevard, the well-worn route through the heart of Richmond, past the houses of the silent majority, toward the Russian Orthodox church with its onion domes shining in the sun. Tac Squadders in their coveralls, hundreds of photographers, not all of them from Army Intelligence.

At Arguello, a Dixieland band pumping a little life into already sagging arches. At the crest of each rise, marchers paused to look back at the packed street and ask the question that was to be asked 10,000 times that day: "How many?" Everybody had a guess but there never was an accurate count. Whatever it was, it wasn't enough, for the war goes on.

From upstairs windows, oldsters staring down at the marchers with expressionless eyes. With us or against us? Here and there, bartenders standing on the sidewalk, glowering. No doubt where they stand. But the kids—ah, the kids. Leaning out the windows, peeking furtively from behind curtains, they flashed the peace sign. At 26th Ave., a drunk with a glass in his hand shouted "Commies!" over and over as he staggered, lurched and finally fell.

* * *

How motley this throng. "It's great to see so many of us old-timers out today," beamed an old-timer, but it was still a march for the young, as it should be. The uniform was tattered Levis and Army castoffs. At least one example of Radical Chic: a woman in Gucci shoes, carrying a Gucci shoulder bag, and around her neck a locket containing a baby picture of—Lenin! At 27th Ave., Roger Kent, wearing his Navy blouse with its row of World War II battle ribbons. Poet Allen Ginsberg, who has lost weight and looks fit, tootling away on a plastic horn. Lawrence Ferlinghetti. But mainly kids, kids, kids, some of whom hadn't been born when the Indochina war began and who now wave red flags in front of bulls on the streets of San Francisco . . . A memorable friendly sign outside a little house on 27th Ave.: "Please Use Our Bathroom."

* * *

The thousands filed into Golden Gate Park, past a row of legless and one-legged Vietnam veterans watching impassively from wheelchairs. On the grass of the polo field, the great crowd settled down for a huge picnic. Out came the salami, the cheese, the jugs of wine. "What are all these PEASANTS doing on my POLO field?" lisped a young man with hand on hip, camping it up. A skinny short-haired guy walked through the mob, carrying a sign reading "Tell It To Hanoi!" Everybody admired his guts. In marched the Gay Liberation Front, to smiles and laughter. Their big Viet Cong banner was colored a delicious delirious lavender.

The speeches began, the well-meaning cliches distorted and lost in the brisk Pacific wind. One sensed the absence of a villain like Lyndon Baines Johnson. Nixon is merely an object of derision; it was "Hey, hey, LBJ!" that used to fire up the crowd. At the edge of the Park, the militant Chicanos, in their brown berets and battle jackets, were forming up to disrupt the speeches for keeps. A raggle-taggle army. "They oughta get drafted," scoffed a Vietnam vet, "so's they'd learn how to march at least."

The last peace march, ending in frustration and bitterness. If there is a next one, it will surely be violent. That was the message of last Saturday and it had better be heeded.   *April 27, 1971*

THOSE ENDEARING OLD CHARMS

I keep reading in learned journals that nostalgia is the hottest movement in the land these days, but I'm not buying. It all seems phony to me, just another exercise in merchandising, a high-pressure plot to put our ladies back in wedgies and ankle-strap shoes, not to mention those awful suits with padded shoulders and nipped-in waists (I'll take the beautiful hippie girls who let it all hang out). Not a tear came to my eyes as I read Life's "Nostalgia" issue, and as for the vaunted revival of "No, No, Nanette" on Broadway, that's a bore, too. Can you really get choked up in 1971 over a song with such lyrics as "Day will break and you'll awake and start to bake a sugar cake for me to take for all the boys to see"? What's a sugar cake? Why does she have to get up at dawn to bake it? And I'd rather not think about the kind of "boys" who'd want to see it.

★ ★ ★

The main reason I think the Big Nostalgia Kick is synthetic is that we don't see any signs of it in San Francisco. If it were really happening it would have happened here first. We've led the way in so many wonderful things—rock music, Love Children, cirrhosis, bridge-jumpers, bare boobs, junk art, junk clothes, turning on at the Opera House—that it's ridiculous to think we couldn't have kicked off a nostalgia boom if we'd really wanted to. After all, San Francisco practically invented nostalgia. It's just that we played "Remember when?" for so many years—while the rest of the country was going crazy with progress—that we've tired of the game.

★ ★ ★

If there were any future in nostalgia, it figures that we'd be up to our ears in it. We'd have horse-drawn hansoms in Golden Gate Park. That pitiful excuse for a Cliff House would have been torn down years ago, to be replaced by a proper white gingerbread beauty, with strolling violins and acres of red flocking. French restaurants would become "naughty" again, upstairs bedrooms and all. We'd add more curlycues to the cable cars, expand the fleet and make the crewmen wear handlebar moustaches. The Crime Committee says our Police Dept. is living in the 1920s, which scandalizes City Hall. If we were truly nostalgic, we'd shove the Force back to the '90s: helmets, uniforms that button under the chin and horse-drawn paddy wagons. Manure on Market Street! Blessed perfume of yesteryear! Gaslights and lamplighters to light 'em! And honest graft!

★   ★   ★

Well, nobody can accuse San Francisco of living in the past any longer. In fact, where we seem to be is in a mad rush to destroy every vestige of The City That Was, The City That Knows How, Poor Pitiful Pearl of the Pacific. We can't tear down old buildings fast enough to make room for new ones that are every bit as distinctive as Pittsburgh's or Atlanta's. As the man said when he first entered the restaurant atop Bank of America World Headquarters: "Instant Cleveland!" And now the rusty steel bones of the Transamerica pyramid are beginning to rise, its lower extremities already girdled in white Plastic Inevitable that puts you in mind of motel bathrooms. When the pyramid was first announced, Mayor Alioto, drawing on his rich Florentine background, enthused: "It will be our Giotto Tower!" Well, he may have meant Irving Giotto.

★   ★   ★

While nostalgia is said to be sweeping the country, it's a dirty word in San Francisco '71 (watch out, here comes M. Justin Herman again with his swinging steel ball!). Redevelopment is the name of the game, and if you just had your old house shot out from under you, it's for your own good, old-timer. "You have to be realistic," as this big builder said to me just the other day over lunch at Jack's, an old restaurant that survives, miraculously. "Realistic." I didn't know how to answer him. Realism to him apparently means congestion, confusion, sterility. One antiseptic building, bustling by day, stone cold dead by night—replacing dozens of little buildings where mama and papa ran a grocery, Joe had a bar, Sam did the laundry, George owned a bookstore and hundreds of people lived, laughed, loved and rejoiced in a "neighborhood." Gone, all of them, to where?

★   ★   ★

Hard days for nostalgia. If you dare to talk of the past—and San Francisco had a glorious one—the icy eyes stares at you as if you were some kind of addlehead. So you remember Lincoln Beachey flying inside the Palace of Fine Arts? Big deal! Dodie Valencia, Ping Bodie, Foghorn Murphy, Izzy Gomez—who are they? A new crowd has taken over the city, people who walk through Waverly Place in Chinatown without giving a thought to Little Pete, who pass the Bohemian Club without thinking even once about George

Sterling, who couldn't care less that Isadora Duncan was born here—without so much as a plaque to mark the spot—and who have no time to read Jack London.

★　★　★

Maybe nostalgia is out here because it's too painful to contemplate the dreams and consider the reality. Once there were giants who built well—for the ages, they thought—but their landmarks, the solid evidence of their achievements, could disappear overnight, and did. Now, it's only when the fog steals in to blot out their ersatz replacements that you dare think of the past— alone in a bittersweet reverie. *June 27, 1971*

A Remarkable Joe: Yesterday, they buried Silvio Zorzi, 84. You knew him better as Joe Vanessi, restaurateur, character, North Beach powerhouse and a Broadway institution for 61 years (in 1910, he got off a streetcar at Columbus and Broadway, heard everybody speaking Italian and said "I'm gonna stay here") . . . Somewhere along the line, he changed his name to Vanessi "because it sounds like Venice and who'd wanna eat in a place called Zorzi's?" He ran a great restaurant, and when he was in his prime, the place stayed open till 4 a.m., crowded with insomniac people . . . He was a wonderful garbler of names. "Hello, there, Mr. Hoppe!" he'd say to Bob Hope. Once he got sued because he refused to serve a black man who turned out to be Paul Robeson: "Would I have kicked him out if I'd known it was Paul Robinson?" he apologized. "Robinson is welcome here any time" . . . One night, Marlene Dietrich was seated alone at the counter and along came Joe: "You know, Marion, I saw you last week at the Cocoanut Grove and it cost me 22 bucks. Now you get to see ME for a 35-cent hamburger!" . . . And he came back from a trip to Rome to announce he'd had an audience with the Pope. How come? "Nothin' to it," said Joe grandly. "I tipped the headwaiter—I gave 50 bucks to some guy in a red hat and he took me right in" . . . Joe died rich and well-loved. St. Peter is due for a fat tip. *July 8, 1971*

Point counterpoint: About the Pan American jumbo jet that struck a landing light pier on takeoff here, Senator Ted Kennedy announced in Washington a couple of days ago that "it was overweight and on a runway too short for its load." Upon reading that, an angry airline employee here fired off this telegram to the Senator: "The night you were overloaded you went into the water. Pan Am did not. Please hold remarks till all facts are in."

August 11, 1971

. . . Mrs. Nathan Bentz continues to be my favorite 100-yr-old San Franciscan. During the late unlamented heat wave, you'll recall, she was seen downtown, coolly shopping for a pantsuit. And a couple of days ago, she knocked on the door of a Green St. neighbor, Mrs. Kathleen Swan, who just had a baby, to smile "I'm going out to do some shopping and have my hair done—can I do any shopping for you?" Mrs. Swan shook her head. Two hours later, Mrs. Bentz was back with two dozen roses for Mrs. Swan, who shook her head again, this time in wonderment.   *September 22, 1971*

TAPING AN INTERVIEW

She (the young journalist from the nearby university) started her Japanese tape recorder and pointed the microphone in my direction. With a glance at her list of questions she began, "How do you feel about San Francisco?"

"I think it was a good idea," I replied. "In fact, San Francisco was one of the best ideas of Western man—Western in the American sense, of course. An oasis at the end of the long Overland trail, a sensibly sized city favored by God and Nature, spiced by the Italians, French and Chinese, run by the Irish, its cultural life enriched by remarkably philanthropic German Jews, a cultivated and European place at the edge of the American frontier. Imagine an outpost city that had Caruso in its opera company 65 years ago, Tetrazzini singing at Third and Market only a few years later and the Barrymores gracing its theaters."

Q: "What went wrong?"

A: "We allowed the world to intrude on paradise. Dorothy and the Wizard and all the other Kansans from everywhere discovered the Land of Oz and they brought a fatal disease called progress. The exclusive club opened its doors and in came the final wrecker, the automobile. We built bridges instead of barriers. Where we should have transformed San Francisco into a true island by building a deep moat along the San Mateo County line, we built free-ways. We traded greatness for bigness, and where the winds blew free there is only smog. Now comes the subway that will speed the flight from the city."

★ ★ ★

Q: "But surely there are some good things about the city today."

A: "Of course. The waterfront may yet be saved from itself. The food is still remarkably rich and varied—and expensive. There is no shortage of bars or people to drink in them with so many good reasons to get drunk. The life in the streets is fasci-nating—more so than in any other American city. We have some remarkably good-looking hookers, some remarkably talented street musicians. The museums are much less mediocre than they used to be. However, I see more people talking to themselves on the streets than I used to—a very bad sign. Union Street gets more plastic by the day, but Polk Street improves. However, we may all live to see the end of the cable cars—by attrition if not intent—and Golden Gate Park turned into a mini-park, with the rest devoted to underground parking."

★ ★ ★

Q: "You seem to think there are too many tall buildings, but haven't some of them provided open spaces—plazas—that weren't there before?"

A: "They have indeed, but have you ever tried to lounge in front of Bank of America? Guards run you off. Most of the new spaces are wasted by day and deserted by night. The Downtown Association, in its wisdom, circulates the startling news that there is more crime in the New York ghettos and slums than in the high-rise districts—meaning we should have more tall buildings and vote against Mr. Duskin's six-story height limit. Of course there is less crime among the high-rises—they are devoid of all life at night, even that. The Chamber of Commerce is spending a for-tune—perhaps $40,000—to defeat the height limit when it should be spending an equal amount to support it. Tourism is our biggest industry, but will the tourists continue to come here to look at more tall buildings? Every indication is that they won't."

★ ★ ★

Q: "When did San Francisco begin to change—for the worse, in your opinion?"

A: "Comparatively recently. Only 15 or so years ago, the city was still comparatively uncluttered and open. The skyline had a

209

decent proportion—graceful and light. When you look at photos of the skyline of 1957 and compare it with today's it is hard to believe you are looking at the same city, which of course you aren't. The old city grew more beautiful by accident, the new one is growing ugly by design. One turning point may have been when the Montgomery Block, one of our few truly historic buildings, was allowed to be torn down for a parking lot. Another may have occurred just the other day when a team of Soviet architects, touring the country, said that we have 'too many tall buildings' and that they preferred St. Louis. My God, St. Louis! We always took it for granted—as we took the Bay, the hills and the views for granted—that visiting Europeans would name San Francisco as their favorite American city. Now we can no longer count on that pat on the ego."

★   ★   ★

Q: "Do you have any solutions?"

A: "Only the usual ones, I'm afraid. We have to keep reminding ourselves that San Francisco is a small and precious place that has, or had, a special reputation all over the world. The quality of life is what is important, not the profits of promoters who look upon this enchanted city as just another hunk of real estate. We need a fresh viewpoint in City Hall—not that Mayor Alioto is an evil man who has lined his pockets. But he comes from a generation that still thinks bigness is greatness, whose idea of real success is a penthouse office on the 60th floor. There is still time, but like parking space, it's running out. I must agree with Ogden Nash that 'Progress was a good thing once but it went on too long.' "

October 10, 1971

By the way: Mission High is celebrating its 75th birthday with a big to-do at the school Nov. 12, organized by a group that includes Nelder, Geracimos and The Incomparable George Lemont . . . George: "All that talk about Mission being a tough school is hooey. Admission to the party will be four hubcaps from any late model car" . . . Nick: "The hard part is getting the word out to all the alumni" . . . George: "It's not hard to find them. They're still around working as cops, firemen or bartenders. It's the girls who are hard to find. The ones who aren't working as waitresses in tamale parlors or as meter maids in Grand Rapids are sitting over at Sweet's Ballroom, wondering where everybody went" . . . Nelder: "Didn't any Mission High grads go on to college?" . . . George: "I knew one and he's still a lousy barber" . . . Nelder: "Well, see you on the night of Nov. 12. I'm arriving in an unmarked car." And fully armed?   *October 22, 1971*

Fan-tastic: His daughter, Marcia, nominates her distinguished father, Dr. Adolphus A. Berger, for Football Nut of the Year, not that the competition for this title isn't keen . . . Monday night, in their comfortable digs on Buchanan near Pacific, Dr. Berger was watching ABC's Game of the Week while Woody Allen and his crew were in the street outside, filming "Play It Again, Sam." The entire neighborhood was gawking, but not Dr. Berger. He remained glued to the set . . . A few minutes later, Woody walked in and said "Could I use the phone?" "It's in there," motioned Dr. Berger without taking his eyes off the screen . . . During a commercial, the doctor called out "Say, Marcia, I think the kitchen is on fire." It was, and pretty soon 10 firemen trooped in and then out as Dr. Berger remained rooted to the set . . . I think he wins the title, all right, especially since the game was about as dull as they come.

November 19, 1971

1972

Here it's only Jan. 4, and we have a Loser of the Year, nominated by Judge Wayne Kanemoto of San Jose. Depressed because his wife left him over the holidays, this Loser ran a hose from his exhaust into his car and prepared to die. However, the hose caught fire and set the car ablaze, which attracted the attention of a passerby, who phoned police. At the emergency hospital, where the Loser was treated for slight burns, some marijuana fell out of his pocket, so he was taken to Judge Kanemoto's court, fined $100 and turned loose to face the new year.   *January 4, 1972*

BALLAD OF DIRTY HARRY

At the premiere of "Dirty Harry," the old Bay Mayor (he ain't what he used to be) rushed the stage to assure all filmmakers everywhere that they are welcome to go on using San Francisco as the setting for their epics. Mr. Alioto's remarks were occasioned by various complaints from old grumps, including this one, that the visiting hams clutter up the streets, damage landmarks (like the Alta Plaza steps) and require all manner of police assistance, in return for which S.F. gets a lot of free publicity of dubious value. In fairness, one should add that local extras are hired, and that the "Dirty Harry" opening raised $10,000 for the Police Activities League . . . "The Mayor of Los Angeles was recently complaining that San Francisco is stealing too much production from there," beamed the Mayor. "Well, I want to say that we'll continue to make pictures in San Francisco and we're not going to worry about a couple of chipped steps in Alta Plaza." Okay—54 Yorty or fight.

★ ★ ★

So I went to "Dirty Harry" to see what we're getting for their money. The title role is played by Clint Eastwood and that's good. How many cities have cops who look like Clint Eastwood? However, he has the same thing for lunch every day—a hot dog. That's bad for our image as a gourmet's paradise. He doesn't have a lady friend, which is good or bad, depending on your taste (his wife died in an auto crash "for no particular reason," he explains for no particular reason). He is called "Dirty Harry" in the department because he takes all the dirty jobs in homicide. He takes them because he likes them. He also prefers to work alone because he hates everybody, especially members of minority races.

★ ★ ★

The first thing you find out in "Dirty Harry" is that you're not safe anywhere in San Francisco. The opening shot shows a pretty girl swimming in the pool on the roof of the new Holiday Inn on Kearny. She is killed by one perfect shot from a sniper using a rifle with a scope on the roof of the Bank of America building. You can't get onto the roof of BofA without a pass, and a security guard remains with you at all times, but it's only a movie, isn't it?

The sniper wears a peace symbol on his belt, establishing him as a bad guy right there. He didn't know the girl he shot. He is out to terrorize San Francisco by killing people at random unless, he warns the Mayor, he gets $200,000 in those small bills. Next, he says, he will kill "a priest or two niggers," which sets a precise value on priests and blacks. To Dirty Harry's disgust, the Mayor is ready to pay. The Mayor of S.F. is a trim fellow with a full head of hair, one of the miracles that result from re-election.

★ ★ ★

Here's the sniper on a North Beach rooftop. He's about to shoot a black fag licking an ice cream cone he bought at Mama's and is eating in Washington Square, but the police helicopter spots him. He flees. That night he kills a priest from Peter & Paul, the only church named after two-thirds of a pop singing group (Mary is inside). The Mayor panics and tells Harry to deliver the $200,000 and the sniper tells Harry how to deliver it.

First our hero has to go to the Forest Hill Muni Station—on foot. Then he has to run to the hot dog stand at Aquatic Park (maybe this picture should've been called "Hot Dog"). From there, Harry is instructed to pant his way to the cross on Mt. Davidson, where, for a bit of local color, a homosexual makes a pass at him. The sniper shows up with a machine gun and kicks the hell out of

213

Harry, breaking ribs. Harry knifes the sniper in the leg, leading to a great shot of the sniper pulling out the knife for about 30 minutes.

Now you really have to pay attention. The sniper goes to an emergency hospital, gets fixed up and limps away (in real life, whatever that is, he'd have been held right there for the police). Then Harry finds out where the sniper lives—in Kezar Stadium, of course—and breaks into his hideout. He also tortures the sniper just a little bit to find out where he hid the kidnaped girl. I think I forgot to mention the kidnaped girl, but it doesn't matter. She's dead.

★ ★ ★

For this, Harry is summoned by the District Attorney (John Ferdon lives!), the kind of guy who wears his suit jacket but has his collar unbuttoned. If he's warm why doesn't he take his jacket off? In a pitch to the lawnorder types, the D.A. barks to Harry "Where you been? You never heard of Miranda and Escobedo? After what you did, we couldn't hold that guy even if you catch him." (Snorts a real-life member of Ferdon's staff: "Hogwash. He could be held on half a dozen charges, starting with assault on a police officer.")

So Harry tracks the sniper to Marin, pulls out his Magnum 44 and snarls "This is the most powerful handgun in the world, punk. It can blow your head off." It does the job. Then Harry throws his S.F. Police Badge into the Bay, but don't ask me why.

It's good publicity for San Francisco, isn't it? What more do you have to know?   *January 9, 1972*

Bookie bit: The unlisted phone in her office rang yesterday and Mrs. Alta Russell picked it up, said "Hello" and heard a voice rattle off "Chocolate Tree in the first—the usual—see ya later, honey," click. A moment longer and Mrs. Russell would have been able to say "Boy oh boy, do YOU have a wrong number!" for she happens to be secretary to Atty. Gen. Evelle Younger . . . Curious, Mrs. Russell checked the Racing Form and sure enough, Chocolate Tree was running in the first at Santa Anita. Not only that, the horse won, paying $13.60, $6.40, $3.40—and now she's worried: "Suppose he calls again and wants his money?"

January 12, 1972

SAN FRANCISCO NOW

A letter from an old-time native San Franciscan begins: "My wife and I have moved to Calistoga. It isn't much of a place but it never was. It's less painful to live here than in a place that was something once and never will be again."

★   ★   ★

My old friend wasn't trying to be chic—he's not the type. I say that hastily because it's currently fashionable to knock San Francisco, "The City That Was Fun While It Lasted" (title of a magazine piece). As I said a few Sundays ago, writers who used to lavish praise on this city are now criticizing it, a remark that drew some angry "Et tu, Brute" letters from San Franciscans. I plead guilty, although, as Nelson Algren once said as he belted Chicago, "You have to have loved a city a long time before you earn the right to knock it." I've loved this city a long time, and still do, although my credentials are suspect: I was born in Sacramento. However, I was conceived at the 1915 Exposition on the Marina; my parents spent the summer here and I was born next April. Not as good as being born in Golden Gate Park in April '06, but not too bad, either.

★   ★   ★

"The worst San Francisco can get is still better than any place else."

★   ★   ★

These words were uttered about 25 years ago by a native, Jerry Johnstone, and a lot of people cheered when he uttered them. They struck me as boosterism of the worst kind—the kind of statement that makes a city smug, complacent and indolent. All of which we are. Why, it was only a short time back that Mayor Alioto beamed, "The city has never been in better shape!" Maybe he meant Vancouver, Wash., or Missoula, Mont., but I doubt it. And yet, and yet:

★   ★   ★

Messrs. Johnstone and Alioto may not be so wide of the mark (or fairmont). In truth, it seems to be the very old and the very young who complain about San Francisco—the old because they remember what it was, the young because they don't like what it is. The in-betweens—the latecomers like Wells Twombly, who knows what Detroit is like, and Allan Jacobs, who knows what Cleveland is like—are better able to see San Francisco whole and they like what they see. And the more sophisticated the tourist, the more likely he is to be charmed and fascinated. It's the narrow minds from the dry valleys who raise blue-nosed hell about "the dirty hippies" and "the filth" of Broadway, holler about the prices and write to the editor that they'll never set foot here again. (I believe them.)

★   ★   ★

I don't think it's possible to complain too much about the disastrous direction this city is taking, but it is also refreshing—and healthy for the perspective—to listen to outsiders. Last week, a Baroness from Paris and a publisher's wife from London were here for the first time, and since they have been almost everywhere else in the world, and appeared to be women of great candor, it was impossible to discount their enthusiasm. In short, they were "mad for this city." They thought Gump's was "the greatest store of its kind" they'd seen anywhere, and spent plenty to back up the opinion. Chinatown charmed them, as did the baby quail at Empress of China. They giggled over tales of Lillie Coit's firemen and her nozzle atop Telegraph Hill, they couldn't wait to visit what's left of the Barbary Coast, they "adored" the street musicians, they "can't wait" to come back . . .

★   ★   ★

Your next impatient comment is absolutely true: What a tourist, especially a rich one, sees of San Francisco, especially from a suite at the Fairmont, is not what San Francisco is all about—except in one not-so-small way. If we are going to continue to throw up— phrase used advisedly—these new buildings and hotels and maintain some position in the great race for the tourist dollar, it IS reassuring that these sophisticated, well-heeled visitors still find San Francisco no end fascinating. However, we may have gone about as fur as we can go, to employ an old Kansas City observation (Kansas City equals Mr. Haas equals two towers on Russian Hill). There is a 12 per cent vacancy rate in our office buildings right now, and emptiness in many a hotel hallway. Even Donald Pritzker of Hyatt House, an "up" kind of a guy, looks worried. A new convention center will help, the problem being where to house the people still living in Yerba Buena, right? Where you house them is in the empty hotel rooms that have been built for the delegates who aren't coming because the convention center can't be built until the city finds housing for the ————. Right?

★   ★   ★

San Francisco today, suffering from a San Andreas of the mind: We can't be what we were but we don't like what we are. This rich city that (shame!) is closing branch libraries, curtailing bus service, running rotten jails, letting the amenities go to hell and remodeling Candlestick Park. Fat cat city where the sky is the limit for

216

some (the builders) and the gutter is too good for the others (the losers). It was on the Bay Bridge the other day that a young man studied the San Francisco skyline and then Oakland's and murmured, "You know, San Francisco doesn't look as different as it used to"—and that's a fact. *February 13, 1972*

The spirit of adventure lives on! Last Tuesday night, two young brothers named Don and Gary Wieneke, who work for Earth magazine, lowered their bicycles by rope into a manhole at Main and Market, and then rode across the Bay through the BART tube, emerging 90 minutes later at the Naval Supply Depot in Oakland! "We rode part of the way on the three-foot walkway," reports Don, "and the rest of the way between the tracks. Nothing to it. And we didn't see a soul" (they then phoned a friend in S.F. to pick them up in his car) . . . A BART spokesman, sounding agitated, confirms that the trip was possible "but only because the big gate at the Embarcadero entrance to the tube was down for a couple of days last week. No, I don't know where the guards were—but what really bothers us is that the alarm system apparently didn't work." *February 28, 1972*

ADAM'S RIB TO WOMEN'S LIB

Last Sunday I wrote about bores and succeeded only in being boring. To paraphrase the sainted McLuhan, the tedium is the message—and today's is Women's Liberation, the subject that won't go away. Whatever anyone writes about it is likely to be wrong, as I have shown on many a painful occasion. Praise the movement and you hear from male chauvinist pigs, to be referred to hereinafter as MCP's. Knock it and you hear from the women, and a more articulate bunch of Mss., or whatever the plural is, has never raised Hugh N. Cry. Make jokes about Women's Lib—and you are battered from both sides. A losing proposition.

* * *

Like everybody else, I think of myself as a person who is prejudiced against nobody except prejudiced people. "Some of my best friends are" and have been all kinds, especially women, and that goes for my best enemies, too. But it is difficult to throw off the shackles of an older generation, and even if I don't watch it, I find myself falling into the trap of stereotyped thinking. For example, I grew up with, and have been the butt of, ethnic jokes all my life and developed a tolerance for them early in the game; it was the only way to survive in my Irish-Catholic neighborhood. One outgrowth of this was the acquisition of a thick skin about jokes that more sensitive people find offensive. If the joke is on me, I can laugh in defensive reflex. That doesn't mean I should, or that others can.

★ ★ ★

Which brings us to women, liberated, M-1. I'm with them all the way, which needn't be said; actions speak louder, and so on. Also due to the benign teachings of FemLib, I can no longer say truthfully, "I have always liked women better than men." Today, that is condescending and a non sequitur. The sentence now reads: "I have always liked people better than people." An entire vocabulary must be unlearned, starting with that nice word, "girl"; having learned my lesson well. I snickered at Trader Vic's last week to hear an 80-year-old woman ask the waiter, "Where's the little girl's room?" Dumb old unliberated b——d and I don't mean blond.

★ ★ ★

Okay, we have come to the crux. "Broad." It's a word that women seem to find more offensive than most anti-feminist terms that sound harsher, to male ears. Having used and heard it in connotations ranging from love to ridicule I find it comparatively innocuous—especially since the most cultivated woman I know describes someone as "a great broad" who is warm, salty and big-hearted. However, Women's Lib is young and its more militant members are not ready for the long view. Since man does not live by broad alone, I respect that.

★ ★ ★

The biggest batch of angry mail I have received in years resulted from my printing a bumper strip that I described as pretty funny: "Support Women's Lib—Take a Broad To Lunch." In finding that amusing in any way whatsoever, my generation gap was showing. Still, that dumb strip has all the elements of a certain kind of American humor: irreverence, vulgarity, shock value, terseness. Of the shock value there is no doubt, for an avalanche of mail poured in from Libbers, most of them wanting to know if I thought "Support Civil Rights—Take A Nigger To Lunch" is funny, too. I then made a really big mistake and lost my temper. "If those broads think they have the same problems in this society as blacks, they still haven't got their heads on straight."

218

The next ton of mail was appropriately abusive. "You have achieved a low in social criticism previously attained only by Eric Hoffer" (Ms. Nancy Musser). "If even my morning cup of coffee with my trusted friend Herb Caen must taste of intolerance then there really is no hope" (Georgia Seibert). "My husband's reaction: 'If Herb Caen thinks that he, as a white male, understands the problems of either blacks or women, he doesn't have his head on straight' (LaVonne Bergman). "I suggest to you 'Support Male Chauvinism—Take A Pig To Lunch'" (Jeanne Whitehouse). "You have revealed yourself for what you are, Count Marco in a clever disguise . . . It so happens that the problems of women are much worse than the problems of blacks and have been for thousands of years" (Mean Dana). "As long as three-dot perverts refer to women as broads, those women are niggers . . . they are object-defined, thanks to the coercive power of the mindless typists who carry the in-human line to the people via greedia-media, and what's your price, fritz?" (Frank Scott).

And so on by the hundreds, some of them amused (Catherine Sang found the offending strip "a satire on pseudo-liberal hypocrisy"), most of them intelligent and a very few speaking up for Men's Lib ("Let a Broad Take YOU To Lunch"). But there is no doubt that I gave offense and I apologize. Meanwhile, I was impressed-depressed by the tone of bleak certitude and self-righteousness in most of the letters. Maybe some day we can all relax and enjoy being people together even unto laughing at ourselves.

April 30, 1972

Superstars: There was adulation in the air at Enrico's Coffee House a midnight ago. At a sidewalk table sat John Lennon and Yoko Ono, dressed in somber black, drinking Ukrainian coffee. Freaks stood around, a few yards away, and simply stared. A girl dashed to the table to present a flower to John. A not-at-all-young stockbroker grabbed Lennon's arm and said unexpectedly, "You're a great guy!" The inescapable panhandlers sidled up for handouts and got them at $5 a crack. Every few seconds, a young person would approach the Lennons, murmur "We love you," and vanish. Bob Stafford, the street clarinetist, wailed "The Saints" as John observed in Liverpudlian: "It's nice, i'n't, that yoong fellers still take up the clareenet." When the Lennons drove off, a young girl ran after the car, vainly offering a joint as a Police Sergeant drifted past on a motorcycle . . . A very San Francisco scene.

★ ★ ★

Earlier that evening, the Lennons, and their local close friend, Craig Pyes, the co-editor of SunDance magazine, had dined sumptuously at Mme. Cecilia Chiang's Mandarin in Ghirardelli Square, looking out over the quiet Bay and the old ships at rest.

"We're crazy about this city," said John, peering at the view through his bottle-thick glasses. "First time we came here, we walked the streets all day—all over town—and nobody hassled us. People smiled, friendly-like, and we knew we could live here. We'd like to keep our place in Greenwich Village and have an apartment here, God and the Immigration Service willing . . . Los Angeles? That's just a big parking lot where you buy a hamburger for the trip to San Francisco."

They raved over Mme. Chiang's newest delicacy, scallop soup. "The food in this city is fantastic," John went on. "Better than London. You know, more variety. And the beautiful old houses and the strange light. We've never been in a city with light like this. We sit in our hotel room for hours, watching the fog come in, the light change."

Peking duck, mandarin style, came wrapped in paper thin pancakes. "We drove here from New York," John continued. "Yoko and I probably have seen more of the United States than most Americans. United Statesians? When I was a Beatle, I didn't see anything—whoosh-whoosh-whoosh. In Nevada, we got out of the car and rolled in the sand. We'd never seen a desert before."

In answer to a question: "Yes, we want to live here permanently. There's violence, sure, and it's scary, sometimes, but there are so many good people, so many chances for change. Not like England, which is dead. Sure, we'd be happy to become American citizens. We're not here on a tax dodge, you know."

The Immigration Service will make a decision in November on whether the Lennons can stay here. "We're in limbo till then," lamented Yoko. "It's hard to settle down, to write, to work, when you don't know where home will be." A kind, gentle, soft-spoken couple. I think we'd be lucky to get them.   *July 21, 1972*

A CAN OF WORMS

The Yerba Buena Center project is a scandal, of course. Any project that has been stuck on dead center for this many years would have to be a scandal—although in this case, nobody has been caught with his hand in the till. This is a superstinker of a peculiarly San Francisco type: a scandal of ineptitude. And the only "heroes" had their job made easy for them by the unbelievable performances of the "villains."

★　★　★

Yerba Buena Center, a tourist-geared dream of a convention center and sports arena surrounded by forests of hotels and office buildings (and garages), has been a dream for decades. Wipe out the crummy old dumps South of Market, get rid of those disgraceful winos, clean up Skid Road and replace these sightsores with The World of Tomorrow! It began as the Swig Plan in the Fifties (Ben owns a little property in the area). Shelley and Alioto improved on it. The late Justin Herman and his Redevelopment Agency carried it a bit farther. New hotels sprang up overnight to take care of the huge conventions that would flock in . . .

So what went wrong?

★　★　★

Forgive me if I'm about to go over familiar ground, but I get a little sick of hearing people say, as a society woman said the other night: "Who cares about those old drunks? Kick 'em out and start building." I think she would have voted for gas chambers. I get a little tired of hearing Supervisors say "Wolinsky and Kline are unreasonable. A couple of punks. Who are they to make major policy decisions? Every time we have a deal they up the ante." And it's annoying to hear conservative lawyers, pals of the Mayor, state publicly that "(Judge) Stanley Weigel is incompetent and emotionally disturbed" . . . The last refuge of the sore loser is character assassination.

★　★　★

Okay, here we go: The Feds (represented by HUD) have thrown $43 million into Yerba Buena for acquiring the land—but there's a humanitarian quirk in the Federal law: you can't kick people out of their homes, EVEN IF THEY'RE POOR AND DRUNK, without supplying other housing, in this case low-cost. And not the same kind of housing, either. The law says it must be "decent, safe and sanitary." The Redevelopment Agency pledged itself to build 1,500 units, already a compromise figure. In one of the major minor mysteries of the modern world, Redevelopment did not build the units. So in 1969, Sidney Wolinsky and J. Anthony Kline, public advocacy lawyers, representing the displaced tenants, filed suit in Federal Court to stop the project. A Judge could do no less than uphold them, no matter how he felt about Yerba Buena. The law was and is the law.

★ ★ ★

Riddle upon enigma: the late Justin Herman, the Chamber of Commerce, the hotel people, the Convention Bureau, the Mayor all consider Yerba Buena to be of the highest priority. So why, back in 1969, wasn't work begun on the 1,500 units of housing to guarantee a green light from HUD?

Says J. Anthony Kline: "The city doesn't want poor people. Do tourists want to look at poor people?" Says a high city official who knew Justin Herman well: "If there's a villain, it's Justin. He was damned if he was going to build those units. He never believed the Feds would make him. Bear in mind that Redevelopment has never been interested in housing—only in industrial and commercial properties."

Says Bob Rumsey, Herman's successor: "We think low cost housing is a good idea. It just takes time, you know, and money." Note: The Feds will pay for 700 units in Yerba Buena for displacees. "We have found enough decent housing to take care of everybody—at least we think it is." Wolinksy: "It isn't." James Price, local HUD chief: "It's like an onion; you just keep peeling and peeling."

Henri Lewin, prominent hotel man: "For Heaven's sake, build the 1,500 units! Where's the Mayor on this? The law is the law and if we don't get Yerba Buena pretty soon we're all in big trouble."

★ ★ ★

Enter Supreme Court Justice William O. Douglas. Early in July, he ruled that work on Yerba Buena must halt because once more the law has been ignored: a study of Yerba Buena's impact on the environment—a requirement of the National Environmental Policy Act—has not been made. In defiance, our Supervisors voted $2.7 million to relocate the perfectly good Howard St. sewer line because—Catch 22!—the sewer would interfere with an underground convention hall that can't be built until 1,500 low-cost units are available. Death wishes all over the place.

You may also have forgotten that "your" Supervisors—not you—voted a $225 million bond issue for Yerba Buena's many wonders, a project that objective observers figure will cost $400 million when finished, if ever.

The latest insanity came last Monday when the Supervisors (Kopp and Molinari sanely objecting) voted $22,000 for a model of Yerba Buena and $29,000 for printing and mailing to attract future conventions to the Center that isn't there. Oh, doctor!

July 23, 1972

Most farfetched press release of the week, from the Warner-Elektra-Atlantic recording people here: "Tower of Power, a 10-member rock group, will make their last Bay Area appearance prior to the nationwide tour at the Frank Lloyd Wright–designed Marin Veterans' Memorial Theater in the Marin Civic Center where the sounds of last year's fatal shootout which catapulted Angela Davis to international fame still reverberate." Take the man who wrote that off whatever he's on.

July 30, 1972

ONCE AND FUTURE KING

Oh, there were giants on the earth in those days, child—giants of jazz, roistering their way from one end of the land to the other, making love to their instruments, killing themselves with bad booze, sleeping the sleep of the dead on all-night buses, yet somehow managing to become immortal while dying young . . .

There was Bunny Berigan with the fat tone and the vibrato that could make you cry, especially in "I Can't Get Started," passion in his heart and bad gin in the pitcher under his chair. Tommy Dorsey, who had an incomparably sweet tone on the trombone (so what if he couldn't improvise), dead in his prime of a piece of steak stuck in his gullet. Brother Jimmy, a fine saxman and two-fisted juicer. The beguiling clarinetist, Artie Shaw, who didn't care all that much about the business; he made his pile, lost his hair and got out, seven wives later.

And then there was and is the king of them all, the most dazzling of clarinetists, builder of powerful bands, perfectionist, the only one remaining of his golden era (back to Bix) who is still playing, still able to get around his difficult instrument, still willing to blow in an age that considers him as an anachronism till he picks up his horn . . .

★　★　★

Right, Benny Goodman, 63-or-something. He comes to mind (he is often on the mind of our generation) because he is playing next Saturday night at the Concord Music Festival. King Benny the Good, the kid who came up from the South Side of Chicago and began recording while he was still in knee pants, the leader who rescued us from what might have been a lifetime of Guy Lombardo. He did for jazz what the Beatles did for rock—popularized it without cheapening it. Without Goodman, there may never have been the so-called "swing-era"—with the big bands that—sorry, old-timer!—are never coming back.

★   ★   ★

The Swing era: how short it really was, and how strange its pied pipers. T. Dorsey was mean, Glenn Miller square, and Jimmy would as soon swing on you as shake your hand, Bunny was sozzled at all times, Artie insulted his fans as "idiots," and as for Benny—well, the word "dour" was invented for him. When a musician in his band played badly, Benny froze him with an infamous glare known as "The Ray." He was tight and a little uptight but the years have been kind and he is now much more relaxed.

Those old fans who first heard BG during the "Let's Dance" programs of 1934 will never forget the experience. The theme, a clever adaptation of von Weber's "Invitation to the Dance," was first played by Al (The Wrong) Goodman and his Mantovani-type orchestra. Then Xavier Cugat played the theme Latin-style—after which came the moment we all waited for: the BG band, with Krupa, Bunny, Toots Mondello, Hymie Shertzer, playing the same tune in the pulsating style that soon came to epitomize "swing" (never before had we heard a studio audience scream).

★   ★   ★

A Goodmaniac, a clarinut: I coined those words in 1934 to describe—me. In my basement, I have Benny preserved in wax, the hundreds upon hundreds of 78s I bought as fast as they came out. In '35, I was part of the awestruck crowd that heard the Goodman band in person at McFadden's ballroom in Oakland. The summer of '36 I spent at the Palomar ballroom at Third and Vermont (who could forget?) in L.A., bellied up to the bandstand, falling in love with Singer Helen Ward, dying a little as she disappeared into the night with Announcer Ken Frogley . . . On a one-nighter in Sacramento in '37, the high point of my life: Benny allowed me to drive him to the gig—a ballroom several miles out of town—while Gene Krupa sat on my friend Jerry Bundsen's lap in my tiny Plymouth coupe. "Careful," Jerry would gasp to me at every corner. "I don't care about us, but—."

★   ★   ★

We Goodman fans were a fiercely loyal, narrow-minded lot. We disliked Glenn Miller because his band did all sorts of mickey mouse tricks—"a funny-hat band," BG called it—and also because he was passing Benny in popularity. We sneered at Tommy because he featured wan singers like Sinatra and dumb vocal groups. Benny was always pure. No tricks, no trumpet sections turning this way and that, no standup sax sections. Just hard, driving music.

Memories: sitting on the dance floor in the Mark's Peacock Court ('40) for an hour's nightly recital by Benny and a sextet that included the unforgettable Charlie Christian, so soon to die. Benny at the '39 Fair with one of his lesser bands but still, on the seventh riffing chorus of "One O'Clock," moving the needle on the UC seismograph. And now ('72) Benny at the Concord Music Festival with a small group that may or may not be worthy . . .

Not that it matters. When he starts playing, we Goodmaniacs and clarinuts will be back in another world, listening to the distant drums of Krupa and that incomparable clarinet rising higher and higher out of a band that could truly make the earth move.

August 6, 1972

Licentiousness: They're getting sloppier and sloppier over there at Motor Vehicles about "dirty" personalized license plates. The best or worst yet appears on Wallace Reed's new Toyota, and since this is still a family newspaper (whose?) I can only say that it's The Word That Won The War in pig Latin.

More car sports: Vince Perrin, the Stockton newsman who has "BYLINE" on his Continental, says he applied originally for "ANGST" but "that had already been claimed by a San Franciscan, naturally." Touche! . . . The local car with license plates VXX 954, notes Marilyn Borovy, bears a sign reading "Mafia Staff Car— Keepa U Hands Offa." Over in Sausalito, Eleanor Cruikshank saw a beautiful blue Rolls-Royce filled with hip types and license-plated "GREED." "GIDIUP" isn't a bad license plate for a Pinto and George Widener spotted it on 19th Avenue. And I happened to see a "Bald Is Beautiful" bumper strip on a car driven by a man who was bald, period.

Other mild weirdies: On Corbett Ave., Robin Jones sees this red Mach 1 Mustang with plates "IM1 RU2," and one what? Is it the old Army joke? Meanwhile, don't bother to ask Financier Dean Dillman why his plates read "BOGEY"; if you do he chortles "Because I'm not up to par!" Har . . . And I'm really fond of this sign noticed by Sharon McClure on the back of a VW bus: "Mach Turtle."

August 29, 1972

WE'LL NEVER GO THERE ANYMORE

Since it closes forever after today, I decided to give Playland-at-the-Beach one more chance to kill me.

Parking my Mazda Rotary where the city meets the sea, I stepped up to that familiar open window at the corner of Balboa and ordered a Bull Pupp Enchilada, "Famous for 49 Years." This one tasted a little younger and had plenty of zing. Bull Pupps are not for kids.

Then I walked up the block to the It's It place and had a 40-cent corn dog, with plenty of mustard and catsup, and topped that with an It's It itself: the fabled sweetmeat made of two oatmeal cookies with vanilla ice cream between, the whole covered with chocolate sauce and frozen.

The It's It didn't taste as good as I remembered it from years past but hardly anything does. For one thing, the ice cream between the cookies should be flat. This was round, scooped out like a golf ball and never did soften into a manageable mess.

Still, as junk food, it's right up there with Taco Bell and Shakey's Pizza, and dyspepsia was fast setting in. I had planned to get a little heartsick over the closing of Playland, but heartburn would have to do.

★   ★   ★

I wouldn't want to keep you away from today's last rites, but Playland looks awful. Along with the familiar aroma of salt air, popcorn, tobacco and greasy food there is the smell of death. Somebody along the way must have bled the place dry, letting it fall apart like railroad owners trying to discourage the passenger trade.

As I stood on the sidewalk, gnawing at my It's It, a station wagon with Oregon plates pulled up to the curb and out stepped a Norman Rockwell family—youngish parents and three neat little pigtailed girls. They stared in dismay at the fading and fallen signs, the grimy windows, the debris on streets and sidewalks. After a long silence, one of the little girls took her father's hand and said "Let's go, Daddy."

They got back in the wagon and drove off. As a San Franciscan I felt embarrassed. "When Playland closes," an old-timer points out, "San Francisco will be the last major city in the country without an amusement park." It has been for some time now.

★   ★   ★

I ran into Marty Davis, a friendly fellow whose fate it is to be Playland's last operator; he has done the best he can but the business hasn't been there and now Jeremy Ets-Hokin takes over the huge property for an apartment complex. When I told Davis what I had just ingested for lunch he whooped "Nobody has ever eaten a Bull Pupp Enchilada, a corn dog, an It's It, ridden on our merry-go-round and lived!"

Accepting the challenge, I boarded a painted wooden horse on the 56-year-old Loof merry-go-round, one of the world's best and certainly the dizziest. "This thing goes so fast," said Davis, bobbing up and down on an adjoining steed, "that my kids are afraid to ride it. About 20 miles an hour. Just think, 68 moving animals, wood, not plastic, and four chariots, a thing of beauty."

★   ★   ★

The fading midway, barely alive with yesterday's laughter. The Diving Bell, a ride I never did like, stood suspended in rust over a pool of fetid water and beer cans. At the old rifle range, George Whitney's first concession 50 years ago, I emptied a load of .22 shells at moving targets so grimy you could barely see them. But the Dodgers—Dodgems or Bump'ems in other parks—were still running, crashing around amid the familiar smell of graphite to keep the metal floor slippery.

In the corner of the Fun House, hideous Laughin' Sal (already bought by Ets-Hokin) bobbed up and down, cackling. As kids, we used to cover our ears as we passed Sal, and we did so again. Inside, I began the long three-story climb to the top of the finest, longest, humpiest wooden slide in the world. On the lane next to me sat a little blonde girl, staring down the long slide and screaming in terror as her mother tried to get her going.

"Tell her it's safe," the mother implored me. "It isn't kid," I said as I whooshed off. "You gotta be crazy to ride this thing," slide, bump, slide, bump, crash into the wall at the bottom.

★   ★   ★

Old Playland. I suppose only those who knew it in the glory days will really miss it, and part of the glory disappeared when the scary, rickety roller coaster, the Big Dipper, was torn down in the late 1950s, for what is an amusement park without a roller coaster? After a show or on a weekend, we'd ride the Dipper in clouds of shrieks, losing our breath on the first dizzying descent and never finding it again till the end, when it was "Let's go again!" There was the slide that you took into Topsy's Roost to dance to Ellis Kimball, the milk bottles that wouldn't fall over even when you hit them, Skee Ball (delightful game) and the prizes you gave your girl in return for her admiring gaze . . .

Goodbye to all that, to part of our youth, and like that youth, we expected Playland to last forever. It is an odd, sad feeling to have outlived it.   *September 4, 1972*

THE MOVING FINGER

He had beaten the odds so many times that I thought he might even win The Big One, but nobody does, even multimillionaires, and so Louis Lurie lies dead at 84. His sycophantic acquaintances, and he had many, called him "Uncle Louie." The late A.P. Giannini, who paternalized him while supplying easy loans, called him "Luigi." He would announce himself on the phone as "Doctor Lurie," for reasons never explained. In many ways, he was a baffling man, this epitome of the Horatio Alger Legend, an easy laugher whose eyes suddenly could turn cold, a man who enjoyed seeing his name and picture in the newspapers and yet was essentially private and lonely. He knew who his real friends were, and they were few. There were many after his money and he knew who they were, too.

★   ★   ★

A rich man has died, and what is the significance? The cliché about an era ending is true, as always, and not all that interesting. The San Francisco Louis Lurie helped to build as a real estate tycoon has changed almost beyond recognition and, not surprisingly, he resented the change. He was conservative to the core—the stubborn conservatism of the poor boy who struck it rich. His interests, aside from money, were few. In unguarded moments, the eyes that usually twinkled would look back for a moment at his impoverished past. The fear of being broke again never leaves those who experienced it at a time when to be poor was a disgrace. It explains a lot about the very rich of a certain age.

★   ★   ★

Hollywood's central casting, in its palmiest days, could not have created a millionaire who looked more like one. The facade was perfect: the pince-nez perched on his nose with those engaging Foxy Grandpa eyes behind them. The homburg was worn at a rakish angle, the shirts were tailored of Sulka's finest silk, and the suits never varied: black or dark gray with silk piping on the vests, lapels and cuffs—his only sartorial foible. The suits were made, year after year for half a century, by the firm of Edlin & Regolo in the Russ Building, which, ironically, went out of business only two months ago. The Lurie limousine was a nine-passenger leather-topped 1960 Cadillac driven by Chauffeur Herman Cameron. The Lurie hobby was backing Broadway shows that smelled like hits. He had little interest, financial or otherwise, in opera, the symphony or museums. "Too high-tone," he'd say. "Not my people."

       ★   ★   ★

Louis Lurie, creature of habit and habitat, a colorful figure, humorous in manner. In his day, getting up in the world was to be taken literally. When I first met him, he was living in mirrored and gilded splendor in the penthouse of the Sir Francis Drake (in fact, his luncheon guest that day was his old friend, Herbert Hoover). Still moving up, he selected 2100 Pacific, an elegant apartment building, as his next abode. The fact that 2100 Pacific was filled didn't stop him: he simply bought the building and kicked out the people occupying the floor he desired.

       ★   ★   ★

The Lurie legend, the legendary Lurie who lunched at Jack's restaurant almost daily since 1916, presiding like a proud papa over his table under the stairs, ordering for everyone (yesterday and last night, the table stood empty, a floral arrangement on it). Whenever you walked into Jack's, you peeked to the right to see who Lurie had as guests that day—Gertrude Lawrence or Noel Coward, Somerset Maugham or Arthur Godfrey, Maurice Chevalier or Sammy Davis. Sometimes it was only politicians or newspaper bums, as he called us. He was unabashed about his love for publicity—getting your name and picture in the paper was a sign of success. When he was angry with me, which was quite often, he would call me "Herbert." We had a bad falling-out over a proposed cultural center, and he barked on the phone one morning: "Herbert, I never want to see my name in your goddam column again"—pause—"for the next few days."

       ★   ★   ★

Louis Lurie, a man to be missed. He had this thing about riding alone in the elevator of 333 Montgomery, the building he built. "Get out," he'd snap at people trying to enter with him. The building itself, torn down for the new Bank of America, was a replica of 333 No. Michigan in Chicago, in front of which, according to Lurie legend, he sold Chicago's first Hearst newspaper as a crippled newsboy. In some versions, the Imperial Hearst himself came by and bought the first copy with a $20 gold piece. When his son, Bobby, was 10, Father Lurie gave him a $10 check for being a good boy; Bobby went from store to store in the neighborhood, but nobody would cash a check for such a small boy. "Dad," said Bobby, handing it back, "your credit is no good."

★   ★   ★

And so it ends. The story of his death and his picture were on the front page—he would have liked that. And when we go to Jack's for lunch, we will still instinctively glance over toward that table under the stairs. But from now on, it will be occupied by mere mortals. *September 8, 1972*

THE OCTOBER CITY

Thick slabs of midday sunshine between layers of misty gray, dried leaves crackling underfoot like potato chips, Sunday picnics in secret corners of Golden Gate Park with only the squirrels to spy and beg, daisies growing in white profusion around well-kept houses on Terrific Heights corners, and out in the Bay, an aircraft carrier fresh from Vietnam sliding slowly past the Marina, harbinger of death casting ugly shadows across the white sailboats . . .

★   ★   ★

October, best of all months in this city where it is always October, opera and football sounds, autumn leaves on mantelpieces above crackling logs, antique mirrors reflecting candlelight and good wine—this rich city, San Francisco, this great eating and entertaining place spread across the hills, indolent, self-gratifying, glorying in past triumphs, hiding the poverty behind velvet skirts and down alleys where even the police are afraid to go, living its little ingrown life . . . A terrific city for the well-to-do, not even such a bad city to be a failure in, there's this tradition of largesse, of noblesse oblige, of "Here, my good man, take this quarter, and spend it wisely."

★   ★   ★

A good walking city. You can stroll in the Mission, near the dry and dying palm trees, and sniff the tortillas. In Chinatown, mingle with the tourists, drink an Orange Julius, buy a toy cable car, eat a nickel sugar doughnut made right there. Near Mt. Sutro, the walking is good along middle-class streets with lawns and gardens and the kids playing at dusk with badminton racquets and shuttlecocks ("They don't roll under the cars like balls do"). Superstud young men, stripped to the waist, play touch football in

Lafayette Square while the uniformed nannies parade past, pushing expensive babies in expensive prams . . . Only Haight St., poor Haight, still seems unalive, forgotten, menacing as Ashbury climbs the hill into lush greenery.

★　★　★

October morn, the foghorns blowing, good old Chron on the doorstep, coffee bubbling in one of Tom Cara's Italian espresso makers. For years I arose at the crack of dawn to the cracks of Don, but Mr. Sherwood has seen fit to retire, leaving some of us bereft. Now I get by with KMPX-FM, which now and then rewards us with a little of Benny the Good and Fats, the wonderful Waller. But remember, on those dark mornings, how Don used to remind us to turn our headlights off after we got to work? Think of the batteries he kept from running down. It was his own that finally went.

I joined the rat race down Geary Blvd., a street that looks like it belongs somewhere else. On gray mornings, ghosts of dead Victorians stir; gone forever the beautiful handiwork of anonymous carpenters with Gothic souls. In the Tenderloin, slim-hipped black dudes in wild threads and rakish hats getting in and out of $25,000 custom-made Cads and Continentals—how do they do it, what's the story?

★　★　★

I park at the Pickwick and start walking. A good day: a stranger smiles at you for no particular reason, a car stops to let you by and you feel warm about the driver. A drunk finds a dollar bill on the sidewalk—terrific. You drop a quarter into a can held by a Black Panther who says "Free breakfasts for kids." How can you be against free breakfasts for kids?

On Market, the noise is maddening. Every few feet, a hardhat is jamming a pneumatic drill into the pavement, beatific smile on face. Is he getting his jollies, does the rhythmic pounding turn him on? It's a thought. A sloppy-looking teen-age girl slips me a card for a massage parlor where there's "more than a massage, you oughta try it." If the place also had a fortune teller would the medium be the massage or the masseur? A Little Old Lady cooed at a pigeon that cooed back, and a midnight cowboy minced past, looking middle-aged at midday.

I crossed Market, wondering how it will look when all the trees are planted and presumably growing and BART is rumbling underfoot and the beautiful old Arthur Putnam lampposts are glowing. Meanwhile, the holes dug for the trees are filling up with trash because this rich city with its $35 million worth of Market St.

231

beautification can't afford trash receptacles. How much can they cost?

*　*　*

A terrific October dusk, with just enough smog to make the sunset fiery, cataclysmic, dangerous. The craggy top of Bank of America's World (Yet) Headquarters caught the rays and turned into a pillar of gold. Is this a golden age for the golden city by the Gate? Will somebody look back someday on San Francisco October 1972 and say "Wasn't it great?" or "You should have been there"? The lights brightened on the great bridges and I stepped into a bar to ponder the problem over a martini. It was a fine martini, of course. They've always made good martinis in this town. After two I agreed with myself that yes, this is a golden age, and watched the cool blondes and the young bucks appraising each other. October night, and the city coming to life as it has through all the Octobers . . .   *October 8, 1972*

Add ceteras: Penny Patterson, a graduate student in psychology, is embarked on a fascinating project at the S.F. Zoo, teaching deaf mute sign language to Koko, the zoo's youngest gorilla. After three months, Koko can give clearly the signs for "Food," "Drink" and "More"—vocabulary enough for a full life, wouldn't you say? . . .

*　*　*

Bagatelle: William Randolph Hearst Jr. dropped into the Post-Powell Roos-Atkins the other day and bought a suit from Dave Falk, who said "Y'know, I sold your father an Inverness cape for the opera opening in 1939, down at the old Roos store on Market." At this, Hearst Jr. turned to his son, William Randolph Hearst III, and grinned "Billy, buy yourself a suit so Mr. Falk can go down in history as the only salesman who sold clothes to three William Randolph Hearsts." Done and done.   *November 20, 1972*

1973

Here in Action City West, Rudolph Nureyev is still going strong on the post-midnight scene but he's wearing everybody else out. At 3 a.m., he is in Bali's, his favorite hangout, looking like a Tartar prince as he chews on lamb bones and tosses them aside. He dances on a table, then grabs his dear friend, Armen Bali, to whirl her around to a wild Armenian tune. Worn out: Impresario John Kornfeld, who is napping in a tiny room above the restaurant. A policeman pokes his head in: "What's going on?" "Is private party!" snaps Armenia's Armen. "Join it or get out!" After a moment's thought, the officer gets . . . Rudy's top-secret retreat, by the way, is the Ritch St. Health Club. The tales they tell!

February 23, 1973

I HATE THE SUNDAY COLUMN

Quite a few polite people ask me why the Sunday column is different from the daily one. Being polite, they don't say it's better or worse, just "different," and of course it is. That's because it's written on the preceding Tuesday, for technological reasons I've never understood, and goes to press on Wednesday, so by the time it lands on your doorstep it's flat as a flounder and twice as smelly. I wouldn't be caught dead reading it. Writing it is bad enough. I use the time-honored hunt 'n' peck system and the hunting hasn't been all that good lately. Ditto the pecking.

* * *

With this five-day lead time, or whatever it's called, I can't stud the column with those red-hot last-second one-line zingers that for years have caused presses to stop and editors to pale. Especially our own presses as the editor barks "Get that dumb zinger out of the paper!" All editors bark, in an effort to command doglike devotion, but mine has been known to barf, especially at my attempts to play Charlie Baxter, Cub Reporter, phoning in a story that will rock City Hall. (Cub reporter is a silly phrase, come to think of it; what can a cub possibly do that's worth reporting?) Anyway, now you know why I hate the Sunday column. Deadline Dick, working five days in advance.

*   *   *

The old bag of tricks, getting older and baggier. Some kindly types suggest: "Why don't you write more about the old days?" but there's no future in it; those who care to read about the San Francisco of yesteryore are dying in droves and winding up in Colma while their friends toast their demise at Coattail Molloy's, one of the great lugubrious saloons. Besides, it's a fact that not all old-timers are interested in reading about old times. Even the seldom-discussed story that Sunny Jim Rolph, saintly Mayor, had a Hollywood actress, Anita Page, as his lady friend is of little interest today. Mourn the passing of Bay shrimp and Hangtown Fry and every eye remains dry, even rheumy ones. As Vincent Hallinan said just the other day, "I've been reading your column lately and let me say one thing—you've got to stop living in the past." When a 78-year-old, which Hallinan is, says that you had better listen.

*   *   *

Baghdad-by-the-Bay, that's what we used to call it in the first flush of puppy (or cubby) love, but there may be a diminishing market for that, too. The symmetry of peopled hills, the gracious relationship between tower and sky, the foaming wakes left by criss-crossing ferryboats, these things are gone. There is still poetry under wet eucalypti and dreams at the end of leafy streets opening on uncluttered views, but now you have to squint a little to shut out reality (desperation grows noisier, reality uglier). When you see a photograph of the downtown skyline today, it looks like a photoquiz that asks "Can you find the Ferry Building?" As far as some of our leading architects are concerned, the answer to that is "Who cares?" For some of the rest of us, the Ferry Building is where we draw the line. We could both be wrong.

*   *   *

City of St. Francis, less gentle than it once was, but still mysterious as we contemplate it for a Sunday column, five days from deadline. "There used to be magic here," an old friend, R.L. Duffus,

234

once said, "but we're no longer sure where it is." I wander the hard new plazas, the rooftop restaurants, the pop-plastic lobbies, feeling like a stranger. Most of my contemporaries live in an alcohol-hazed glow, snapping their fingers to songs nobody remembers; tapping their toes to a ghostly beat, turning their back on the present tense. To the young people, this may be just another city, who can tell? They don't appear to react to San Francisco the way we did, all rapture and adoration, terribly pleased with ourselves for having the exquisite taste to be San Franciscans. Perhaps I underestimate them; maybe they do know this is a special place and that they are among the favored few in a world growing cold.

★   ★   ★

The Sunday mood, five days in advance, mind's eye roving about the familiar outlines of the city, floating over snaggle-toothed piers that now stand rotting and empty (how can this be?) and across Candlestick Park, where millions have been squandered to transform the third-rate into the second class. City of bikes and bagels, the noisiest buses anywhere (and the quietest streetcars), headstones from long-gone cemeteries in the curbstones around Buena Vista Park, and the Haight-Ashbury slowly stirring back to life after the death of summer love so many eons ago, back when Pig Pen was sassy-young and fat and the answer to all questions rose in the smoke of the good grass that turned bad and finally evil . . . Out at Playland, seagulls swoop vulture-like over the debris where laughter once ruled. The fog lies offshore like a beast, crouching.

★   ★   ★

Sunday in the city, the paper fat, red, pink and blue, this column written by a stranger who was me five days ago, trying to find answers in deadlines and failing. Again.   *March 18, 1973*

RUNNING AROUND IN CIRCLES

It was a sentimental weekend or a weekend filled with sensations, whichever comes first. Blame it on the full moon. Police, bartenders and other observers of the human condition have always been aware that the full moon brings out the loonies, that being a corruption of the term lunatic, which itself is derived from the Latin "luna" meaning moon. But you looniebirds already knew that, correct?

Saturday evening, the moon shone down with furious intensity on slanty old Powell between Sutter and Bush, illuminating a steady stream of freaks and nonfreaks inching their way up or down to the new International Museum of Erotic Art. You know, dirty pictures, about 1,500 of them, setting a pornograph record at whatever speed you have in mind, and if you have a dirty mind, relax and enjoy it. That's where it all is, anyway.

This Phallus in Wonderland, occupying the former S.F. State Extension building (ah, Doc Hayakawa, semanticist, what fun to play with the word "extension"!), is the creation of Drs. Phyllis and Eberhard Kronhausen, whose names are household words in certain houses from here to Munich and on to Stockholm. "The only museum of its kind in the world," states Eberhard firmly. Why in San Francisco? "The most liberal city in the United States," he replied, adding a second later, "It is, isn't it?" I assured him it is, despite the plainclothes police plainly in view across the street.

Three floors and a basement crammed with erotica, artistic and otherwise, is a dizzying experience, especially when you have to fight your way through several thousand guests, all swilling and spilling champagne. "It looks like a gynecologist's office," decided Gloria Vollmayer. No gynecologists were in view, but there were skin doctors, like Herb Lawrence, and ticker docs (Hill Katz) and psychiatrists, such as Richard Kunin, plus several obstetricians musing over the museum's message: "Sex Is For Pleasure And Recreation, Not Procreation."

★ ★ ★

Aside from these proper people, the crowd was so freaky that even the queen of the vestal virgins, Margo St. James, appeared demure. Jerry Rubin, gold earring flashing, featured the Choir Boy Look in a white shirt open to the navel, not necessarily his. Shirley MacLaine, an old friend of the Kronhausens, popped in from Honi Soit Qui Malibu to act as unofficial hostess. "I really dig this sort of thing," she said with simple eloquence to Willie Brown. Her friend, Columnist Pete Hamill of the New York Post, was with her, as usual; he's her current "old man," a phrase I truly abhor. "Is this a typical San Francisco crowd?" he asked, goggle-eyed behind goggles. "Just like opening night at the opera or closing night at the Bohemian Grove," I said. He nodded and made a note.

Another visiting superstar in the crowd: Author Gay Talese, wearing a Gucci leather overcoat "that cost more than a Ferrari."

He is still engaged in "deep research" on his next book, all about sex in America, and will begin banging it out soon. Meanwhile, he has been living in the widely known Southern California sex commune, Sandstone, with some 35 people who have achieved "deep personal satisfaction and sincere insights through sexual freedom." Like, you know.

Footnote: There are very few women in the world who look attractively dressed without a bra. Not one was present at the opening of the Kronhausens' museum.

★ ★ ★

Well, I mused to myself as I tooled up Powell, at $2.50 a pop the museum should make a pile, especially from visiting Iowans, and some of the art is highly amusing. Playland at the Beach dies, Playland at the Crotch is born on the slotted flank of Nob Hill. Wandering into the Fairmont, I ran smack into Benny Goodman, just back from a tour of Australia. After all those ersatz swingers down the hill, it was nice to see an immortal one.

"Let's go say hello to Vince," BG suggested, so we went into the New Orleans Room, where Vince Cattolica, the blind clarinetist, pays nightly homage to Goodman as part of Jimmy Diamond's band. (Vince recently visited Benny in New York and returned to report solemnly "I have met God.") The crowd roared for BG to play, but Jimmy interrupted "He just flew in from Australia and he's tired." "I am not," grinned Goodman. "I feel great."

With that, he grabbed Vince's beatup old clarinet and swang "Jada," followed by "Georgia Brown," while I sat in on Johnny Markham's drums, playing impeccable triplets on the ride cymbal at the wrong tempo. Vince Cattolica sat in the audience, tears streaming down his cheeks. Later, Benny confided "I played awful, but that's one awful clarinet. Still, Vince makes it sound pretty good and that makes me feel even worse."

Before he left town yesterday, Benny was on the phone, arranging with a clarinet manufacturer to provide Vince with a new one.

★ ★ ★

The full moon still shining down on us loonies, we crossed to Berkeley to hear Bette Midler, new queen of camp, at Berkeley Community Theater ("which," somebody once said, "looks like a building ordered over the phone by Mussolini"). "I'm doing a tour of America's tackiest towns," announced the divine Miss M. "Last night we worked in Los Angeles, which is Numero Uno. The pits! The crowd was full of movie people, all sucking their cheeks." Miss

237

Midler had a capacity turnout, left Tackytown Two with a bundle and earned every nickel of it. She burns enough energy to light Emeryville for a week.   *March 20, 1973*

THEY'RE OFF AND STROLLING

When I was a kid in Sacramento—there's a phrase to glaze the most tolerant eye—I lived and died for baseball. Many was the time I'd awaken the entire household in the middle of the night by shouting "Get him at the plate, the plate!" and at breakfast my father would inquire rather blearily, "So who won?" Sacramento in the '20s: a great town if you were a tree, a pretty place of endless summers and corner lots where a ball game seemed always to be in progress, to the sound of breaking windows and squeal of brakes on passing Chandlers and Chalmers and an occasional Willys-Knight. Windshields were made of glass then, too, and many a one was shattered by a frayed ball covered with black friction tape . . .

★ ★ ★

All this by the way of observing that another season opens here today, here where the last beloved teams were called Seals (and sometimes played like seals) and to acknowledge it's hard to recapture the old tingle. Of course, these are not good days for baseball. To my knowledge, not a single POW returned to announce he had dropped bombs on Asians to make the world safe for baseball, or even, for that matter, Mom's frozen apple pie. The President is a football freak, being the kind of man who equates strength with joy. A lot of good gray heads are even ready to concede that we may live long enough to see the end of baseball as we know it. Chances are we already have and don't know it.

★ ★ ★

Apparently we have been so overstimulated by the media and the message that we can no longer loll at the ballpark for a couple of hours, watching (occasionally) a couple of dozen "illiterates" playing a child's game, as Scott Fitzgerald mercilessly put it. It makes us feel guilty and nervous. Besides, all the changes in the game have been for the worse: cozy wooden ballyards have been replaced by concrete mixing bowls, hot dogs cost twice as much and are half as good, the players have been taken out of baggy flannels and stuffed into stretchies that disclose every inch of flab. Further, baseball is for hot days on God's grass. If you're my age,

238

I'll bet you'll never forget the thrill of coming out of the dark entry-way into the golden sunshine of your first professional game, the grass greener than green, the uniforms whiter than white as you walked in a trance to your seat, close enough to the field to smell the liniment.

★   ★   ★

I've never understood why, exactly, but baseball has always had a stronger appeal for writers, F. Scott excepted, than football. Ring Lardner, a most sensitive intellect, loved the game, much to Fitzgerald's baffled annoyance. Hemingway was forever using its jargon to describe his own writing: "I really hummed my high hard one in on 'em (the critics) with that yarn." One reason may be that baseball is a sentimental game, living always in the past, and most writers are sentimental slobs. Furthermore, Ted Williams to the contrary, almost anybody, even a lardassed writer, can play at baseball. Williams once said that hitting a baseball (round) with a bat (round) is the most difficult feat in any sport. Maybe, but there's all that standing around, too. No other sport involves so much standing around, watching grass grow. Or spitting, although artificial grass may bring a stop to that.

★   ★   ★

For me, a former shifty-footed first-sacker, the downgrading of baseball began with the decline and fall of first base. There used to be dazzlers at the initial hassock: Prince Hal Chase, Peerless Frank Chance, Gorgeous George Sisler, Lou Gehrig and the flawless Dolph Camilli. Now, when a manager doesn't know what to do with some aging rummy, he puts him on first base. Frevvinsakes, I've even seen PITCHERS playing first. Another mistake was bringing the major leagues to the West, where we could see that the Giants weren't gigantic, after all. Sometimes they were even Seal-like. One of the few heroes left is Phil Wrigley, who still won't allow night baseball at Wrigley Field. He was also the last to succumb to the nonsense of playing the National Anthem before every game, a brutish idea conceived during World War II to delude the public into regarding a ball game as "patriotic."

★   ★   ★

True, baseball is slow. When such old-pro sportswriters as Charlie Einstein and Leonard Shecter had to cover games every day, they'd bring a book to read in the press box. "We'd only look up from whatever we were doing," Shecter recalls, "when we heard the sound of bat hitting ball." Most of the action at a baseball game takes place before the game starts. If you're really a fan, you go out

239

there at least an hour before game time, to watch infield practice, incredibly swift and beautiful, and coaches hitting amazing fungo flies to the outfield. Now the American League, in danger of having to recruit designated fans for its empty parks, is going in for beer-belly pinchhitters, while Sal Bando, may his white shoes turn puce, says let's stop throwing the ball around the horn between outs to speed up the game. Dumbo Lives!

At Vanessi's the other day, an American League exec cut me short in the middle of a recitation about the '29 Philadelphia Athletics to say coldly: "We don't want old fans, mister, we want new spectators." Poor fellow. He doesn't understand that in baseball, unlike any other sport, it's always wait till last year.

April 9, 1973

Streetscene: If "It could only happen in San Francisco!" was heard once Thursday afternoon, it was heard a dozen times at the corner of Geary and Taylor, where something that could only happen in San Francisco took place. As hundreds of people spilled out into the street, their lives endangered by onrushing cars, the ghost of Isadora Duncan hovered over the site, her birthplace on May 27, 1873.

A handsome bronze plaque recording this was affixed to the building now on that corner; it is owned by Bert Tonkin, who had never heard of Isadora Duncan. Several old-timers wondered if she had been Vivian and Rosetta Duncan's sister (no). A Clean Old Man sneered, "Typical phony San Francisco stuff—Isadora Duncan was born in Oakland" (he may have her confused with Gertrude Stein, Jack London or Charlie Finley).

Barefoot women in togas did "The Isadora Duncan Walk" along Taylor in their bare feet, which takes courage and dedication in the Year of the Dog. Isadora's adopted daughter, Irma Duncan Rogers, gave a touching, eloquent speech. At last the purple silk covering was whisked off the plaque and gray heads and young beards applauded. Good vibes were everywhere. "It could only happen in San Francisco," said George Cory, composer of "I Left My Toga In Calistoga."

Now let's do something about replacing the plaque to our poet laureate, the late George Sterling, at his shabby memorial on Russian Hill, for in the annals of his "cool grey city of love," he means even more than Isadora. "At the end of my street are stars!" he once exulted, in the quiet nights before the high-rises came,

and now he is almost forgotten, even the plaque to his memory
having been stolen. *June 4, 1973*

Caenfetti: Consternation at the Dept. of Motor Vehicles! Personalized license plates reading "FK NXN" got past everybody, including the computer, and are now out in the open, adorning the front
and back bumpers of a Bay Area car . . . *September 10, 1973*

ANOTHER WORLD

Nightmare alley: I dreamed I was wearing a double-knit suit and
white shoes and having lunch in the Clift Hotel's Redwood
Room—and I woke up screaming?

Not exactly, for the dream was only partly true. I was not wearing crummy crochets and albino alligators, but I was standing at
the gates of the Redwood Room, contemplating entrance for the
first time in several years.

Don't get me wrong: I don't think that boycotting that place
is any kind of blow for freedom. It's just that there was something
distasteful about the way they denied entrance to men—especially
young boys and elderly codgers—whose hair was "too long," result-
ing at times in great embarrassment to nice people.

Now you are about to say that the owner of a place—in this
case, Robert Odell, recently deceased—has a right to set standards
of style and taste and impose them upon his customers. Well, yes
and no. The law doesn't see it that way: if you're catering to the
public in a public place, the only legal standard is your behavior,
not whether your hair falls an inch over your collar.

If you dance on the tabletops, set fire to the waiter, drink wine
out of your lady's wedgies, pour ice water down the dresses of Little Old Ladies and make loud and unmannerly noises, you should
indeed be thrown out. But to be asked to leave because you wear
your hair in a style more suited to the 1970s than the 1950s is a
bit much.

★ ★ ★

Okay, the subject is a cliche and academic besides, since the late
Mr. Odell's philosophy allegedly has been interred with him. Since
his death, the caveat posted outside the Redwood Room has been
altered slightly to remove any references to hair length, warning

241

only that those wearing "extreme or unconventional dress" would not be served.

This, of course, opens up a new can of escargots. What's extreme or unconventional and who says so? I was wearing a plaid Brioni suit, Gucci (pronounced "gucky") shoes and a Cerruti tie that might be considered extreme by someone who doesn't like Italians, and the total effect was definitely unconventional by Pacific Union Club standards.

Nevertheless, the head waiter flinched only slightly when I walked in and ordered a Campari. Drink the way you dress, I always say. When I mentioned the warning at the door, the Clift's demon public relations counselor, Herbert Cerwin, said mollifyingly, "You know what that means—like people in Levis. "Not even Wally Haas?" I asked, naming the Levi Strauss head man.

"Not even Wally Haas," said Mr. Cerwin firmly. "He has too much taste to wear Levis to lunch downtown. Further, I would say your attire is more suited to the country and I'll think of which country in a moment."

★　★　★

I was there in the Redwood Room, breaking vows and bread, because of the blandishments of Mr. Cerwin, a superflack I have known and respected since the Boer War, which he handled. He grows his own wine, a respectable Johannisberg Riesling, on his property in Sonoma, and brought along a couple of bottles for this historic occasion. You can't hate a man like that.

As the wine cooled in silver buckets, I looked around the room, with its handsome redwood walls, long bar, plush booths and impressive hush. Or rather, depressing hush, for not too many people were there. I examined them with some interest, for they seemed quite at home and therefore must have represented the type approved of by the late Mr. Odell.

They had that vaguely Santa Barbara aura I always associate with the Clift. Some looked retired, others resigned, and a couple may have been dead. One stoutish matron, who could have stepped straight out of the windows of Lane Bryant, on the fifth floor, was smoking a cigarette and drinking a martini straight up. The cigarette appeared to be straight, too, its tip smudged by her Ultra-Brite lipstick. She stared steadfastly at the opposite wall, which returned the stare.

Several of the male customers were in the approved double-knits and white shoes, their hair so short I wondered if they had just been prepared for prefrontal lobotomy. I have nothing against double-knits, personally or politically, but esthetically they are an affront and in various shades of red, definitely an incitement to riot.

"These people certainly dress in an extreme and unconventional manner," I commented to Mr. Cerwin, who mumbled something about chacun a son choucroute.

★ ★ ★

Considering the funereal atmosphere, the waiters were amazingly lively and pleasant, but the food was like everything else in the room. Bland. The asparagus were watery, the mustard-mayonnaise sauce tasteless, the salmon like pink cardboard, the Hollandaise as dry as the Sahara but without the texture. Mr. Cerwin's wine saved the day.

As I left, having broken the redwood barrier, I recalled Comedian Dick Gregory's remark after liberating a segregated lunch counter in the South: "All these years of battling, and when we finally get in and get served, the food is no good!"

October 14, 1973

In response to a tepid query from one of my few surviving readers, I stated recently that "phlug" is the stuff that collects in the pockets of old suits and overcoats, and once again controversy rages! For one thing, an infinitely more learned fellow, the late Robert Benchley, called it "gnir," and described it as being "specially constructed for adhering to candies." In Gretchen Herbkersman's lexicon, it's "nuff-nuff," while several sources quote H. Allen Smith as labeling it "phlerd," adding that it collects in pants cuffs as well. You know those little rolls and balls of crud that form under beds? Those, Harriet Ainsworth reminds us, are "gerfingles," whereas "curdles" are the curly hairs found in bathrooms . . . Getting back to H. Allen for a moment, G. Hodder reports that Smith collected navel lint and placed it on his windowsill for birds to use in nest-building, a generous thing to do. None of these experts mention the term "phlug," so perhaps I simply made it up. You know the stuff that collects on what's left of the chewing gum you can't scrape off your shoe? Maybe that's phlug.

December 2, 1973

Now then, about the pronunciation of everybody's favorite comet. "It's KO-hou-tek," says Charles Susskind. "All Czech words are

243

accented on the first syllable." Julius J. Frnjak: "Ko-WHO-tek." Grant Wallace: "Kaw-HOE-tek." Al Cerny: "Ko-hoe-THEK." Nat'l Geographic, quoted by Mrs. R.N. Shiras: "KAH-hoe-tek" . . . Last word to George Poggi: "I HATE comets! When Kohoutek goes away, I hope I never see it again."   *December 19, 1973*

1974

★ ★ ★

PLEASE CALL IT FRISCO?

A few of us were sitting around the other night, discussing our third favorite subject, after sex and weather, and Rex Adkins came up with a truly original thought. "San Francisco," he ventured over the Mountain Red, "is a city that wishes people would call her Frisco again," a remark that caused the rest of us to nod with sad half-smiles. Only a few years ago, Adkins' aphorism wouldn't have crossed his mind, and it occurred to me later that I no longer hear people say either "Frisco" or in automatic reproof, "Don't call it Frisco." An ominous sign, but any old portent in a storm, especially at deadline time.

★ ★ ★

It was the sailors who first called this port "Frisco," as they called San Diego "Dago," San Pedro "Pedro" and Oakland several unprintable epithets (that has changed, too). They also thought of this city as the best liberty this side of Port Said, by which they meant they could get juiced and tattooed and tarted and maybe even shanghied but never bored. Why, on Kearny, pronounced "Carney" in old Frisco, you could raise a crew to sail for the Galapagos in the course of one block and lose every man jack of them in the next. Frisco was a place for heroic hangovers, prodigious deeds and herculean lies, all printed immediately by fuzz-cheeked reporters, and only the pompous asses of Nob Hill insisted on "San Francisco, sir, if you please."

★ ★ ★

There's no doubt that it's San Francisco today. They're selling health food sandwiches at the Cliff House, out there where you

245

could once dance all night and sleep all day, with a different belle for each shift, and Playland has disappeared into two big holes surrounded by rickety fences. If the seagulls seem to be crying as they wheel over the breakers, and the sea lions sound more mournful than foghorns at midnight, there's reason enough and blame for all. For in spite of the brave young beards, the faded jeans and the mucho macho boots, the city has gone straight and its soul belongs to innkeepers and snake-oil salesmen selling corny porn.

★   ★   ★

It's San Francisco now, a matchless harbor crowded with the ghosts of ships that have gone elsewhere while a superannuated Port Commission tries to make up its mind about something. Anything. San Francisco, with black blockbuster buildings and pointy-headed novelties and plastic towers that house commuters who don't call it "Frisco" because they never heard of the word and wouldn't know what it represents anyway. Goodbye, Frisco, goodbye, and hello, San Francisco, where a one-time giant of the waterfront, Harry Bridges, a man who once fought fascists, scoffs at those who would save what's left as "hard-nosed" environmentalists, surely one of the great phrases of the decade. If the nose grows hard, consider the smell.

★   ★   ★

There's a pun there somewhere—does the smell of the past evoke nostalgia?—but it's hard to make even feeble jokes as a beloved city wanders off in all directions, having lost its way. "Don't call it Frisco!" was the battle cry of The Respectables, and they appear to have won. The city of legends is being carved up by thieves in the night, and the money-grubbers grow fatter (and grubbier) in the high-rising marketplaces. This is no place for dreamers. Weavers of spells, come not here, to paraphrase the Bohemian Club motto. Jack London would look around and retreat to the First and Last Chance Saloon. The shade of George Sterling stands askance at his despoiled, vandalized monument on Russian Hill. Saroyan stays in Fresno.

★   ★   ★

Frisco. Surely something of it persists, for there is an unquenchable spirit here, as Saroyan is unquenchable. We feel it stirring on foggy mornings, when the mind's ear catches the faroff chunk-chunk of ferry paddles and the blasts of "The Lark's" hooters at Third and Townsend. In the old streets, steam rises from a thousand underground pipes, the hot breath of a city whose pulse still beats in cable slots. On Telegraph Hill, once Tellygraft, Tom Cara

246

reminds us that Mother Nature continues to fight "progress": after each heavy rain, Italian parsley sprouts from the street curbings in Edgardo Place. And on the rooftops above tawdry North Beach, a glass-roofed garret here and there where a young artist lives, even today, la vie boheme.

* * *

At Fisherman's Wharf, a little Frisco lives in the form of seagulls on pilings and the "helldriver" grebes disappearing soundlessly into the murky waters after a quarry only they can see. Sunset brings the brave figure of moustachioed William May at the wheel of his faded fishing boat, the Belle of Dixie, with five dogs yapping on the afterdeck. Lovely old William, one of the last of the great fisherfolk, who squints up at the Russian Hill skyline and says "Been livin' 68 years here in Frisco—pardon me, San Francisco." No, William. Pardon us. *February 3, 1974*

Far in: "This is going to be a religious experience," the young man seated in front assured me, but what the heck, we've all been bored in church at times. Still, nobody sleeps when Bob Dylan is on, and he was on most of the time at Oakland's Arena Monday night, a birdlike scarecrow treated with due reverence by the middle-aged, young, white and affluent. A whiff of patchouli, a lot of grass, an occasional clenched fist and V-sign, but rest easy, fat burghers. There ain't gonna be no revolution, that's what ain't happenin', Mr. Jones, but a lot of $400 cameras were flashing. "Dylan is the new Jesus," whispered the young man to my left. Jesus. Looking out over the serried ranks of the Silent Seventies (they did bestir themselves, finally, for "Rolling Stone"), I could only decide that the fat kid with the provocative waddle, the Maharaj Ji, may make it big with these old young people. The Sixties seem light years in the past. *February 13, 1974*

Loss: It was odd not to see the flags at half-staff above Hotel St. Francis yesterday, in honor of Dan London. His unexpected death at 69 leaves an unfillable gap in the San Francisco skyline: he was at home under a homburg and at ease with the great of the world; he turned the St. Francis, with its many foreign banners, into what we used to call San Francisco's "American Embassy," with Dan as Ambassador Plenty Potent. In his glory days, hotel managers were famously part of the scene; one talked of Dan London in the same breath with Jimmy McCabe, Halsey Manwaring, Archie Price, Baron Edmund Rieder, George Smith and a few others with individual styles . . . Today, aside from an occasional Henri Lewin or John Carrodus, you can't tell them apart without their name tags. Dan was VIP all the way, before the term and the hotel world went plastic. *May 21, 1974*

How red the tape: Darryl Cohen and Stan Roth, who sell hot pretzels at a pushcart in Ghirardelli Square, can't get a license for a variety of bureaucratic reasons, one being that the Health Dept. says they have to have "hot and cold running water" (on a pushcart?). Meanwhile, they are in imminent danger of being busted despite their ingenious solution. Under Proposition J, which passed in the June election and OK's street artists, Darryl and Stan are peddling their pretzels as 'artistic dough sculptures'! *July 23, 1974*

TAKE A TOURIST TO LUNCH

Don't look now (business of swiveling head cautiously) but I think they're here again. The tourists, I mean. Our principal source of income. The people upon whom we rest our hopes and half-aspirations. The apple-knockers and hay-shakers for the taking of whom we have overbuilt hotel rooms and restaurants and razed half the city. Has the city that long looked askance at tourist traps become one itself? The cowled monk with his hand extended for alms on Powell, is he a Tourist Trappist? Only asking.

Not that there really are apple-knockers, hay-shakers and dung-scuffers any longer in this broad and bounteous land. The hick, once rough as a cob, has been smoothed out and slicked up. Well, maybe a few survive. In the Hyatt Regency the other day, Jan Seibert found herself descending from the Equinox in an elevator with three farmer types who stared at the vast, incredible lobby with awe, Adam's apples bobbing.

"Biggest corncrib I evva saw," twanged the first. "Yeah," nodded the second. "Got to be the damndest silo in the world." The third was at a loss for a few seconds. "I mean, man," he finally exploded, "this here is a BARN!"

★ ★ ★

Every year, the same neurotic worry about the tourist. Will he come back again, or did we do it to him too fast and often last year? Did he leave his wallet here and take his heart elsewhere? Now the sightings and soundings are in, and the evidence is reassuring. The tourist may be an endangered species, but unlike the Monterey sardine and the Bay shrimp, he is not yet extinct . . . For this, we deserve no credit. Give thanks to Nature for providing the hills, the vistas, the Bay and ocean. Let's hear it for our unpredictable weather: misty mornings, romantically foggy evenings and in between, blue skies washed clean by the same wind that dirties our streets, but you can't have everything. Blue skies, I must remind you, are a phenomenon not to be seen in too many other major cities of the world . . . As for our man-made objects, let us never stop paying humble respect to the makers of Golden Gate Park, the cable cars and the bridges. Ghirardelli Square and the Cannery, si! Fisherman's Wharf, not so si but lots to see nevertheless. And for people who tear down places like Sutro Baths and Playland without being ready to replace them, a curl of the lip. These are the diggers of holes, the heroes of zeroes, the minus men in a city of pluses.

★　★　★

I know, we're not supposed to call them tourists. They're "visitors," as in Convention & Visitors Bureau, but tourist seems more precise. A visitor sounds like somebody who stays with his Auntie Millie in the Richmond and takes all his meals in. Pfaw. A pox on him. What we want and need and love are tourists, elbowing onto the cables, waiting in line for restaurant tables, paying too much for a weak drink in a topless joint to see a person with fake frontage, staying in a hotel room with a view overlooking a parking lot, and walking up Powell and around Union Square, snapping their Instamatics and giggling and shaking their heads at the freaks. The veritable true White-Shod Head Shakers.

In all truth, the old-time San Franciscan cares about the tourist and frets over his reaction. "The worst San Francisco can get is still better than anyplace else" is an article of faith here, but does the tourist agree or does he think the town has slipped? Is the tourist getting to the good stores, the good restaurants, the good places to view the city? Are the bartenders pouring him a decent drink, are the cab drivers being helpful, is the cable car gripman putting on a proper show? Truly, the San Franciscan hopes so; he still thinks his city is the best but now, in this era of great change, he needs reassurance.

★　★　★

I never tire of the tourists and their observations. I remember the woman standing near the Powell turntable, looking at a cable car for the first time and snapping in disgust: "Is that all? I thought they'd be SUSPENDED from cables!" . . . It was tourists who said "I love this hilly city—when you get tired of walking around in it you can lean against it" and "How I pity the children of San Francisco when they grow up and find out that other cities are not like theirs" . . . Of course, it was a tourist child who watched a paisan throw a crab into a pot of boiling water and yelled, "Mommy, mommy, they cook in garbage cans down here!" And I was with Phil Baker, another tourist, on the day he looked down from his St. Francis hotel window and coined the line that "San Francisco without its cable cars would be like a kid without his yo-yo."

★   ★   ★

The tourists. They used to beat a path from the Ferry Building to the Cliff House. Now they roam around the Vaillancourt Fountain, making funnies, and stay in Hyatts and Holiday Inns, eat at whatever place is handy and ask plaintively: "Where do the real San Franciscans go?" There is no satisfactory answer, for the San Franciscan is forever a tourist in his own hometown, mingling with the tourists from elsewhere and usually having just as good, or rotten, a time as they . . . Come let us play and pay together.

August 4, 1974

Well, BART may be good for a few laughs. Monday night, Phil Grosse was aboard a Concord-Daly City train whose operator announced "You are now entering the transbay tube, which is 3.6 miles long, and we're traveling at a speed of 80 miles per hour. Please enjoy your trip"—following which he piped in the Jeanette MacDonald recording of "San Francisco" from the earthquake movie classic, thereby cracking up the crowd. Adds Buck Rannels: "I kept waiting for a stewardess to appear to explain how Scuba gear tumbles out of the overhead compartment in case the tube springs a leak . . . "

September 18, 1974

Atty. Colin Claxon, who was part of the whole ugly messsss, reports a massive tieup on the Golden Gate Bridge a few nights back that had him and a lot of other San Francisco-bound drivers stalled inside the Waldo Tunnel for a good or bad 45 minutes. "After a short while," he says, "people began wandering around, striking up conversations. A bunch of long-hairs produced Frisbees and began slinging them back and forth, half the length of the tunnel. The people in the car ahead of mine opened the trunk, got out the bottles and ice, and began mixing martinis. Nicely dry, I thought. Radios were tuned to the same rock station and people began keeping time with their horns. A bit of dancing ensued. It was all very San Francisco. Not a tunnel of love, exactly, but definitely a tunnel of like."   *October 10, 1974*

A cheery face wreathed in cigar smoke, a voice redolent of tafelspitz and gemutlichkeit, a twinkling eye for the ladies (his first wife, Mitzi, described him admiringly as "The Bull of the Vienna Opera!"), that was Maestro Josef Krips, who died Saturday. Not only was he a fine musician and good fun to be around—everybody was "My dear" to him—he may be said to have saved the San Francisco Symphony, taking over the orchestra as it was disintegrating after years of neglect. It's a tribute to his charm that he was able to beat this almost dead horse back to life without killing the beast or making its members his enemies; his booming optimism was contagious: "Grrreat, chust grreat!" he would beam to the orchestra even when it wasn't. "Beethoven lifts you to Heaven," he once remarked to Bill Bernell, "but Mozart is there to greet you," and if this is true, Josef was warmly welcomed by Wolfgang.

October 15, 1974

How shabby we now feel for having made fun of Mr. Nixon's alleged fondness for cottage cheese and ketchup. Did you see what President Ford served for breakfast to his old Michigan football buddies on Thanksgiving morn? Eggs Benedict and apple pie a la mode! This is indeed the end of civilization as we have known it.

December 2, 1974

Superman: If you're among the old-timers who insist that San Francisco's sourdough French bread isn't as sour as it used to be, you'll want to mourn Giovanni Fontana, who died last week at 92 without a line. of recognition . . . Giovanni, a founder of the Parisian Bakery, was a baker himself for many years, working stripped to the waist and, at the last moment, brushing the dough across his hairy, sweaty chest before popping it into the oven. That, according to fond legend, is what gave his bread, then known as Fontana's, "it's real fine sour flavor," but Pecksniffs from the Health Dept. thought otherwise and made him desist . . . Giovanni himself would never go into detail, other than to agree the bread was sweetened considerably since his chest was placed out of bounds. "The secret died with him," sighs his nephew, Ed Croce, "and maybe it's just as well." *January 23, 1975*

THE RAMBLING WRECK

"You are no bigger than the things that annoy you," read the slip in the Chinese New Year's fortune cookie, and I was immediately annoyed because I knew there was some truth in the statement but who needs philosophy from a fortune cookie? A fortune cookie should be funny or silly but never wise. All I want from a cracked fortune cookie is the news that I'm about to take a long trip and meet somebody dark and mysterious who will make me rich. Like maybe run into Sammy Davis in Las Vegas and he's feeling especially expansive and lays a million bucks on me. That would be mysterious, all right.

Drat that cookie. I sat at the window table in Kan's, looked down into teeming Grant Avenfoo, and made a list of all the little things that annoy me, thereby making me a small person. What dreckerei, that fine Mandarin word, or maybe Manischewitz. I'm annoyed by Astroturf on traffic islands, politicians who clap you on the back and say "Good to see ya!" because they can't recall your name, shoeshine boys who get brown polish on your black socks, "You don't remember me but"ters, gasoline described as "Super Regular," alleged progressives who look at you pityingly and murmur "You can't live in the past, fella." Who says?

I'm annoyed by dogs dirtying the streets when it's really Their Masters' Vice (dog owners hate people and encourage their dogs to poop on the stoop of people they pooticularly dislike—you have noticed that, haven't you?). I could kick people who spit in public and cheerfully throttle every Clean Old Man who blows his nose in the street via thumb and forefinger. No jury in the world would convict me. Acquittal by acclamation would be followed by a medal which I would accept modestly.

Color me picky-picky, call me just another pretty face, but I sometimes get the urge to run over oafs who stand 10 feet off the curb against the light and grandiloquently wave you through, as though they're doing YOU a favor. I don't run them over because of my already well-known sensitivity; deep down inside I know they're ecologically sound because they're on foot while I'm at the wheel of my Italian benzina burner, contributing my pittance to 11 ongoing world crises. I get annoyed at meter maids and yet They're Only Doing Their Job, is it not so? Maybe it's because they seem to ENJOY their job, or maybe it's those horrible uniforms. Some of those meter maids are quite nice looking, too, and could even have excellent legs, but I digress.

*   *   *

There is no limit to what annoys you when you reach September or whatever this is. I went to a literary tea party (wine and cheese) at Minerva's Owl the other night in honor of somebody's new and probably annoying book, and this elderly chap, in his 50s, introduced me to a woman as "my new old lady." She looked annoyed. Maybe she didn't want me to know she was his old lady (translation: living and presumably "sleeping" together). I was annoyed because it was more unnecessary information for my already overloaded memory banks. Besides, he was too old to be indulging in such young people's jargon as "old lady."

That's another thing: young beards who call their 18-year-old girl friends "my old lady," or the girl who points out that callow yout' as "my old man." Who started this and why and when will it go away? When will it go away? When I was a kid (dread phrase, annoying), "my old lady" was my mother, naturally, and "so's your old man" was a snappy rejoinder referring to your father. I do realize that whereas "necking" and "petting" somehow have survived from the days of innocence, our vocabulary is still limited when it comes to describing those we live with in unmarried cliche.

"Mistress" and "lover" are of course unacceptable for various sexist reasons. The terms are also imprecise since a mistress can be a lover, too, whereas a lover who has a mistress may not necessarily be a lover but is believed to be paying the bills. In this egalitarian (ha) world, that will never do, although I have yet to see a human being of the female persuasion make a lunge for the luncheon check. I still say "chum" is the best word to describe the person one lives with. "This is my chum" gives offense to no one and is redolent of sachets, potpourri, samplers, hot water bottles, comforters and other warm niceties that make life worth sharing.

★　★　★

Judging from my mail and phone calls, everybody in this town is annoyed about something, if it's only high prices and the difficulty of deciding who's to blame. Don't say something annoying like "Look in the mirror," frevvinsakes. It's Ford's fault, or that dopey Simon's, or Arthur Burns, who may actually be bananas. Who can tell these days? The unions claim they're not making enough—the statement comes from $100,000 a year international presidents—and the employers are all losing money except those whose profits are up 3,000 per cent over last year and—

Well, it's all most annoying but thankgawd we're all living in San Francisco. I'd hate to be this annoyed anywhere else, wouldn't you?   *February 23, 1975*

Wondering muse: is there still time to cancel those $950 trash "receptacles" planned for The New & Improved Market St.? (At those prices you don't call them cans, except in Louis Quinze.) I prefer the present battered old oil cans, which have a certain jaunty funkiness. Painted by some starving artists at $5 each, they could even be quite sightly. Maybe we could also get a refund on the five lightpoles around the cable car turntable. They cost $11,000 EACH and wouldn't be acceptable for a shopping center parking lot in Cucamonga. Hell, you can't even fly a flag off'n 'em

and they don't look strong enough for a lynching party, hang
it all . . . *March 9, 1975*

KALEIDOSCOPE

What a week, what a world: live infants and dead ones in a black
travesty of a "Baby Parade," plane crashes and calla lilies, Ted the
Boston Strong-boy roughed up by his own people in his own con-
stituency as Irish cops smile at the camera, spring and baseball
and skimpy bathing suits in department store windows . . . But not
to feel guilty, guilt-ridden Americans. They are still sunbathing on
the beaches of South Vietnam as the red tide inches closer, and
tennis was only lately banned in Saigon, artificial capital of the
artificial republic, a terminal case kept alive long past its time by
transfusions of blood and money. South Vietnam, a freak invented
by the mad doctors in Washington, none of whom will admit that
a mistake might have been made. When in doubt, close ranks and
mouths, or let a platitude drop on the sidewalk, to be circled war-
ily by the fastidious. Hold your nose, here comes Walt Rostow
again to suggest sending troops to Vietnam, and can McGeorge
Bundy be far behind? Just think, if McBundy sat in a bathtub and
opened his veins, he'd freeze to death.

*   *   *

Operation Babylift, and where is Lenny Bruce? You can see him
now under the spotlight at Ann's 440, discussing it, stopping now
and then to hum a few bars of theme music from "The High and
the Mighty." Politicians and babies: they go together like ham and
eggs, power and corruption. Right up the old media alley, the President nuzzling an orphan as the windbag TV commentators charge
through thickets of cliches, wild bulls of the pompous (only good
old Andy Park of Ch. 5 tried to keep some perspective, reminding
the viewers of the thousands of children left behind, the thousands of dead and wounded, the thousands bombed and
napalmed and strafed and corrupted). After a decade, the TV war
is winding down—or, more literally, winding up the miles and
miles of videotape that recorded the death throes of helpless people. How would you like to die face down in a rice paddy so Lyndon Johnson could go on regarding himself as a real ballsy Texan
who wasn't about to be pushed around by no Commie gooks,
y'hear?

*   *   *

So at last it has come to this, the end of the long journey through lies and duplicity, Ike and Jack, hell no we won't go, a new vocabulary called Pentagonese. Christmas bombings, Cambodian "incursions" and Herr Doktor Kissinger's "moral commitments" that turned out to be not worth the paper they weren't written on. War without heroes, as David Douglas Duncan termed it, a war without even a good song, a good joke or a good story. A war that dirtied everyone who touched it, and now The Sentimental American, direct descendant of The Ugly American, is fondling babies, washing diapers and guilt, and still, with indifferent arrogance, making the same mistake all over again: trying to tell other people how to live and die, fighting to the last Vietnamese.

★   ★   ★

San Francisco is a long way from Vietnam—San Francisco is a long way from anywhere, fortunately—but it is a city with sound instincts. San Francisco smelled something sour about this "crusade" early in the going. By 1965, there were marches and demonstrations. The first really big one was here, at Kezar in '67, and the ripples were felt in Washington and New York. The driving force came from the young and the hairy and the unwashed, from the rock musicians and the "radical" politicos, from old lefties and bohemians, from the labor guys (not the big names, interestingly) who were not afraid to stand up and be counted—by the FBI and the CIA, as it turns out. The real radicals were the limousine conservatives with their cocktail hour talk of "nuking Hanoi." Why is it they knew so little, these addlepates with the martini brains, when even the street people could foresee what is now in sight, a unified Vietnam run by Hanoi?

★   ★   ★

Ho-Ho-Ho Chi Minh, with the goatlike whiskers on your chin-chin-chin . . . A sad irony you're not around to take over your wounded nation, though you would be heartsick at the plight of so many of your people. Thieu and Ky, it is useful to remember, fought with the French against their own people, but let us not indulge in recriminations. No blame, no blood baths, no purges. Maybe Gerald Ford, who so loves infants, can find it in his heart to love grownups, too, even those who were right in the first place about the war. Let the boys come home from all over the world, let there be peace, let there be amnesty, let us even forgive Dean Rusk and Arthur Schlesinger Jr., and let there be an end to the hawklike croaks of the Reagans and the John Waynes, who love to watch other people fight. From a safe distance. Strange people,

256

these: they've never been bombed (except by booze), never been burned out of their houses by an enemy, never been refugees, and yet they hate those who have suffered through all that while fighting for their own land IN their own land. Why?

★ ★ ★

The Bicentennial year is almost upon us. In our short history, there is much to celebrate, much to lament. Flags, parades and cannon are all very well, but a little silence and humility might go good right now, too.   *April 13, 1975*

Walk softly and carry a big salami!: After leaving the North of Market Senior Center's press conference to publicize assaults on oldsters in the Tenderloin, 79-year-old Eva Heartman stopped at a grocery store for a bit of shopping. Then, heading for her hotel room, she was grabbed by a young mugger who attempted to rip off her handbag—at which she whipped a salami out of her grocery bag and jabbed it into his groin (OH, how that smarts) . . . As he doubled up on the sidewalk, four large locals sat on him till the police arrived. Salami: intact.   *April 30, 1975*

BAGHDAD-BY-THE-BAY

August foghorns at midnight, misty puffs drifting across Nob Hill as though plucked from a vast box of cotton just over the horizon, a human sandwich wrapped in old overcoats Sleeping It Off on a discarded sofa outside the Eagle Cafe on the waterfront, shadowy figures in doorways on Polk and on Eddy whispering "Wanna have a good time?" in joyless voices, a fat raccoon dragging itself up and over a garden fence in Terrific Pacific Heights, its cheeks and belly puffed out with a flowery feast of petunias and geraniums, and always the sirens making white fingernail scratches across the blackboard of another bloodstained night . . .

★ ★ ★

In his apartment in the Fontana, overlooking Ghirardelli Square and bay and bridge, Scott Newhall, the one-time S.F. newspaper editor, is pounding out an editorial for his L.A. county paper, the Newhall Signal. Like many a native of taste and background, he finds himself obsessed with and disenchanted by Mayor Alioto, whom he describes variously as the Grand Duke, His Eminence, the Dodge, Il Magnifico.

At the moment we are concerned with, Newhall is typing "While 'Il Magnifico' held court in his City Hall fortress, skyscrapers rose like giant sequoias and towered over San Francisco and the waterfront crumbled into ruin. He provided jobs for his blue-collar workers by digging holes and trenches in the city streets, until much of the downtown area was cratered like the moon. The streets filled up with gypsies, fortune-tellers, vagabonds, drag queens, cutpurses, muggers, homicidal maniacs and old-fashioned beggars. Street crime is a common pastime."

At this very point, the doorbell rings. Newhall opens the door and in walked a man and woman, armed, who proceeded to rob him and his secretary of all the valuables in the apartment. The bandits then placed pillowcases over the heads of their victims, "which," says Newhall, "convinced me they were going to kill us." But they didn't, of course, and Newhall was able to complete his chronicle of his beloved city's decline and fall under "the reign of this fastidious garrulous master of political fakery."

★   ★   ★

Baghdad-by-the-Bay: candlelight and red checkered tablecloths in good little restaurants along Clement and on Chestnut, folksingers entertaining crowds waiting under Golden Gate Park trees for their turn to gasp over the Asian Art Museum's treasures from Old China, the morning paper hitting your front door simultaneously with the age-old "karrrrump" of the Presidio's 6 a.m. cannon, deep-throated blast of a ship's horn outward bound, thousands of shoppers thronging the "new Hong Kong" markets of Stockton near Broadway, where the smell of fish and ducks and foreign bodies makes your nose hold its breath.

★   ★   ★

What we need, writes Kenneth Rexroth in San Francisco magazine, is "a new Golden Age here." Mr. Waxwroth, who spends most of his time in Santa Barbara when he isn't in Japan, is the closest thing we have to a resident philosopher, which tells you how tough things are. I'm not quite sure what old Golden Ages he has in mind, unless he means himself reading poetry to jazz. He demonstrates a fondness for Lawrence Ferlinghetti, Enrico Banducci, the old hungry i, and Broadway when it consisted of inexpensive "family" cafes, and who can argue with that.

But one man's golden age is another man's dross, and I would think that for a lot of San Franciscans—Jann Wenner of Rolling Stone, Bill Graham and Mr. Coppola come immediately to mind— THIS is a golden age. Besides, the Great Days of Yesteryore are all

258

mixed up with one's youth, and maybe the kids of today are having every bit as much fun as Rexroth and I had, even though the six-bit full-course Italian dinner is now ten times six-bits and there is no Big Dipper to ride screamingly at Playland—no Playland, in fact—and the Fillmore jazz scene, where even ofays were welcome, comparatively, is as dead as Billie Holliday.

Come to think of it, have you seen the Fillmore lately? Once, in a brassy if not precisely golden age, it was alive alive-o with singing and dancing and growling trumpets and well-honked tenor saxes and all the little eating and drinking (and pawn-broking) joints that make up what they call a "community." Now it is a city of the dead, a fenced-off world of dusty lots, a cold place where danger lurks without even a landmark to warm the heart.

Baghdad-by-the-Bay: don't get us wrong, we love it come hell or high taxes. It is still the best of all possible cities, am I right, Dr. Pangloss, you old fraud? Belly dancers gyrating at the Powell St. turntable, the small change still washed all new and shiny at Hotel St. Francis, tourists clinging to cables and little houses clinging to hillsides and a dwindling number of us clinging to dreams of golden ages past, present, and maybe even future.

August 3, 1975

THOUGHTS ON INTERSTATE 80

Roadside signs. "Reduce Speed When Wet." What's that for, drivers who wear diapers? Reduce speed when changing diapers. "Slippery When Wet," with a nice drawing of a skidding car. What isn't slippery when wet? A blotter, maybe. Strange little satellite communities just off the road, "Easy Access to Freeway." Smoggy world of Denny's, A&W Root Beer stands, three kinds of service stations, liquor store, and back to the freeway. "Eat Here and Get Gas." People have been sending me sightings of that sign for 30 years. Scatological humor. America's finest. "We Buy Junk and Sell Antiques." That sign has been around 20 years. Still cracks people up.

★   ★   ★

End of summer. Hot in the valleys of our life—Vaca, Sacramento, Napa, Sonoma, middle age—but you can tell another summer is dying. Where now the promises of spring, a pennant for the Giants? Gone with the gas. Green hills of summer now tawny as Hemingway's Africa. Fall approaches, teetering on high heels after a season of loafers. Bobby Short, the Hildegarde of our time, opening soon at the Fairmont, sure sign of autumn. Herr Adler's wandering minstrels rehearsing, putting more cracks in the Opera House walls. Spring has a perky sound, fall sounds like something about to topple over into winter, Thanksgiving, Christmas, there went 1975 and still no pennant, no Stupid Bowl, no President, no Mayor . . .

★ ★ ★

Roadside Signs. "Slower Traffic Keep Right." That's traffic going a legal 55. Not much of a crowd keeping right. The average: 70. If you've got it, burn it, baby. Best roadside sign I saw this year was in Ireland, coastal town, sign showing a car shooting off a pier into the ocean. Message loud and clear. Heading for Tahoe, crossed the Carquinez twin bridge, marveling again at its height. Memories of the old highway, then called 40 (even numbers East and West, odd numbers North and South), and the funny little ferry that carried your car across Carquinez Straits. First bridge was called "a miracle." Now there are two miracles at 35 cents per crossing, a bargain.

★ ★ ★

Vaca Valley, smell of onions, looking in rear view mirror for highway patrolmen, nudging 70. Guilty as charged. Ran the AM radio dial from front to back. Nothing. Is anything worse than AM radio? I mean except for the classical stations, which are a bit too Pops (sorry Mr. Fiedler), and the occasional news bulletin that is actually news. Bubble-gum rock, bubble-head dee-jays, commercials written by and for morons. Thankgawd for tape decks and Mahler's Fifth by the Chicago, greatest classical recording of the decade. Thankgawd for Benny the Good noodling around on "Tea for.Two," Gene adding something epic every four bars. Why can't there be an AM station, 50,000 watts, that even plays Sinatra, Riddle, Ella, Oscar, Shearing, good big bands? Has to be a market for that and those.

★ ★ ★

Cars passing by with roof racks carrying water skis. Soon, snow skis. I know some phonies who put ski racks on their cars and they don't even ski. Like when TV first came out: a neighbor put a TV aerial on his roof to make people think he had a set when he didn't. Status symbols. Few left. Gucci copied to death, Cartier cheapening its own classic tank watch with a tacky imitation, and as Betsy Bloomingdale says, "Who wants a Rolls-Royce when every hairdresser in Beverly Hills has one?" S.F.'s best status symbol, a parking space behind the Opera House, will disappear when the

260

backstage area is extended. Good. Would white Earth shoes be a status symbol?

★ ★ ★

Whizzing along the Sacramento bypass, greatest invention since Scotchguard. Into the Sierra foothills. Roadside signs. "Deer Crossing." "Falling Rocks." Have never seen either but maybe someday I'll see a falling rock hit a crossing deer. Through gold country toward silver country, lodes of luck. The narrow road past Squaw Valley along the boiling Truckee, kids in rafts. Enjoy, kids! Soon it's back to school, where they will try to teach you the world is round. Don't believe it. The world is flat, flatter than the Sacramento Valley. The world is the center of the universe and the sun goes around it. We say the sun rises and sets, don't we? We don't say the earth rises and sets. Ergo, the earth is flat and man is god.

★ ★ ★

A house at Lake Tahoe. That's status. Not a new pizzelegant house but a sort of tackyrich one that has been in the family three generations. With photos on the wall of the train arriving at Tahoe Tavern from San Francisco. Only way to travel. (It's still a crummy drive despite the great road.) Status is a tackyrich house on the northwest side of Tahoe, a place no effete decorator would even be allowed to touch, Indian blankets, logs crackling, an old Gar Wood speedboat out of the Thirties bobbing at the pier, which should be falling down a little. Status is belonging to Secret Harbor, a picnic-overnight place on the Nevada side, started by five S.F. families a decade ago. Winter status is Sugar Bowl, so secret it isn't even marked by a highway sign. But the right people know where it is. They always do.

★ ★ ★

Repeat after me: Old is good, new is bad. Tahoe is old, almost as old as some of the families whose domain it will always be, and that's not bad, considering the all too visible alternatives.

August 24, 1975

Of human interest: She was young and persuasive and even fairly attractive, so she succeeded in talking her way past the various security people and into the chambers of U.S. District Judge Charles Renfrew at the Federal Bldg. here. "My father is in San Quentin," she lamented, "and they won't let me in to see him. Can't you help me?" . . . Judge Renfrew, a sympathetic man, began listing the prison lawyers who would be of assistance, but she shook her head impatiently: "They won't help. They only help blacks. I'm white and ignorant and the family is breaking up." The Judge sighed and ushered her out . . . For the next several days, she hung around the courtroom, till Renfrew said to his chief clerk: "Please get rid of her—she's making me nervous." As the clerk led her to the exit, with orders to stay away, he asked "By the way, did you ever get to see your dad?" "He's not my dad," she snapped. "He's my FATHER—Charles Manson." And with that Lynette "Squeaky" Fromme stomped out, heading for her eventual moment of madness in Sacramento . . . By the way, didn't it fry your elbow to see her picture on the covers of both Time and Newsweek? Exactly what she wanted—and what too many other like her are seeking.

September 17, 1975

YOU ARE WHAT YOU READ

That was the week that was and too bad it wasn't, in most ways— The President weaving and bobbing, sirens screaming 25 hours a day, Patty and Randy, Squeaky and Sara Jane (that flower of the Old South), Steven Weed coming out from behind his soup-strainer, "Sports Activist" Jack Scott performing for the TV cameras, the media racing around like presstitutes and videots, straining for the elusive "scoop." In the case of the kidnapped heiress and her "elimination" problems, the inside story purveyed to the presumably bug-eyed reader may have been a little more literal than necessary. The Patty Hearst doll that wets its pants is even now on the drawing boards at any number of major toy factories, you may be sure.

Bulletins, flashes, dots and dashes, the entire arsenal of journalism firing at will, or whoever. Interviews with eye-witnesses who saw other eye-witnesses who described in some detail the capture of Patty Hearst at Geary and Larkin when the actual event took place on the other side of town. Power of the press, the press of deadlines, the powerful pressure of suggestion, the cobra-like fascination of a microphone waving back and forth in front of your Eyewitness News.

Whoever first called California "the land of fruits and nuts," back there in the 1920s, was not wide of the mark, even though fruit had only one connotation then. Updating the thought only slightly, a Presidential aide describes Northern California as "the kook capital of the world—kooks with guns and placards. I've traveled all over the world with the President and the only place we've seen demonstrations is Sacramento and San Francisco." A little cofusion there, Presidential Aide. Assassinations are not popular to our part of the world, nor are placards illegal around here. Yet.

★   ★   ★

More nuts than we care to think about—or kooks, if you will—are walking the streets. We see them every day, talking to themselves in loud voices, gyrating among the crowds, darting in front of cars, trying to direct traffic, bumping into people, hoping to start a fight. The center is not holding, as some Irish poet no doubt said, and the debris is flying in all directions. On Ellis St. I watched a man drinking white port in the hot sun and then collapsing amid the debris piling up at the entrance of the padlocked Ambassador Hotel. He used to live there, now he sleeps in the doorway. His slow misery was observed with curiosity by a passerby whose left ear was glued to a radio. He was getting his "news fix," his input, his headline high.

But this shooting at Presidents, who knows? Instant fame, the covers of Newsweek and Time, all those famous newspeople seeking interviews. And the inane questions! Radio reporter to jail-keeper: "What did Miss Hearst have for breakfast?" He wanted to hear "prune," you just knew. "The usual," said the jailer. "What the other prisoners get." "What is she wearing?" "Prison garb." "How does she feel about being free?" (In jail?) "I haven't asked her."

All this preoccupation with clothes and "feelings." "How do you feel about your daughter being captured, Mrs. Hearst?" How do you answer a dumb question like that? (Have a nice day). Clothes are a big deal, don't ask me why: "Sara Jane Moore wore a neatly pressed turquoise raincoat over her bulky body." Thankhevvin, it wasn't sloppily pressed. "Miss Hearst, who was wearing shower thongs, brown cord slacks, a striped jersey and chic large rimmed glasses." Good thing they were chic, otherwise nobody would ever speak to her again at the Burlingame Club. "'Hello comrades,' cried William Harris, who was wearing dark glasses and a green T-shirt." That leaves something to the imagination, at least.

★   ★   ★

"In other news," as they say on the air, there was the miraculous media rehabilitation of Charles Bates from good old wishy-washy Charlie Bates, the FBI bumbler ("She'll be home for her birthday, I have a feeling in the seat of my pants!"), into, and I quote, "Charles Bates, cool, efficient chief of the FBI." The New York

263

Times found him to be a man "who had triumphed over adversities that would have crushed a lesser man," an "upward-striver" graced with patience and understanding. Sainthood may be just around the corner. Actually, he's the same old Charlie Bates, a good man in a pinch.

Amid all this, it was considered worthy of front page space that "a group of California researchers" (kooks and nuts, no doubt) have discovered the obvious—people who don't smoke, drink moderately, eat regularly and get eight hours of sleep live longer than people who do the opposite. Flash! But don't stop the presses, they may never start again. In the same edition, we were told by the Nat'l Association for Mental Health (more nuts and kooks) that "depression now rivals schizophrenia as the nation's No. 1 health problem." Scoop! My feeling is that if you're not depressed these days you have to be crazy, but I'm schizofrantic.

Then there was and is the brouhaha over CBS' "The Guns of Autumn," which puts hunters in a bad light. Poor hunters. In their defense I quote from the Winchester Rifle, published by guess which rifle company: "For many men, it (hunting) is the truest, most personal exercise in freedom that is available today—and we support wildlife populations not just so we will have something to kill, but in order to have a reason to hunt. Put another way, we do not hunt for the joy of killing, but for the joy of living."

Got that? It's all yours.   *September 28, 1975*

THE LAST GASP

Aboard the N Judah trolley last Friday, reports Passenger Alexander Katten, the motorman called out cheerily at Market and Van Ness: "You heard about Ali Baba and the 40 Thieves? Get off here for City Hall, starring Ali Oto and the 11 pickpockets!" (General laughter, shaking of heads, assorted mutters and mumbles) . . . Later that day, at the M&M Saloon at Fifth and Howard, a newsman was heard to sigh, "We won't have Alioto to kick around much longer," to which a cynic responded, "That works both ways."

Either way, he may have been a bad Mayor but he was good copy. In almost eight years, nobody ever heard him say publicly, "I don't know." He had answers to questions that weren't even asked. What a waste of talent and energy: a bright man—"too smart by half," in the British cockney phrase—whose facade is shiny with self-confidence (but what is he like in the middle of the night,

Angelina?). Eight years ago, there was hardly anybody in town who wasn't for him and who didn't wish him well, and how rapidly he used up that credit. Eight years later it's the other way around.

Maybe we all expected too much from him, this man thrust into the race when Gene McAteer died unexpectedly. To the public at large, he was simply a personable, back-slapping, flesh-pressing millionaire lawyer, an anti-trust specialist. "I'm convinced," a wag was to say a year after his election. "He lost my trust almost immediately." If his image was favorably vague at first, it soon became clear: big builders, big labor, big buildings, big ambitions.

No sooner had he been installed than he was off and running for Governor, then Vice-President. He spent more time away from his desk than at it. When the Mike Nevin scandal broke, he was in New York "on private business." Here was the Alioto-backed candidate for Sheriff, Alioto's own chauffeur and an S.F. policeman to boot, being arrested on a felony charge of vote fraud, and all an Alioto spokesman could say was "So what, it has been going on for years." So has murder but it's still illegal.

"This city," says a knowledgeable City Hall old-timer, "is in the middle of a bloodless civil war." You could deduce that from the dirty fight over the Propositions. You can feel it when you see the grim faces of the old Alioto cronies, who know they are on the way out. You can read it in the angry letters from local taxpayers—the ones who LIVE here—who feel they have been HAD by those they trusted most, those policemen and firemen who, it turns out, pay their taxes elsewhere, vote here at phony addresses, and swing elections.

The Alioto years have provided an expensive education for thousands of San Franciscans who once were content to say, "I never think about politics." He forced them to, and the police-fire strike, which he settled so precipitously, not to mention unilaterally, turned out to be a political error of the first magnitude. "Why, I had no IDEA we were paying so much pension money," was the refrain heard time and again, "and they want MORE?" Suddenly, it was "they," the beloved firemen a city had admired, without question, since 1906.

For decades, ballot measures to fatten the paychecks and pensions of police and firemen passed automatically. Nothing was too good for "our boys" who are now "they," strangers living across county lines and voting illegally. Nor has the lesson of New York's lavish pensions been lost. The bloodless civil war erupts in the polling booths today, and this city will never be the same.

And so, in "the cool grey city of love," hate on election day. A tax-payers' revolt is in the air. Questions to be answered: is there still a "labor vote" in this labor town, a "downtown vote" in this big business city, or has power shifted to the neighborhoods? Now faces and fresh ideas are needed: Yerba Buena and "redevelopment" generally are the dying proof of that. Given the lessons of the past few years, it seems appropriate to sound the old battle cry of many a corrupt political machine on election day: "Vote early and often!" *November 4, 1975*

FUNNY OLD WORLD

Christopher, age 10, had a classroom assignment. "I have to make a list of the things that hadn't been invented yet when YOU were 10," he said, pencil poised over paper.

"Well, for starters, the wheel," I replied, waiting patiently for the laugh that never came. I felt even worse when he wrote it down. "Okay, the wheel," he said briskly. "What else?"

The child psychiatrists are right after all: you shouldn't make jokes with kids. They don't understand whimsy, sarcasm or subtleties. They expect straight answers to straight questions. All kids are grown-up Jerry Fords.

I thought back over the eons—the Ice Age, Stone Age, Cro-Magnon Man, Joe Magnon Woman—that separated his 10th year from mine. "No hair transplants, no capped teeth, no novocaine, no elevator shoes, no hormone shots," I began. That sounded a bit as though I worry about my appearance, which is of course ridiculous (my appearance, I mean), so I said "Scratch that. We'll start over."

He sighed and looked out the window. "Be serious, Daddy," he said. Why, I asked myself, doesn't he have my sense of fun, my panache, my lower backache, my arthritis? "Okay, kid," I said, "when I was 10, we didn't have any Band-aids—just cotton and adhesive plaster—got that?—no penicillin—just moldy bread—no atom bomb, no jets, no missiles, no smog, no television, no McDonald's, no nylon, no air-conditioning, no transistors, no Kleenex—."

"No Kleenex?" That blew his nose, I'll tellya. "That's right," I said, having captured his attention at last. "We poor kids used hankies made out of old BVD's." "BVD's?" he gasped. "Go on"—but I

266

was already lost, heading for yesteryear in my Buster Browns, immersed in such immemorial jokes as "My father was a Confederate but he wore a union suit," not to mention "She was only a stableman's daughter but all the horse manure." Anyone for "Many men smoke but Fu Manchu"?

★   ★   ★

As Strange de Jim might say, "The only exercise I get these days is jogging my memory." I don't even remember people exercising much in the old days. For one thing, we didn't have the clothes for it. Bill Tilden played tennis in heavy white flannels. Helen Wills wore a long skirt with box pleats, yet. Suzanne Lenglen cavorted about the courts draped in enough finery for a debutante's party. In the summer, we wore pongee shirts, heavy linen pants and wool socks.

Come to think of it, I don't think deodorants had been invented when I was 10 (make a note, Christopher). We must have smelled as ripe as an old Roquefort. The first under-arm deodorant I remember was called O-do-ro-no, or was it Odor-O-No? My sister used some sort of hot wax depilatory that was only slightly less bothersome than tar and feathers. We all got bad sunburns, too, because Tanfastic, one of my favorite coined words, hadn't been invented, either.

Baseball players wore real flannel uniforms, wool socks, and, for some reason, heavy cotton sweatshirts, but they ran around on real grass instead of a green carpet. The summer uniform for the well-dressed man-about-town was a flannel blazer that weighed about 11 pounds, over pegged white flannels that bottomed out onto white buck shoes you cleaned with a thick fluid and a wire brush. The women at least had chiffon and headbands and could cool themselves with ornate fans, looking as glamorous as Jetta Goudal or Barbara LaMarr.

I suppose the "miracle fibers" are an improvement, if you can stand the humidity along with the heat.

★   ★   ★

Oh, and another thing, Christopher. There weren't any loudspeaker systems. Politicians had to orate at the top of their lungs but not too many people listened anyway. Announcers at sporting events used megaphones: "Playing firrrrrst baaaaaase, Berrrt Ellllison!" (Cheers.) Singers with dance bands used miniature megaphones. If you never heard and saw The Three Rhythm Boys—Bing Crosby, Harry Barris and Al Rinker—doing "Mississippi Mud" through their little meggies, you didn't miss much, as

267

you may remind yourself by replaying the old Whiteman record.

And, Christopher: phonograph records were made of some kind of shellac and had to be handled the way porcupines make love or they shattered into a jillion pieces. Not that the records lasted too long at best. Needles were of steel and wore through the shellac in no time. Real collectors used cactus needles which had to be sharpened regularly with a complicated doo-hickey.

Start reminiscing, a dangerous pastime, and you are lost in a cloud of ghosts in no time. I miss the old silver 50-cent pieces with the swinging, long-legged, goddess-like Miss Liberty, and the buffalo nickel, and the silver dollar with the milled edges that you could throw on the bar with a clang. I miss proper mailmen and streetcar conductors with wicker caps and Little Old Lady elevator operators who wore one glove only, on the hand they used to open the door. It was a much simpler world, Christopher, and we had "rising expectations." You might write that down, too, even though Governor Jerry Brown and Tom Hayden wouldn't agree. The American Dream of a better life has gone down the drain, but now we have Dran-o if that helps. *November 16, 1975*

EASY COME, EASY GO

News item from Las Vegas in Tuesday's papers: "Joe Bernstein, 'The Silver Fox of Turk Street,' died here at the age of 76."

And so another familiar name bites the dust-thou-art-to-dust-returneth. Still, he lived to an overripe old age, a little thick in the middle, a daily double around the chinline. As a gambler, which he was all his life, he didn't figure to make 76. He would have bet against it.

I named Joe "The Silver Fox" in 1939. I was pretty new at the column racket and not above stealing stale nicknames. Still, Joe did have silvery gray hair, premature then. He also had "an eye for redheads with bad teeth and good legs," usually chorus girls. They had chorus girls then, too, most of them from families that couldn't afford orthodontists.

Joe had a dazzling (till you looked closer) all-white apartment in an unlikely location—above Tiny's Waffle Shop and across from the Sir Francis Drake on Powell. That's why he liked red-haired girls. "They look nice against the white, you know what I mean?" he would say. Everybody nodded when Joe spoke. Why not? He never listened, anyway. Strictly a talker.

*　*　*

When I first met him, he ran a gambling joint behind a bar on Turk. I was so bug-eyed by the action there, running fullblast all night, that I saw fit to mention the place in my shiny new column. I had broken an unwritten law: San Francisco was wide open but you never mentioned it.

So the police, looking disgusted, had to raid Joe's place and haul in a few gamblers. "Jeez, that dumb kid from Sackamenna, hasta blow the whistle." Then they padlocked the joint for a while. Joe took it nicely. A real gent. Next time I walked past the bar, he said "Come on in and have a drink, pal." He mickied me. I made it home just in time and spent the worst night of my life but I never let him have the satisfaction. "How ya feelin', pal?" "Fine, just fine." "Really?" Really, pal. "Pal" is what he called everybody, especially those who weren't.

He was no better or worse than he had to be. In the parlance of the Tenderloin, he "went to his pocket pretty good," picking up tabs, overtipping waitresses and pinching their bottoms. "For five bucks I'm entitled, pal." He wore the uniform of the day for downtown gamblers: polished nails, polished shoes, diamond pinky ring, double-breasted suits with padded shoulders, Charvet ties, white shirts with Barrymore collars, wraparound polo coats. A dude. When he smiled he showed lots of teeth but his eyes were colder than a hooker's heart, as he might have put it and did. Often.

He made friends, enemies, millions. He kept his enemies but also lost friends and millions.

*　*　*

In his weird Powell St. digs, the walls covered with autographed photos from old girls like Libby Holman and Helen Morgan and Gertrude Niesen, he would play poker at stratospheric stakes for days in a row. The exhausted players would sleep on the tables. The dirty white apartment was a mess of half-eaten club sandwiches sent up from Tiny's and coffee mugs studded with cigarette butts. The red-headed girls got lost. No action. Just "Whose deal?" and the click of chips.

Money meant nothing to him. It was just a commodity, stock in trade. One night, after he'd won $150,000 in a four-day session, he had dinner at Larry's (now Swiss Louis) on Broadway with lawyer Jake "The Master" Ehrlich. I named Joe "The Silver Fox" but Jake named himself "The Master" and meant every word of it.

269

"Joe," said Jake, "you're not getting any younger and you can't win 'em all." "You haven't said anything yet, pal," observed Joe. "Do you want to die old and broke?" Jake went on. "It beats dying young and rich," said Joe, examining his nails. They reflected the candlelight satisfactorily.

"Give me $100,000 of that $150,000 you won," said Jake, "and I'll buy you an apartment house. You'll never have to worry again." The Silver Fox shook his head. "Never in a million years, pal," he said. "Why not?" inquired The Master. "Because, pal," said Joe, "you can't shove an apartment house into a pot."

★   ★   ★

Joe had a remarkable memory for cards. He could have been the best bridge player ever except "the game's too slow and too many bores play it." The story goes that he was barred from several Las Vegas blackjack tables because he remembered every card and won thousands. Now they use the "shoe" at blackjack tables, all because of Joe. He'd bet on anything. Once, when Bernstein's Fish Grotto on Powell had a tank of live fish in the window, he said loudly, "That's the biggest Spanish mackerel I ever saw." "Sea bass," said a bystander. "Spanish mackerel," insisted Joe. "Look," said the mark, "I'll bet you $20 that's a sea bass." They walked inside where Mr. Fish Grotto said it was a sea bass.

"Unbelievable," said Joe, paying off. "Here I have every fish in the sea except a bass running for me—and I lose."

Joe was part of the good old days, when the police ran the town and the newspapers ran the police. Then the reformers moved in and Joe moved out. "They can change the town but I can't change me," he said, heading for Nevada. "So long, pal. Ever get to Vegas, call me." He knew I wouldn't.   *November 23, 1975*

HOLIDAY CITY

Financial district at dusk, hard-edged buildings turning soft in the moonrise, a wall of lights rising toward the stars, patter of tiny feet (and gunboat-sized) hurrying to favorite bars. At the North Beach end of Montgomery, dear old Coit Tower glowing dimly under a flashing Christmas tree. From high in the Wells Fargo building, you can look down on the austere, formidable Bush St. head-quarters of one of the "Seven Sisters" that control the world's oil—Standard of Cal, with its satellite towers across Market. Christmas lights glow in the cathedral-like Russ Building, once the mightiest in town, long since eclipsed by the new Bankamonstrosities, yet still dignified, impressive, historic: in bonanza days, the Russ House stood there, housing the new rich in a city too raw for the old rich—they would come later. The most exciting slice of Sanfranciscana as the sun goes down and the lights come up, this Wall Street of the West, lawyers and bankers, con men and entrepreneurs, wheelers and dealers, the power and the glory—and what profiteth it a man if he lose his soul? Temporally speaking, looking around at the chauffeured limousines waiting outside plush offices, it profiteth him plenty.

★ ★ ★

The weather: sensational. "Don't talk about it, you'll jinx it." All our guilt comes out at Christmas. Let him who has not sinned against the Lord step forward. (All sit.) If it comes to the Lord's attention that we are having such good Christmas weather, he will cause it to rain for 40 days and 40 nights. On the 41st day, the stores will advertise a "Post-Deluge Sale." Good weather is good for business and the merchants are smiling, which is also good. They all laughed when Calvin Coolidge said, "The business of America is business," but Cal was right on the money.

★ ★ ★

Beautiful Baghdad-by-the-Bay, aglow. On the streets, strangers actually smiling at one another, and isn't that what Christmas is all about? It makes us feel a little kinder. A fiver for the kid who throws your Chronicle into the bushes—a good kid, a splendid little chap. A tenner for the garage man who dented your favorite fender last July, and a bottle for the postman, who always rings twice to announce the junk mail has arrived. Actually, our maligned postal service is pretty damn good, given its vagaries. A few days before Christmas, Atty. Bob Feyer was at the Bush-Montgomery post office as a woman called frantically over the counter: "Please help me— I put all my San Francisco cards into the out-of-town slot by mistake." Postal worker, loudly: "Forget it—they all go in the same bag anyway" . . . And UPS, the United Parcel Service, with its neat brown trucks and friendly drivers. Is there a better outfit anywhere?

★ ★ ★

The two Christmases, sacred and—well, not profane. Mundane? At Grace Cathedral, the mighty organ rattling the stained-glass windows, its treble and bass pipes fully a block apart (joy to the world). In Huntington Square, lights in the trees atop the hill of the robber barons, and parties, parties everywhere, followed by

271